No Ordinary Landmark

LANDMARK LAW CASES & AMERICAN SOCIETY

Julie Novkov and Victoria Woeste
Series Editors

Peter Charles Hoffer
N. E. H. Hull
Founding Series Editors

RECENT TITLES IN THE SERIES

Prigg v. Pennsylvania, H. Robert Baker
The Detroit School Busing Case, Joyce A. Baugh
Lizzie Borden on Trial, Joseph A. Conforti
The Japanese American Cases, Roger Daniels
Judging the Boy Scouts of America, Richard J. Ellis
Fighting Foreclosure, John A. Fliter and Derek S. Hoff
The Passenger Cases and the Commerce Clause, Tony A. Freyer
Discrediting the Red Scare, Robert Justin Goldstein
The Great Yazoo Lands Sale, Charles F. Hobson
The Free Press Crisis of 1800, Peter Charles Hoffer
Rutgers v. Waddington, Peter Charles Hoffer
The Woman Who Dared to Vote, N. E. H. Hull
Plessy v. Ferguson, Williamjames Hull Hoffer
Goldwater v. Carter, Joshua E. Kastenberg
The Tokyo Rose Case, Yasuhide Kawashima
Gitlow v. New York, Marc Lendler
The Unusual Story of the Pocket Veto Case, 1926–1929, Jonathan Lurie
Opposing Lincoln, Thomas C. Mackey
Medellín v. Texas, Alan Mygatt-Tauber
American by Birth, abridged ed., Carol Nackenoff and Julie Novkov
The Supreme Court and Tribal Gaming, Ralph A. Rossum
The 9/11 Terror Cases, Allan A. Ryan
Obscenity Rules, Whitney Strub
On Account of Sex, Philippa Strum
Speaking Freely, Philippa Strum
The Campaign Finance Cases, Melvin I. Urofsky
Race, Sex, and the Freedom to Marry, Peter Wallenstein
Bush v. Gore, *3rd expanded ed.*, Charles L. Zelden

For a complete list of titles in the series go to www.kansaspress.ku.edu.

LOUIS HULL HOFFER

No Ordinary Landmark

How New York City Saved Grand Central
Terminal and Preserved Urban Spaces

UNIVERSITY PRESS OF KANSAS

© 2026 by the University Press of Kansas
All rights reserved

Published by the University Press of Kansas (Lawrence, Kansas 66045), which was organized by the Kansas Board of Regents and is operated and funded by Emporia State University, Fort Hays State University, Kansas State University, Pittsburg State University, the University of Kansas, and Wichita State University.

Library of Congress Cataloging-in-Publication Data

LCCN: 2025032301
ISBN: 9780700640980 (cloth)
ISBN: 9780700640997 (paper)
ISBN: 9780700641000 (ebook)

British Library Cataloguing-in-Publication Data is available.

Jacket design by Karl Janssen
Cover photographs of Grand Central Terminal: Top: circa 1915, Library of Congress. Bottom: 1985, Metro Transit Authority.

CONTENTS

Series Foreword vii

Introduction 1

1. The Railroad City 3

2. Grand Central Terminal and Penn Station 28

3. The Terminal in Post–World War II New York City 50

4. Landmark Law 67

5. Landmark Status for Grand Central Terminal 100

6. Penn Central Strikes Back 124

7. Appeals in the New York State Courts 156

8. Briefs and Oral Argument in the US Supreme Court 179

9. The High Court Decides 210

10. The Terminal After *Penn Central* 230

Conclusion 242

Chronology 245

Bibliographic Essay 247

Index 253

A photo gallery follows page 146.

SERIES FOREWORD

The railroad, invented in the nineteenth century, made twentieth-century America possible. Transportation was the key to westward expansion, the development of markets, and the rise of industrialization. Railroads quickened the pace of American development, and, for good or ill, the American judiciary rewrote the common law to subsidize the growth of rail networks and to socialize the costs of accidents.

The hegemony of transportation over the American economy was scarcely questioned during the heyday of the "iron horse." The obvious benefits of moving passengers and freight at speeds previously unknown to humanity outweighed their obvious costs: property and crops burned by embers from passing engines, loss of life and limb due to accidents on trains and between trains and people on the ground, and the dedication of important overland routes to rail construction instead of other, perhaps more equally, productive uses. New legal inventions such as the fellow-servant rule, which denied employees recovery against the railroads if a coworker was even slightly at fault, were downright cruel.

The first half of *No Ordinary Landmark* sets out this narrative with admirable efficiency. It foregrounds the position of New York City as the center of East Coast transportation while explaining the push of railroads to Chicago and the Mississippi River. We also learn about the swift consolidation of the railroads in corporate hands, as railroad barons quickly realized the economies of scale that near-monopoly control provided. But the most important development, from the vantage of New York City, was the rise of the commuter, who traveled from the boroughs outside Manhattan and the suburbs to the west to work in the city by day and return home at night. It was to serve this slice of the transportation market that city officials authorized the construction of railroad stations above and below ground. As we learn, the two most important of these—the Grand Central Station and Pennsylvania Station—were architectural masterpieces that beautifully married form and function. Penn Station was designed by the famous firm of McKim, Mead & White in a beautiful expression of Beaux-Arts design, and completed in 1910. Grand Central, also a Beaux-Arts building, opened its doors in 1913.

But progress thundered on, and as Manhattan grew in economic importance, so too did the value of real estate—on the ground, underneath it, and in the air above it. New York's Penn Station did not survive the post-war expansion blitz; it was torn down in 1963. Its loss precipitated the modern architectural and historical preservation movement, which found its greatest initial cause in saving Grand Central from a similar fate.

Working with the records of the New York City Landmarks Preservation Commission, Louis Hoffer recounts the political and legal battles spurred by the drive to defend Grand Central from powerful real estate interests. His lens begins at the micro level, where Grand Central's owners—by midcentury, ironically, the Penn Central Transportation Company—first fought the designation of the terminal as a historic landmark. We are walked through New York City's municipal politics, dominated by fights between mayors and developers as the conflict became more heated and monied interests chose sides. Once the Landmarks Preservation Commission succeeded in protecting Grand Central, the macro-level jurisprudential battles emerged in the New York state courts. Penn's victory in the trial court, however, did not bode well for the case's appellate journey.

Yet the city's victories on appeal, all the way up to and including the US Supreme Court, did not turn solely on whether it was constitutional for New York City to designate a particular property with protected landmark status. Eventually, the stakes broadened to pose a threat to the existence and legitimacy of zoning itself. The Supreme Court famously recognized the constitutionality of zoning in *Euclid v. Amber* (1926). But the uniqueness of the landmarks preservation concept seemed poised to strike at the heart of land use regulation that was universal in land planning across the country by the late 1970s. The Supreme Court's decision *Penn Central Transportation Co. v. New York City* (1978) cannot be dismissed as a simple triumph of the emerging liberal bloc on the Burger Court. Some of the Court's conservatives voted to uphold the preservation law because Penn Central was left with valuable air rights that it could develop as long as the city approved. One of its liberals dissented, joining an opinion that described the landmarks law as an unconstitutional taking of a property owner's expectations of profit. The majority opinion's central finding was that Penn Central was still free to operate Grand Central Terminal as a railroad station with concessions and offices on site. This outcome can hardly be described as a socialist capture of private property without compensation.

Despite the dissatisfaction expressed by observers on all sides, the *Penn Central* case has withstood the test of time in terms of both jurisprudence and the intangible value to society of historically significant structures. Hoffer notes that in New York, historical preservation began with the designation of buildings and sites that were central to the American Revolution and to New York's time as the new nation's capital. That historical preservation now serves public bodies at all levels is a testament to the lasting relevance to Americans of their history and historical identity. This book tells a fascinating story, emphasizing that preservation itself is a historical process.

Victoria Saker Woeste
Series coeditor,
Landmark Law Cases and American Society

INTRODUCTION

No Ordinary Landmark is the story of the landmarking of Grand Central Terminal—of the railroad company that owned it, the architects and engineers who built it, the city that supported it, and the lawsuit that saved it. It is a story of landmark law at a critical moment in its existence and what property owners ultimately do with their assets. The cast of characters is immense—some familiar, like mayor Robert Wagner and Jacqueline Kennedy Onassis, and some now obscure, like Albert Bard, father of the New York Landmarks Preservation Law. Railroad moguls, real estate barons, politicians, arts experts, and, above all, lawyers and judges played vital roles. It is, finally and not least, the story of one of the greatest cities in the world, in microcosm.

As a legal tale, the suit the railroad brought against the city and its preservation commission pit two core values of American jurisprudence against one another. The first is the absolute right of property owners to full compensation when their land, buildings, and rental rights are taken by the government. This was the takings provision of the Fifth Amendment. The other value is a more amorphous but equally powerful notion that the people's interest in urban spaces might outweigh total control of one's property. That contest is by no means done, but *Penn Central v. New York City* created a new legal framework for a generation of jurists, planners, preservationists, and legal scholars.

This book is divided into two parts—the first five chapters discuss the railroad, the terminal, the city, and the rise of the Landmarks Preservation Commission. The second five follow the case through the courts of New York to the US Supreme Court, and beyond. The last chapter reverses this order, first tracing landmark law in the federal courts, and then describing the restoration of the terminal.

I am greatly indebted to James A. Kushner, whose course in zoning law at Temple University, and whose book *Subdivision Law and Growth Management*, ignited my interest in preservation, and who was kind enough to read the manuscript for the press. His comments were gracious and immensely helpful, as were those of an anonymous reader for the press. I am grateful as well to Peter Charles Hoffer, Williamjames Hull Hoffer, and N. E. H. Hull, who each worked with me on revisions, and to the New York City Preservation Society, for allowing me to use its archives.

CHAPTER ONE

The Railroad City

The legal history of Grand Central Terminal is directly tied to the geography and history of New York City, and the history of the terminal begins with the vision of Cornelius Vanderbilt. If New York did not start out on an island off the Eastern Shore of North America, the New York Central Railroad (NYCRR) would not have had a monopoly on direct train traffic to the city. If New York City had not been the preeminent transportation hub of the United States in the nineteenth century, due to the building of the Erie Canal linking the Atlantic Ocean to the Great Lakes, the NYCRR would not have been so valuable and profitable to require a structure like Grand Central Terminal. And if waves of immigrants did not come to New York from Europe throughout the city's history, the design and construction of the terminal would have been very different.

New York City started on the southern tip of the island of Manhattan in the seventeenth century. It was created as a Dutch trading post called Nieuw Amsterdam, and was renamed New York City when an English naval force in the service of its new proprietor, James Stuart, Duke of York, conquered the city and the surrounding lands. The trading post had grown into the second-largest city in the newly formed United States of America by the opening of the nineteenth century. The city was blessed with a naturally deep harbor for shipping, sheltered from the Atlantic Ocean currents by Staten Island to the south, Long Island to the east, and the mighty Hudson River and New Jersey to the west. The narrow Harlem River separated the top of the island from the mainland. Its eastern boundary was, aptly named, the East River, separating the island of Manhattan from Long Island. The development of the city was thus closely tied to the expansion of transportation into and off the island.

The Erie Canal

The Erie Canal was the first such transportation improvement. It would connect the city via the Hudson River with the potentially rich agricultural heartland of the Great Lakes region. The Hudson's width and deep banks were perfect for shipping raw material a hundred miles downstream from Albany to New York City's harbor. The canal was possible because the Mohawk River Valley, a natural water-level east-west transportation corridor, connected the Hudson to the Great Lakes and lay between the Adirondack Mountains to the north and the Catskills Mountains and Finger Lakes to the south. The Mohawk was too shallow a river to take direct advantage of its location, but the New York state legislature had the foresight to authorize a canal along the Mohawk to allow barge shipping between Lake Erie to the west and the Hudson River. Many thought it was a foolish scheme, calling it "Clinton's Folly" and "Clinton's Big Ditch" after its sponsor, Governor DeWitt Clinton. They were wrong.

Begun on July 4, 1817, the first section of the canal took less than four years to complete. The rest was finished by 1825. While only 4 feet deep, the 363-mile-long, 40-foot-wide strip of water with its locks and flights was a civil engineering marvel and the second-longest canal built to that date, only surpassed by the Grand Canal in China. The impact of the canal on the development of western New York was striking. People and goods moved more efficiently and cheaply from the east coast to the Great Lakes. In nine years the canal had repaid the state loan, and canal tolls were recouping the costs of its construction.

The building of the Erie Canal transformed the economy of the city and the state. The profits from trade with the Great Lakes and, later, Mississippi Valley enabled New York City investors and entrepreneurs to amass great fortunes and capitalize other business ventures. Workers flooded into the city. "A town with an imperial name was about to witness the birth of a project that would turn New York into an imperial state," canal historian Peter Bernstein wrote. The boom allowed the city to grow north along a new street grid, build the very impressive aqueduct system that supplied the city with clean fresh water, and build denser and denser retail, manufacturing, and residential neighborhoods.

The Erie Canal had affirmed the state of New York's political ascendancy over Virginia and the rest of the South (four of the first five presidents were Virginians) and secured its commercial dominance over competing ports not just on the Eastern Seaboard, but all the way to New Orleans. In particular, the canal gave New York City an advantage in competition with Philadelphia, Newport, Baltimore, and Boston, by bringing the trade and investment capital from the middle of the continent to New York. It also gave rise to many cities upstate, including Buffalo, Rochester, and Syracuse.

The Commodore's Railroad

Cornelius Vanderbilt, later known as the Commodore, was one such man who benefited from the Erie Canal and whose transportation empire would later dwarf the canal's economic importance. Born on May 27, 1794, he began his career when he borrowed a hundred dollars from his parents and purchased a pirogue—a small sailing vessel—and started a ferry service from Stapleton on Staten Island to the Battery at the tip of Manhattan Island. Rather than operating a regularly scheduled ferry service, in summer months Vanderbilt, just sixteen years old, hoped for at least one round trip a day hauling passengers and whatever freight fit aboard. Vanderbilt soon expanded his ferry business into Long Island Sound, up the Hudson River to Albany, and entered the coastal trade as far south as Charleston and Savannah.

Railroads were known to be the next booming transportation industry in the United States, in coming years supplanting the canals. The first steam-powered locomotive operating in New York State was even named the DeWitt Clinton, an ironic tribute to the Erie Canal booster. The line that the DeWitt Clinton traveled went from Albany northwest to Schenectady, avoiding some of the locks on the Erie Canal, and was an immediate financial success. The same year it opened, in 1831, the Harlem Railroad received its charter.

Vanderbilt was entranced by the newly constructed railroads in the 1830s and made up his mind to get into the railroad business. The Harlem Railroad, one of the first, was a lackluster and meager performer when it was built. It connected New York City with the village of Chatham Four

Corners, 150 miles to the north. Nevertheless, the route was a franchise of immense value, as it was the only railroad allowed to bring trains directly onto Manhattan Island and thus to New York City. The railroad had completed a line to Harlem in 1837 and then into the Bronx and on to White Plains in Westchester County in 1844. Eventually, the Harlem Railroad extended its line to Chatham, near Albany. In addition, along Fourth Avenue (present-day Park Avenue) at Forty-Second Street, the railroad purchased land for a train yard and wood lot to service its steam engines. The Harlem never made much money, but to Vanderbilt that was beside the point. He recognized its potential.

The Harlem Railroad's charter from the legislature stated that while it might parallel the Hudson in Manhattan, the tracks would have to be laid far to the east of the river between Third Street and Eighth Avenue so as not to threaten the steamboats' passenger and freight monopoly. It allowed for a double-track railroad from Twenty-Third Street, but only as far north as the Harlem River. Even at the groundbreaking on February 23, 1832, the line's founders, including Thomas Emmet, whose younger brother, Robert, was the famous Irish revolutionary, barely masked their ultimate goal. Before adjourning for toasts "drunk in sparkling Champagne with great hilarity and feeling," John Mason, the railroad's vice president (the president was dutifully attending to his day job as a congressman in Washington), showered accolades all around. He revealed that "while the road's principal objectives were necessarily local, the higher importance was to encourage the building of another road to Albany, which is intended to commence where the present road (our New York & Harlem) terminates at the Harlem River." Still, the railroad industry in America was in its early years. The first iron rails had to be ordered from England.

The dangers the railroads posed to the environs and their own passengers were many. Locomotives' boilers exploded, trains derailed, collisions were common, and cinders from smokestacks set fires along the tracks. With the city rushing northward, however, nothing could stop the expansion of the lines. Still, steam power was banned below Forty-Second Street. Only horsepower—literally—was allowed. When the first stretch opened later that year on November 22, from Prince Street and Union Square the carriages, each pulled by horses, more closely resembled streetcars than a railroad. The fare was a penny. The inaugural ceremony did not go off without its own problems. A miscommunication between the drivers of the cars resulted in what the railroad historian Louis V. Grogan speculated "was the first recorded instance of a rear-end collision in America." The Harlem Railroad's cars ran on rails on deeply rutted unpaved avenues or jarring cobblestones, which prompted the *New York Herald* to describe a routine ride on a horse drawn rail car as "modern martyrdom."

Regular service to 125th Street and the opening of a hotel there inspired the *New York Herald* to predict that "this and other improvements will make Harlem a fashionable rival to Hoboken, New Brighton and other summer resorts." Despite its slow start, by 1852 the Harlem line stretched from New York's City Hall over a hundred miles north to Chatham, with connections the last twenty-two miles to Albany. The railroad's owners knew its true usefulness would come with freight travel to the rest of New York State and beyond if the tracks could be extended—and if it could survive competition from other railroads, steamships, and intrigues in the New York state legislature.

The Harlem Railroad's first rival was the Hudson Railroad. By 1851 the Hudson line reached all the way to Albany (actually, at first, to the ferry terminal in Greenbush). The New York train connected with the overnight express to Buffalo, a train that introduced the sleeping car—a vehicle so inferior that it inspired one rider from western New York, a carpenter named George Pullman, to devote the rest of his career to developing the perfect alternative. Whatever the defects of the sleeper from Albany, the daytime passenger business was booming. Within a year, the Hudson was claiming more than 1.1 million passengers annually. The New York & Albany (Hudson) Railroad was still prevented from building its line south of the Bronx in the Harlem Railroad's exclusive Manhattan zone. Even so, the latter was falling on hard times because it could not compete with the Hudson Railroad's faster water-level river route along the east side of the Hudson. Moreover, the line had been fleeced by one of its executives in 1854 and, in part, blamed Vanderbilt, whom the executive had tricked into buying Harlem bonds. In the economic Panic of 1857, after Harlem Railroad stock suddenly dropped to $9 a share, Vanderbilt was invited in as a director. Within a year, when Vanderbilt turned seventy, he was president of the Harlem line.

In the 1850s four giant railroads rose to dominance over all others, consolidating the mismatched pieces of the eastern lines. As early as 1854 they were dubbed the "trunk lines," defined as the primary routes between the Eastern Seaboard and the west, reaching from the main Atlantic ports to the heads of rivers and lake navigation across the Appalachians. They were the Baltimore and Ohio, the Pennsylvania, the Erie, and the New York Central. The latter two were New York State lines, though the Erie terminated in Jersey City.

Passengers heading east from Buffalo had the choice of the Erie line, which ran through barren mountains to a terminal across the Hudson from New York, or the New York Central, which had emerged in 1853 from the consolidation of ten railways that paralleled the Erie Canal from Buffalo to Albany. It and the Erie line were far larger in capitalization and length than any other line in the state. The New York Central merged all the short lines along the Mohawk Valley, connecting a chain of agricultural and manufacturing centers from Buffalo to Albany, which gave it a potential edge over the Erie—if exploited. From the New York Central's terminus in Albany, passengers and freight might travel one of three paths to Manhattan: Daniel Drew's Peoples Line steamboats along the Hudson River, the Hudson River Railroad on the shore's east bank, or the Harlem, later controlled by Vanderbilt (bought in 1864) via a short rail line.

Despite an occasional setback, such was Wall Street's faith in Vanderbilt's business judgment that the stock price promptly rebounded. Vanderbilt had a flair for using national events to promote the railroad. One example was when three months after Robert E. Lee surrendered at Appomattox and ended the Civil War, Vanderbilt and his son William H., the vice president of the line, accompanied General Ulysses S. Grant on the Chatham leg of the general's well-deserved vacation to Saratoga on a train hauled, unsurprisingly, by a flag-decorated engine named W. H. Vanderbilt. At the end of the two-hour, forty-five-minute ride, a *New York Times* reporter pronounced the Harlem line "admirably adapted for rapid travel" and said it "afforded a rich treat to the tourist and lover of nature in the magnificent scenery to be found along the whole route."

The movement of troops and supplies during the Civil War, increased wheat production in the West filling freight trains, and the demand for manufacturing in urban settings made the northeastern and midwestern railroads very wealthy and powerful, changing the world around them.

On September 5, 1864, abolitionist editor William Lloyd Garrison wrote a letter to his wife. He had taken the train to Albany and marveled how much the countryside had changed in thirty years. "Then there were no railroad conveyances; now the whole country is covered in rails . . . and through what enormous expenditure of money, and what incredible efforts of the human brain and hand! . . . So many the modes of communication and the ties of life continue to multiply, until all nations shall feel a common sympathy and worship of a common shrine." It was, one contemporary writer argued, "the most tremendous and far reaching engine of social revolution which has ever either blessed or cursed the earth." It magnified the steamboat's impact by connecting it to new rail stations. The railroads' ability to shrink a monthlong journey to a day instilled a mobility in society that unraveled traditions, gave rise to new communities, and undercut old modes of transportation. Its time shaving integrated markets, creating a truly national economy.

For example, the first all-rail shipments of grain from Chicago to Buffalo began in 1864; within a decade, they would surpass the volume carried over lakes, rivers, and canals. The rise of cities that served as rail hubs was astounding. Kansas City was virtually nonexistent before the Civil War; afterward it rapidly sprouted as a cattle shipment center on the edge of the Great Plains, and soon was a major city after being chosen over neighboring Leavenworth as the site for beginning a second transcontinental railroad.

The railroads had raised up Chicago even earlier, building on its status as a major lake port. Cook County, home to this Midwestern metropolis, grew from 43,385 people in 1850 to 394,966 in 1870. Railways to the Eastern Seaboard allowed Pittsburgh, Pennsylvania, to flourish as an iron and steel center; railways to the oil fields of Pennsylvania permitted Cleveland, Ohio, to emerge as a refining center; eastern railways brought farmers from Ohio to Nebraska into the global market. It is telling that the word "rail" was often dropped from "railroad"; the companies were, indeed, America's roads.

In the meantime, the maturation of the railroad system required standardization. Perhaps the most critical standard was the distance between the parallel rails, called the gauge. Railroads must have the same gauge if cars of one railroad are to travel over the tracks of another. Before the Civil War there were several popular gauges in North America, including 6 feet (the Erie Railroad), 5 feet (in the South), and 4 feet 8 ½ inches (in the North). Legislation enabling the construction of the first transcontinental railroad required that it be built with a gauge of 4 feet 8 ½ inches—partly to freeze the South's 5-foot gauge railroads out of the picture during the Civil War.

On January 27, 1870, the first stockholders' meeting of the New York Central & Hudson River Railroad assembled, the company capitalized at a then astounding $90 million (nearly $2 billion in 2020 dollars). Three months later, the company paid a $3.6 million semiannual 4 percent dividend, which *The New York Times* eagerly wrote was "the very largest single dividend ever paid in this country by any one great corporation or state." The New York Central was no ordinary corporation, and its president was no ordinary man. As one of its historians has written, "The creation of the New York Central & Hudson River stands as a historical landmark . . . showing us where the era of big business—the Vanderbilt era—well and truly began."

Soon after buying the Harlem Railroad, Vanderbilt bought the Hudson Railroad and the Central lines to Buffalo. The Empire State had never seen anything like Vanderbilt's new empire. From Lower Manhattan to the shores of Lake Erie, its tracks stretched 740 miles in length, with lines branching out 300 more miles. It operated 132 baggage cars, 400 locomotives, 445 passenger cars, and 9,026 freight cars. In 1870 the newly consolidated railroad carried over seven million passengers and four million tons of freight. Though the number of employees remains uncertain, the New York Central paid more than $2 million in salaries. No other enterprise in New York came close to these figures—not even its rival trunk line, the Erie, which was three-quarters its size. The Central ran through all of the state's largest cities, with the exception of Brooklyn. Few companies boasted a capitalization as large as one-tenth that of the New York Central & Hudson River; and few if any factories represented an investment equal to what Vanderbilt spent on fuel alone each year ($1,869,000).

The growth of the New York Central & Hudson River (to be called simply the New York Central, or the Central, hereafter) Railroad surpassed all other industries combined. Railroads grew faster and earlier than other businesses. Historian Alfred D. Chandler Jr. counted only forty-one textile mills in the 1850s capitalized at $250,000 or more. Even the largest commercial banks rarely boasted a capitalization of more than $1 million. By contrast, at least ten railroads had a capitalization of $10 million or more even before the war began. The stock of the New York Central alone stood on the books at about $25 million at par in 1865; even excluding its $14 million outstanding bonds, this amazing figure was equal to approximately a quarter of the investment in manufacturing in the United States.

The Commodore made sure the consolidation of his mighty Central went smoothly. He paid hundreds of thousands of dollars out of his own accounts to expedite its cash flow. The Harlem, too, announced it would issue twenty thousand shares to pay for a new Central station at Forty-Second Street, Grand Central Depot. Vanderbilt would buy them. Meanwhile, his son William scheduled new trains to compete directly with the Hudson River steamboats, and also invested in the Hudson line relay tracks with steel rails that were more expensive but were smoother and would last longer than iron ones. Work began on a new double-track bridge at Albany. Historian T. J. Stiles wrote, "There is a double irony to all this. Vanderbilt had first marched onto the economic battlefield like a Viking warrior, storming the ramparts of corporations under the banner of the individual competitor."

Vanderbilt was not finished with his expansion of rail lines, reaching out to Albany and Buffalo with two additional tracks. To construct a quadruple track over the distance of some three hundred miles loomed in the public mind as a monumental undertaking and seemed hardly needed in the short term. Vanderbilt told a reporter, "I got our best people together, and submitted a proposition to them. Suppose all the passenger trains were taken off, and the road given up entirely to freight? How much percent on the current expenses could we save in the transportation of freight?" The quadruple track became a boon to the Central's bottom line. In fact, the Central's freight haulage had risen dramatically since the Civil War, and extra capacity was desperately needed. Freight receipts had climbed by 72 percent, despite the fact that freight rates had fallen by an average of 8 percent per year. Passenger traffic, in comparison, remained flat.

The next target was the Lake Shore Railway. It was considered an excellent road, connecting cities from Erie, Pennsylvania, all the way to Chicago, yet it had only one track for part of its length. Businessman and former congressman Horace Clark, the husband of Maria Louisa Vanderbilt, joined in his father-in-law's initiatives. Clark took over the presidency of the Lake Shore on May 4 and in short order arranged with connecting roads for a passenger through line from Cincinnati, Louisville, and St. Louis, over the Central to New York. Vanderbilt had outmaneuvered his old rival Jay Gould to gain control. In 1872 work began to extend sidings at various points along the line until they met. By the end of the year, seventy-five miles had been completed. Clark died in 1873.

"Come, Ye Sinners, Poor and Needy" was said to be Cornelius Vanderbilt's favorite hymn. Some certainly classify Vanderbilt as a sinner; while others say he had little interest in the poor and needy. Although the Commodore was certainly a wily manipulator of railroad securities when necessary, he at least created real value in profitable railroads. Others had no interest at all in running railroads, only in manipulating their stock price. Daniel Drew, Jay Gould, and Jim Fisk all fell into that latter category. They operated under the principle that good press releases and political contributions were more effective at fortune-building than running trains on time, though Vanderbilt wasn't shy about using politicians to his advantage. The three participated in such fortune-building using Erie Railroad stock.

The Pennsy

The Pennsylvania Railroad, or PRR (and often nicknamed the Pennsy), was the New York Central's main competitor for the lucrative New York–Chicago and Midwest traffic. One cannot understand Vanderbilt's rail achievement without a bow to that of his great rival, for competition pushed the Central and Pennsylvania to greater achievements that reshaped New York and the rest of the country. The Pennsylvania, like the Central, gave handsome rewards to investors, providing a dividend for many years. Its excellent credit rating made it a darling of stockholders even when times were bleak, which facilitated the later-merged Penn Central's ability to continue securing loans in the face of a doomed destiny.

The Pennsy was born through a need by the state of Pennsylvania to maintain a competitive edge against New York's Erie Canal. What started out as a mixed canal and railroad program of public works morphed into something different. It was clear by the 1840s that railroads were the future of transportation, and the PRR was created as a result of growing into an all-rail project. It constructed a well-engineered route from Harrisburg to Pittsburgh and then expanded largely through acquisition. At its peak the Pennsy operated thousands of miles and served millions of travelers. Sadly, history will remember it as also creating the ill-fated Penn Central Transportation Company. Today, many of the Pennsy's key routes carry on under Amtrak and CSX Transportation.

Unlike the other major eastern trunk lines, the Pennsylvania Railroad got off to a relatively late start. The Baltimore & Ohio (B&O), Erie, and New York Central lines could all trace their corporate heritage back to the 1820s and early 1830s. The PRR was not formed until a decade later. The delay was in part due to reliance on construction of a canal (officially known as the Pennsylvania Canal) connecting Harrisburg with Pittsburgh, running nearly the entire length of the state. The "Main Line of Public Works" was a somewhat profitable system for a short time, but faster transportation lines were already under construction. The B&O Railroad was a most worrying rival, as state and business leaders thought Baltimore, Maryland, could pass Philadelphia as the Mid-Atlantic's foremost port. In March 1846 the state legislature established the Pennsylvania Railroad, authorizing it to construct a rail line from the state capital in Harrisburg west to Pittsburgh with already built connections to Philadelphia.

The PRR's first civil engineer was John E. Thomson. He devised a superb route, maintaining moderately gentle grades to what developed into the city of Altoona, the location of important upkeep and repair shops, following the Susquehanna and Juniata Rivers from Harrisburg. The railroad then headed for Pittsburgh, connecting through Johnstown, just west of Altoona. Officially, construction of the PRR initiated in 1847 at Harrisburg, and at the same time, work was embarking east of Pittsburgh and finished in late 1852, with the first train running from the future Steel City to Philadelphia on December 10, 1852.

Direct rail service across the state was now instituted, although much work remained to make the PRR a better-quality railroad. In 1851 it began construction of a new and improved crossing of the Allegheny summit and the engineering achievement that would become Horseshoe Curve. With its completion and opening on February 15, 1854, the PRR blossomed. At around the same time the PRR was already looking beyond Pittsburgh with an eye toward Chicago and St. Louis. In similar fashion to Vanderbilt's New York Central, multiple leases, acquisitions, and new construction all enabled the Pennsy to prosper during the latter nineteenth century.

The PRR's two most important Midwestern acquisitions were the Pittsburgh, Fort Wayne & Chicago Railroad and the Pittsburgh, Cincinnati & St. Louis Railway, which occurred on January 1, 1859. Chicago had become a natural terminus for eastern roads. Situated at the southern end of the wide Lake Michigan, the very flat geography of the land made it easy to build railroads north and west of the city, and it became a boundary that rail lines had to go around. The PRR was the first trunk line from the Eastern Seaboard to reach Chicago, and its growing web of rails soon spread west and north. Naturally, the competing eastern systems had to follow the PRR to Chicago to compete. The B&O did not arrive until 1874, and the New York Central followed in 1877 via stock control of the Lake Shore & Michigan Southern, and then the Erie Railroad in 1883.

The Pennsy had conquered the Midwest but was no longer satisfied with just Philadelphia as an eastern terminus. It wanted its own route to the Port of New York, fast becoming the largest on the East Coast. The PRR swallowed up the Philadelphia & Trenton and United Canal & Railroad companies through leases in 1871 to move northeast of Philadelphia. Those lines fanned across New Jersey and gave the Pennsy access to the budding New Jersey shore resorts as well as New York Harbor via Jersey City, New Jersey. Along the waterfront the PRR opened the colossal Exchange Place Terminal, with ferry service provided across the Hudson River into downtown Manhattan. It was one of many rail depots and freight terminals that sprung up on the riverfront between Edgewater and Bayonne. The straightaway from Trenton to Newark and Jersey City became known as the Northeast Corridor, a route that now boasts four high-speed electric tracks and is the backbone of America's passenger rail system.

Commuter Rail Lines

Adding to the PRR routes from the south, in 1843 the New York, New Haven & Hartford Railroad (the New Haven for short) reached its namesake city from New York. The result was a dense network of village stations, industrial centers, and branch links along Long Island Sound and up the Hudson River. A year later, the *New York Herald* prophesied that within two decades the Harlem line "of this road will be nearly one continuous village as far as White Plains." With Westchester's population ballooning by 75 percent in the 1850s alone, in part from the growth of the Hudson, Harlem, and New Haven lines, an English traveler marveled that suburban homes were "springing up like mushrooms on spots which five years ago were part of the dense and tangled forest; and the value of property everywhere, but especially along the various lines of railroad, has increased by a ratio almost incredible." The reaction of rural residents who overnight evolved into suburbanites was profoundly mixed.

A perceptive railroad superintendent remembered only as M. Sloat noticed a new class of customer: the repeat passenger, whose back-and-forth trips to work and home represented a potential marketing windfall. The railroads originated an imaginative fare structure of tickets based not on a onetime passage or even a round trip, but on unlimited rides for six months or a full year at a steep discount from the single-fare rate. The full fare was commuted, and with one bold entrepreneurial stroke the commuter was officially created. First-class fare between downtown and Harlem was $35 for a year; a second-class ticket, for $25, was good only during prescribed hours and on local trains. Even with the discount, annual commutation rates from Westchester were too high for most wage earners, making commuting into Manhattan a luxury most people could not afford.

While the west side of Manhattan's rail docks flourished, on the east side, the Harlem's main depot was becoming a dump. Built in 1857 and bounded by Fourth and Madison Avenues and East Twenty-Sixth and Twenty-Seventh Streets, it was the nation's first "union" depot, welcoming passengers from multiple lines, in this case shared with the New

Haven line. But it was congested. Adjacent property owners who had been promised they would reap the rewards of modern transportation were instead vexed by noise, sparks, and smoke.

Terrified pedestrians and drivers risked life, limb, and their vehicles by crossing the Fourth Avenue tracks. Complaints were met by a rejoinder from a railroad representative that could just as easily have been issued by ne'er-do-well corporations decades later: railroad use was vital, and anything in their way was hurting the public and progress. This was a version of the "best use" doctrine for competing private property cases that courts developed at the same time. Still, the noise, cinders, and speed of steam locomotives brought the railroad in conflict with residents as the city grew up around it, and in 1854 the Common Council banned locomotives south of Forty-Second Street, establishing a de facto station there. Work sheds, coaling stations, and similar operations grew up around that point.

The Central's Depot

As Vanderbilt expanded his rail empire westward, he wanted to make the New York Central more professional and accountable. He dictated that employees wear uniforms and collect tickets before passengers boarded trains, ideas he took from the British. He also knew the Central needed a great station for New York, a grand central depot. He began expanding his real estate holdings to the west to create a sizable new transportation empire. Traffic expanded so much that a larger, wholly new station and yard complex was required, even if it had to give up its more central location at Madison Square. It stretched 249 feet wide on East Forty-Second Street and north to East Forty-Eighth Street.

The old station featured a "fuel factory," where a treadmill powered by horses teased with a wisp of hay operated the machinery, cutting wood for the steam locomotives north of Forty-Second Street. Horses still pulled the streetcars south of Forty-Second Street through the tunnel under what is now Park Avenue from Thirty-Third to Forty-First Streets, a passageway still used by automobiles. As late as the mid-1870s, the line's stables on Fourth Avenue between Thirty-Second and Thirty-Third Streets could still accommodate 916 horses, and even that number was sometimes insufficient. The old facility on Twenty-Fifth Street was later sold, and became the first Madison Square Garden. (Ironically a later Madison Square Garden would stand on the ruins of the Pennsy's classic McKim Mead and White Penn Station.)

In New York City, nothing got done without political support; certainly nothing as substantial as the Commodore's new depot. Vanderbilt knew the Tammany Hall political machine well. Two appointed city commissioners sold him a parcel of city land, at Fourth Avenue between Forty-Second and Forty-Third Streets, for a very discounted price of $25,000—the actual value was much more like $350,000. Consider that just a year or two earlier, one of the Tweed Ring's local court judges had gone so far as to issue an arrest warrant for Jay Gould when he sought to prevent Vanderbilt from seizing control of the Erie Railroad. But perhaps the commissioners were unaware that the ring was no longer beholden to Vanderbilt, having undoubtedly succumbed to a better offer.

Less than two years after ground was broken, Vanderbilt's $6.4 million depot and rail yard opened for business. His Grand Central Depot—or Union Depot, as the press first styled the massive new complex—lived up to its name and was as grand a building as New York had yet seen, dwarfing other city landmarks. T. J. Stiles's biography of Vanderbilt reported that the new depot was the second-largest structure of its kind in the world. It was intended to be a beautiful building: the enabling state legislation specified that the depot "be substantially constructed of the best materials, and the front of said building on Forty-second street shall be of Philadelphia pressed brick, brown or freestone, or marble and iron, and shall be finished in the best style of architecture."

Vanderbilt aimed to emulate one of the great train terminals of Europe, St. Pancras Station in London. England had pioneered railroad development and monumental railway stations. It was natural for him to look across the Atlantic for inspiration. St. Pancras opened for business in 1868, just one year before the Commodore's new depot took shape. The English station claimed to have the world's largest single-span train shed and the largest interior space. Vanderbilt's architect, John B. Snook, created a version of St. Pancras's shed almost as large as the original at 652 feet long. However, for the design of the head house, the depot's public facade, Snook turned his back on St. Pancras's Victorian Gothic style in favor of the French Second Empire. The depot thus draped French style over British engineering. "Second Empire" design got its name from the mansard apartment blocks being redeveloped in Paris under the Second Empire of Napoléon III. Thirty-one iron trusses supported the depot's resplendent sixty-thousand-square-foot semicircular glass roof.

From 1869 to 1871 the first Grand Central Depot rose, 249 feet wide on Forty-Second Street, and 698 feet long on newly created Vanderbilt Avenue. The station and yards stretched several blocks to the north. The Real Estate Record & Builders Guild in 1870 boasted that "the scaffolding alone, erected for putting these ponderous masses of iron in place, is worth a visit; and the roof, when completed, will be a triumph of mechanical ingenuity." The guild fell in love with "one of those wonders of mechanical design and ingenuity well worthy of attention to all those interested in such matters. The work is proceeding with such extraordinary speed that, to any one who allows the interval of only a week to elapse between his visits, the progress appears almost like the work of enchantment."

When completed, the station had even more admirers. *American Architect & Building News* explained in November 1884, "The train-house portion of this great building was erected with extraordinary rapidity, by means of a travelling stage, upon which the arched girder trusses were successively built and placed in position." Visitors were impressed. "The sweeping lines of their gigantic curves fill the mind with the sense of harmony and repose. Are we to deny to such structures the term true architecture?" *The New York Times* emphasized the engineering advances of the depot. "In this new enterprise are the stone platforms, the steam heating arrangements, gates, and other contrivances for the convenience, safety and comfort of travelers. . . . It will be the largest and most complete depot, in every particular, in the world."

The train shed itself was remarkably quiet and free of smoke. Ringing bells and blowing whistles were banned, and railroad cars minus locomotives coasted to the platforms by gravity. However, the building was far from perfect: The lobby arrangements were peculiar at best. The New York Central, the Harlem, and the New York & New Haven lines each had separate waiting rooms; a passenger transferring from one railroad to another had to leave the building and then reenter. In part, this design issue was by mistake, but it also reflected the decentralized nature of Vanderbilt's empire. This reflected his often-overlooked sensitivity to public opinion, but the Harlem line was also a property of great personal meaning to him. After rescuing the long-scorned company and raising it up to glory, he may well have resisted its consolidation into the Central out of purely sentimental motives.

The new depot reserved its most important waiting room for the New Haven Railroad, fronting East Forty-Second Street. The Harlem and Central lines were relegated to the side entrance on Vanderbilt Avenue. Lost to history was the reasoning behind the arrangement of the tracks. Because outbound trains left from the west side of the train shed and inbound arrived on the east side, trains had to cross each other's paths, which they did first at Fifty-Third Street and later at Spuyten Duyvil along the Harlem River and Woodlawn in the north Bronx. Even with five platforms and fifteen tracks, passengers complained. Particularly vexing was transferring from one line to another, a function of the different needs of commuters from the new suburbs and long-distance travelers with more luggage.

Despite the Hartford & New Haven Railroad having the more prominent waiting room, Grand Central belonged to the Harlem Railroad, in which Vanderbilt senior, William, and William's sons now owned almost all the station's stock. Thus far, it had not been absorbed into the New York Central & Hudson River. Grand Central Depot formally opened on November 1, 1871, receiving about fifteen passenger trains each day and sending fourteen trains up the quadruple track that ran over the surface of Fourth Avenue. The land and construction cost well over $100 million in today's dollars, and Vanderbilt, who was seventy-eight years old when it was completed, paid for the depot out of his own deep pockets. He personally told the board, "I never lease property—always buy."

Miller's *New York / Strangers Guide* proclaimed in 1880, "This is decidedly the largest and handsomest depot in the world. Its exterior is imposing, and its immense size and regularity gives it a marked magnitude in a city where there is so much architectural discord.... It is well worth the time for a stranger in our city to pay a visit to this rightly named 'Grand Depot of the World.'" *Scientific American* told New Yorkers to be proud of the new Union Depot in its July 15, 1871, issue: "Among all our large commercial buildings, the railroad depots are those of which New Yorkers have least cause to be proud.... But at last a building has been erected, where space for business, order and discipline in arrangement, ample ingress and egress, and substantial elegance of interior and exterior, are provided." In an address on the history of American architecture at the tenth annual convention of the American Institute of Architects, one speaker concluded that the terminal "has dominated the superstructures of this whole land as completely as the Greek Temple did at one time."

The interior design promoted the majestic quality of the station. The *Times* waxed eloquent over "the colossal bronze statue, with allegorical accessories, erected in honor of Commodore Vanderbilt, on the summit of the western wall of the new and immense Hudson River Railroad Depot." Interior space usage contributed to the feeling of awe. When the station opened, the *Railroad Gazette* gushed, "The effect of the whole is perfectly gorgeous. At night the interior is lighted up by twelve chandeliers, each provided with one hundred lights and a large reflector."

The station had its fair share of naysayers who noted its flaws in function and location. "The new 'Grand Central Depot' can only by a stretch of courtesy be called either central or grand," one editorial in *The New York Times* moaned, and then "denounced the administration of affairs, not only in regard to the slow and wretched arrangement of time on the horse-cars, but also the inconveniences and outrages suffered by passengers at the Grand Central Depot." Even more than a century later *The New York Times* noted the depot's shortcomings as a station: "the red brick station was awkwardly up-to-the-minute, more cowtown than continental.... It must have made sense in 1871, but the three railroads each had entirely separate sections in the new station and the paths to the trains could be long and tortuous." Another critic complained, "The Forty-second street depot is simply an enormous nuisance where it stands, a source of great public danger; it cuts the city into two parts, and makes traffic from east to west above Forty-second street a matter of imminent peril to life and limb. And as the Commodore has shown no disposition whatever to serve the public, there is no mercy to be shown to him when the question of public convenience impends. All good citizens, from this time forth, will insist that must clear off this island."

True, because the depot was in the middle of nowhere, passengers were "penned in like hogs" on the streetcars that ferried them from the depot to downtown. Dennis McMahon of Morrisania in the Bronx groused, "We lose one hour between the depot and City Hall." C. W. Poole of Mount Vernon invoked the ultimate threat, to "sell out and move to New Jersey." Despite the threats and complaints, Grand Central Depot grew in demand along with the city. The Commodore had seen the city expand from a mere town to a global metropolis during his lifetime; he had every reason to expect it to swell past his new depot, as the population increased from 942,292 in 1870 to 1,206,299 in 1880 due to increase immigration from Europe, and soon *Railway Age* reported 170 trains a day at Grand Central.

The depot sparked the imagination of novelists. Richard Harding Davis's Captain Royal Macklin, returning from his escapade in Honduras, reveled in buying a train ticket to his hometown in Dobbs Ferry. In the afternoon rush one September, in Edith Wharton's *The House of Mirth*, Lawrence Selden began his stroll with Lily Bart—"a figure to arrest even the suburban traveler rushing to his last train. Against the dull tints of the crowd," Wharton wrote, her vivid head "made her more conspicuous than in a ballroom" as she threaded through the throng of returning holiday-makers, past sallow-faced girls in preposterous hats, and flat-chested women struggling with paper bundles."

Though Grand Central was not the busiest passenger terminal at the turn of the twentieth century, it handled an estimated three million passengers a year, and realistically expected that number to rise. Arthur T. Vanderbilt II would later write in his book, *Fortune's Children: The Fall of the House of Vanderbilt*, that "crusty old Cornelius (Commodore) Vanderbilt would sit in his office on the second floor of his Grand Central Depot and listen to his New York Central trains rumble below, secure in the belief that his family would always be the richest in the world." The elder Vanderbilt died on January 4, 1877, as a blizzard's weight shattered the glass roof of the Grand Central Depot, but his fortune did not melt. In total, the Commodore left $100 million—more money than was held by the US Treasury at the time, and $2.5 billion in 2020 dollars. "Any fool can make a fortune," he once said. "It takes a man of brains to hold on to it after it is made." His last words were "keep the money together"—an admonition that went unheeded by his heirs.

When Cornelius died, full ownership of the rail line and the depot passed to his oldest son, William H. Vanderbilt, who greatly increased the scope of his father's empire. Within a few years, William's wealth more than doubled because of his proper management of the Central. William's sons, William K. and Cornelius II, would build Marble House and the Breakers, respectively, in Newport, Rhode Island. Their houses, built for just a six-week party season in the summer, would be inseparably associated with the Gilded Age—an epoch that the Commodore exemplified. "With the death of Cornelius II in 1899 at the age of only 56, the Vanderbilt dynasty at the New York Central really came to an end," Louis Auchincloss concluded, although Vanderbilt's great-grandsons would remain involved with the railroad until the 1950s. "The 10 Vanderbilt mansions that once lined Fifth Avenue were never occupied by the next generation," and one by one they fell to the wrecker's ball or the auctioneer's gavel, Arthur Vanderbilt recalled. Only the grand depot and its glorious successor, Grand Central Terminal, would endure as their legacy.

Sticky Fingers and Traffic Jams

The achievements and the shenanigans of railroad jobbers have filled volumes that only accountants and business historians could love. There was a mixture of boast and cynicism in their attitude that financier and rail consideration backer J. Pierpont Morgan captured. As he consolidated railroads into what would become the Southern Railway, instrumental in the development of the nation's Southeast, Morgan's own words, "I owe the public nothing," summed up the era of the robber barons. For the robber barons looked upon railroad treasuries as their own personal piggy banks. Construction companies—owned by corporate insiders—would profit handsomely from a railroad's construction even while the railroad itself went bankrupt and its stockholders lost everything. For example, a never-completed tunnel west of Denver, Colorado, was to be a link in a transcontinental railroad. If any investor had stood at the tunnel mouth, they would have realized that the only way a train could get to the tunnel was to fly through the air! Nevertheless, it took the collapse of the stock market in 1929 to bring about the establishment of the Securities and Exchange Commission's effort to regulate abuses against public stockholders.

For all the corruption, nothing could stop the rail lines from expanding. Following the completion of the first railroad to the Pacific, almost all railroads standardized on a gauge of 4 feet 8 1/2 inches. Time itself was standardized when the railroads adopted a system of time zones (four across the continental United States) in order to have accurate timetables. Millions had to comply to standard railroad time if they didn't want to miss their train. According to the *Scientific American*, "How many individuals reset their watches is impossible to compute, but they could certainly be reckoned by millions. Probably no such singular incident has ever before happened, or is likely to occur again."

Given the innovations and resulting efficiencies on railroads of Eli Janney's automatic coupler or George Westinghouse's automatic air brake, it is no surprise that growth was substantial. Not quite 31,000 miles of track in 1860 became 93,000 in 1880. Ninety-three thousand miles became 193,000 miles by 1900. US railroads reached their peak in 1916 with enough track, about 254,000 miles, to reach the moon. The peak rate of construction of new railroad track occurred in 1886 and 1887.

In New York City the pressure of growth led to the construction of an extension on the east side of Grand Central Depot. In the Gilded Age, bigger was always better. The press and public were happy to know the depot would be expanded and modernized: "The general public little appreciates the work imposed upon railroad officials in handling a passenger traffic that has grown beyond the facilities of the station where it is received. Travelers . . . will rejoice." "The estimated cost is $200,000," declared the *American Architect & Building News* in November 29, 1884.

Opening in 1885, the annex added seven tracks, on five platforms, to the depot's existing twelve tracks. The depot already stretched east from Vanderbilt Avenue to Fourth Avenue but left Fourth Avenue unobstructed. Expanding farther east meant closing Fourth Avenue between Forty-Second and Forty-Fourth Streets and creating Depew Place—named for New York Central president Chauncey Depew—as an eastern counterpart to Vanderbilt Avenue, to accommodate the redirected traffic flow, an arrangement still in use today.

The terminal complex could barely keep up with the new arrangement of overlapping crossing points. "The Grand Central yard is now one of the most crowded in the country," the *Railway Gazette* reported in December 1889. "The number of trains here are so great that even with a considerable amelioration of the conditions, the yard movements would still be very heavy. Engines are flying around in so many directions that injuries to employees are somewhat frequent, and no financial obstacles should stand in the way of the substantial abatement of the confusion now existing." What was glorious in 1871 was, by the 1890s, "the worst station in New York," according to *Railroad Gazette*, in part because almost five hundred trains a day now used the station, compared to the fifteen daily when it opened.

The annex did not fix the waiting room problem, and passengers using the building still needed a unified facility not broken up among the three railways. In early 1896 the rail companies announced an expansion that would all but create a new building in place of the depot. They turned to their chief engineer, Walter Katte, and brought in architect Bradford L. Gilbert. According to a *Chicago Tribune* article in 1892, Gilbert was "famed throughout America and much of Europe as a designer of railway stations." He had designed Chicago's Illinois Central Station, completed in 1893.

The exterior of the building was to be altered considerably, but Gilbert's aim was to harmonize the new with the old. The entire exterior of the plain brick walls was covered with a Portland cement stucco, "giving the effect of a solid, rough gray background, with trimmings of white.... When completed it will be one of the finest stations in the world in all its appointments," hopefully proclaimed the *American Engineer, Car Builder, and Railroad Journal* in 1897. Optimism ruled, at least in the local newspapers. *The New York Times*, for example, sounded like a local booster when it concluded "When the improvements are all finished, in a year or two, the Grand Central Station will probably be the largest, finest, and most comfortable railroad station in the world."

But the alterations were not as easy as the proposal suggested. The *New York Tribune* noted in an October 3, 1897, edition, "Though the station . . . is not to be pulled down, so far as appearances will go it might just as well be, for all the old towers will be destroyed and the mansard roof taken away, and four stories of red brick and granite composition are to rise on the two stories left standing. Hardly a trace of the old building will seem to remain." And the builders seemed heedless of the flow of traffic in and out of the terminal. Fortunately, no one was killed.

The new structure was also adorned with nine-foot-high cast-iron eagles (two of which, following a nine-decade absence, now adorn the terminal again). Inside, the new station included significant mechanical upgrades, including elevators, steam heat, a new power station, and—a major advance—electric lighting throughout. Gilbert proposed a dramatic barrel-vaulted rotunda waiting room—modeled on the rotunda of his Chicago station—to replace the three separate waiting rooms of the individual railways, but delays, blamed on recalcitrance by the New Haven line, kept the interior work from going forward. Gilbert was replaced by Philadelphia architect Samuel Huckle Jr., and Katte by William J. Wilgus, an engineer who would soon play a major role in creating Grand Central Terminal. The work was complete in 1900, with the inconvenient separate waiting rooms for the three lines merged into one that measured 100 by 200 feet.

The new Grand Central Station was not remembered fondly. Quoted in *The New York Times*, Yale University architecture professor Vincent Scully bemoaned "the abject gateway to New York." He continued, "Nothing pertaining to New York City except its government has been so discreditable to it as its principal railroad station," and concluded, "The waiting rooms constituted an ordeal hardly second to that of the tunnel itself, a waiting in rooms crowded to the limit, heated to more than the temperature of the outer air and not ventilated at all.... It was an ordeal so dreadful that the experienced shirked it at almost any risk." The depot was denounced as cramped, dark, repelling, ugly, and disgraceful, and, in the unkindest cut, as a station "which would be considered adequate in Sandusky, Ohio" (which was home to fewer than 20,000 people that year, compared to New York's population, which O. Henry would immortalize a few years later as "The Four Million").

The critics piled on. One angry letter writer to *The New York Times* complained that someone living on East Forty-Sixth Street near Third Avenue and wishing to go to Forty-Sixth Street and Fifth Avenue has to travel to Forty-Second Street or Forty-Ninth Street, making a detour of a half-mile "because this monopoly has made it unsafe to cross at any other point." Another resident, this one from East Fiftieth Street, was apoplectic, writing, "There is no single thing on New York Island so dangerous to the community and prejudicial to its interests as this Valley of the Shadow of Death, which cuts the city in two its entire length, and stretches, unpaved, ungraded, and is given over to the hundreds of locomotives that continually dash up and down, through the richest district of New York."

The phenomenal increase in traffic not only affected the station. The original right-of-way had to be widened to accommodate four tracks throughout Manhattan to serve the mushrooming number of trains. Work was needed to keep local traffic away from moving trains. Beginning at Forty-Fifth Street, the tracks were lowered below street level so a dozen bridges could be built to connect the two sides of Fourth Avenue between Forty-Fifth and Fifty-Sixth Streets, where a new tunnel would begin (leading to a stone viaduct between Ninety-Eighth and 116th Streets where the land was swampy). Construction finally got underway in 1872. It dragged on for two exhausting years.

New York City was forced by the state legislature to lay out several million of the projected $6 million cost of the so-called Fourth Avenue Improvement. The press was not happy about this. "All charitable persons pity Mr. Vanderbilt as a poor man who is compelled to spend his frugal income in lowering the railway tracks in Fourth Avenue, merely in order that people may not get themselves run over and killed by passing trains," *The New York Times* wrote sarcastically, adding: "The collaboration was a marriage of necessity." Nonetheless, this was one of the earliest examples of collaboration between government and private industry, a public/private partnership that is used many times today. The Central proposed to further mitigate the dangerous congestion by tunneling through solid rock all the way to Ninety-Sixth Street with the sunken tracks flanked by iron fences and plots of grass. After the tracks were buried, Edith Wharton, who lived in a townhouse on Park Avenue at Seventy-Eighth Street, wrote to a friend in 1896 that in any given hour, "seven or eight trains passed without affecting our nervous system. What happens is a short roar & rumble, & a puff of white smoke."

But technology could not alleviate all the problems of the traffic jam. Smoke and ash from steam engines caused two kinds of problems for Grand Central: the aesthetic problem of a smoke-filled and sooty headhouse, and the safety problem of running trains through smoke-filled tunnels. Early on, the railroads' determination to keep smoke out of the station interior gave rise to the flying switch, an extraordinary mechanism meant to keep locomotives out of the train shed itself. An article in *Harpers Young People* captured the public response to these improvements. "While wondering at the speed with which this train approaches the station, you suddenly discover that its locomotive is running alone, and at some distance ahead of its following cars, from which it seems to have broken away. From a certain point the locomotive takes a track that runs outside the station, while from the same point the train follows another line of rails, over which it rolls of its own momentum into the great building. You have witnessed the making of a flying switch and a very neat one at that." Amazingly, this procedure caused no accidents. But no comparable procedure could keep smoke out of the Park Avenue tunnels, where conditions for travelers continued to be almost unbearable.

An electric traction engine had made its experimental debut on the Ninth Avenue El in New York in 1885, but the sparks it generated and its slow speed prevented its wider use for the time being. Electric-powered streetcars proved more successful over short distances in 1889, but using electricity to power trains over long distances was relatively untested. In 1900, coinciding with the internationally influential Paris Exposition Universelle, the French Gare d'Orsay became the first major train station designed for electrically powered trains. The French depot had similar tunnel approaches to Grand Central's. The city's newspapers pushed the New York Central to take note of new technologies. *The New York Times* led the way:

> Paris is a civilized city.... A piece of ground on the river front happened to come into the market, and electrical development, allowing of electrical traction, synchronized with this opportunity. The result is that the railway has built a station which is one of the architectural ornaments of Paris, on the Quai d'Orsay.... Would it not be within the financial power of the "Vanderbilt system" to send a competent electrical engineer out to Paris to find out just how this feat has been performed which the system keeps on repeating is beyond the power of man?

Planning for transforming Grand Central's operations by switching from steam to electricity had begun as early 1899, although it would take a deadly accident to force the issue.

Could the future of the railroads, in particular the Central and its great rival, the Pennsy, lie not in the lines themselves, but in their monumental reimagining as stations? Could innovations and investment in engineering, architecture, and financing come together to turn the image of the railroad hubs from fierce machine warehouses to awe-inspiring urban space? For that is just what happened in the first decades of the new century.

CHAPTER TWO

Grand Central Terminal and Penn Station

The nineteenth-century Grand Central Station was a geospatial nightmare. It spanned more than twelve blocks of what was becoming prime real estate, cheek by jowl with the Gilded Age mansions on Fifth Avenue. At a city's edge, the station would have been far less intrusive, but that was not where Vanderbilt wanted it. The Grand Central Depot and Station had pulled the center of New York north from the port of lower Manhattan. At the same time, running steam engines through smoke-filled tunnels under Park Avenue—tunnels once welcomed as a solution to the problem of train traffic—became ever more controversial and dangerous.

In 1871 the depot averaged about twelve thousand passengers a day. By 1902 the revamped station moved forty-four thousand passengers every day on more than five hundred trains, sixteen million passengers a year on three railroads. On a total of 177,450 trains, the traffic was about one departure or arrival every forty-five seconds during rush hours! An expanded yard and tracks to meet the demand was a nonstarter. The existing yard already took up too much expensive Manhattan real estate.

And the trains were getting too long. Travelers were required to walk interminable distances to reach their seats. In five instances it was more than a thousand feet from street to train. Some within the corporation thought it was just a matter of time before the station relocated to somewhere further up the line, like the Mott Haven section of the Bronx, once again putting it at the city's periphery.

The station and the yard space were not even the most pressing problems for the Central. The steam locomotives were dirty, sooty, smoky machines. With hundreds of trains a day rolling in and out of the station, the smoke problem had become unbearable and dangerous. The greatest concern was the approach to Grand Central Station through the Park Avenue Tunnel, where smoke threatened to asphyxiate passengers, particularly during rush hours when trains paraded in and out of the station on short headways. Locomotives spewed smoke and ash as they ran beneath Park Avenue, inside a thirty-year-old tunnel meant to handle a fraction of the train traffic now pouring in and out of the city. After all, since the Park Avenue Tunnel was built in 1875, three railroad companies had shared the four-track main line down Manhattan's spine. The situation was horrific: "Let a car with doors and windows tightly closed stand in the burning sun for an hour or two until to its inmost recesses it is quivering with heat, then crowd it full of perspiring humanity, keep the doors and windows closed and drag it through several miles of hot, smoky, gas reeking tunnel, and you will have a pretty effective imitation of the Black Hole of Calcutta," wrote one railroad historian. The *New York Tribune* lamented the situation, inflicted on thousands every day.

New, grander train stations were built in the growing cities of the Atlantic coast, in the Midwest and New England. The Pennsylvania Railroad, the Reading, and the Baltimore & Ohio all constructed elegant depots, including Reading Terminal in Harrisburg, Philadelphia, and Pittsburgh's Penn Station. The New York Central built new stations in Albany, Utica, and Rochester. The number of tracks on the main railroad lines was doubled on Grand Central rights-of-way, and the Pennsylvania Railroad copied the Central in building four parallel tracks in 1903 between Pittsburgh and Philadelphia. Grand Central Station run by the New York Central was looking less and less competitive.

As sometimes happens in rapidly changing technologies, improvement came not from steady innovation, but from a sudden and unexpected (though not unpredictable) direction. On Wednesday morning, January 8, 1902, Train 118, the local from White Plains, was late. It was due at Grand Central Station at 8:15 a.m., but, already behind schedule, it was delayed at 110th Street for nearly five minutes to let another southbound local, this one from Croton, pass ahead of it, a common occurrence during rush hour. At the same time an incoming New Haven train came to a halt in the Park Avenue Tunnel. Moments later, the Harlem-line train plowed into it, killing fifteen passengers and seriously injuring thirty-six others, of whom two subsequently died. "The tunnel, the dreadful smoke-filled tunnel, against which all New York has long stormed and protested, is responsible for the murderous collision of yesterday. . . . Having no warning that the train ahead of him had come to a standstill, the Harlem engineer ran as if he had a clear track, and the collision and slaughter resulted," wailed *The New York Times.*

Three days later, on January 11, 1902, the *Times* reported that the New York Central would be switching to electric power. And the following year, after a series of hearings and meetings, an indignant state legislature ordered the railroad to give up steam by July 1, 1908. "No existing railroad electrification anywhere in the world," Kurt C. Schlichting wrote in his biography of civil engineer William J. Wilgus, "approached the scale of the Central's project or provided a model to duplicate." The railroad set up an Electric Traction Commission, calling on many authorities in the field to assist in the planning of practical electrification. Work began in 1903, a prototype locomotive was built in 1904, and the first scheduled electric trains debuted in 1906.

The New York Central developed a 660-volt, direct-current third rail to power trains. (Trains received power from third-rail shoes that collected current from the bottom side of the rail. The top was covered with a safety shield to minimize the chance of people or animals being accidentally electrocuted on the tracks.) By the time the new Grand Central was underway in 1906, all routes to the station were fully electrified, completely eliminating the use of polluting steam engines in Manhattan. Plans to convert from steam to electric power necessitated the building of electric power generating plants and an elaborate distribution system through the areas to be electrified in Manhattan, the Bronx, and Westchester, after which travel was made with the usual speed and a great deal more comfort.

Plans for a New Terminal

In the meantime, Chief Engineer Wilgus's conception of a new and improved headhouse was gaining traction, with four firms submitting proposals. Wilgus's experience and training was the story of American railroading in microcosm. His father was a railroad foreman in Buffalo. Young William apprenticed to a Marsden Davey, a civil engineer with the railroads, took a correspondence course in engineering at Cornell University, and then went to Minneapolis to ply his new trade. He soon moved to New York City, the focus of national railroading.

There, the competition for the design of the new terminal was held in the exceedingly short time of two months, with some of the best known firms applying, among them D. H. Burnham of Chicago, and Stanford White, of McKim, Mead & White of New York, nationally prominent architects with major monuments to their credit. All the competitors had railroad experience of some kind.

Both Burnham and McKim, Mead & White had just taken on projects for enormous new terminals for the New York Central's great rival, the Pennsylvania Railroad—Burnham's Union Station in Washington, DC, and McKim, Mead & White's Pennsylvania Station on the west side of Manhattan. Reed & Stem had a lower national profile, but also a great number of railroad stations to their credit—as well as a personal connection to the board.

No record of Burnham's proposal appears to have survived. McKim, Mead & White and Reed & Stem each proposed grand projects reflecting the current American fashion of classically inspired Beaux-Arts architecture as idealized in the City Beautiful movement, inspired by the Chicago World's Fair of 1893, with clean lines and boulevards. They featured a monumental tower over the terminal itself as their centerpiece. All three proposed lowering the railyard out of sight and developing the land on top with income-producing office buildings above and around the terminal. The competition went to Reed & Stem of St. Paul, Minnesota. The firm began with two big advantages over rival bidders. Charles H. Reed and Allen H. Stem had designed other stations for the Central, and Reed was Wilgus's brother-in-law. Yet in the highly charged world of real estate development in New York, another firm's connections trumped Reed & Stem's.

William K. Vanderbilt, who in 1903 played a role on the board, thought that the architects might not be up to the task of designing such a grand monument, and insisted on bringing in, as collaborators, Warren & Wetmore—a firm that had not entered the competition. Whitney Warren and Charles Wetmore were respected; however, Warren was Vanderbilt's cousin. The Central's chairman officiated at a shotgun marriage of the two firms, pronouncing them the Associated Architects of Grand Central Terminal.

Reed & Stem then offered a novel suggestion of an elevated exterior circumferential driveway with a bridge across Forty-Second Street for the interior extension of Park Avenue to deal with local street traffic. Warren & Wetmore instead proposed a low, broad building with no wraparound roadway or internal ramps but did add refined elements to the design. Warren & Wetmore's additional contributions included replacing the twelve-story revenue-producing building proposed by Wilgus and planned by Reed & Stem with a lower but more immense structure devoted to railroad functions, with limited commercial space. The focus was clearly on the monumental side, much like Penn Station's design, instead of on revenue-generating elements. Wilgus, angered at the decision to abandon both the revenue-producing building and the elevated roadways, maintained that Warren & Wetmore's design involved only the exterior treatment of the station and kept the wraparound roadway and commercial space, but all of them managed to work together.

The City Beautiful design was complementary to the Beaux-Arts architectural style, both incorporating an eclectic variety of elements. Beaux-Arts developed at the same time in France. Although primarily classical, it included Gothic and Renaissance details. The École des Beaux-Arts in Paris had been churning out some of the finest classically educated architects for decades, such as Richard Morris Hunt, Louis Sullivan, and Charles McKim. Warren was among them, having attended the École des Beaux-Arts from 1888 to 1891 before forming the architectural firm of Warren & Wetmore. Earlier in his career, Warren had worked for McKim, Mead & White, masters of domestic Beaux-Arts. His design reflected all the elements the Beaux-Arts sought to achieve. Grand Central also embodied the goals of the City Beautiful—systematic neighborhood planning and building on a grand scale of a new district with a conscious effort to beautify as well as to provide the most modern railroad terminal in the world.

Reed & Stem, now working in close accord with Warren & Wetmore, produced a nearly perfect master plan. Its form was not only exquisite Beaux-Arts but also took into account the intricate mix of rail traffic—suburban, intercity, elevated, and subway—with pedestrian and vehicular access. The terminal itself became a sort of grand pedestrian thoroughfare from one building to another, with ramps and open spaces providing easy circulation. Around the outside, the two firms developed the circumferential roadway that took traffic between Forty-Sixth and

Fortieth Streets, bridging busy Forty-Second Street. The terminal was a collaborative effort, just as Beaux-Arts combined distinct architectural features.

A Working Terminal

The new terminal fused engineering innovations with its architectural novelties. Wilgus formally wrote to the president of the New York Central in March 1903, in which he laid out, in detail, all the component parts of the immensely complicated project. In all, there were thirteen points (listed below) that Wilgus wanted the new Terminal to adopt. One hundred years later, the Grand Central Terminal complex still embodies almost all of the elements Wilgus proposed in 1903:

First, a double-level underground terminal with a loop track at the suburban (lower) level; second, an elevated driveway around the twelve-story building connecting Park Avenue north and south of the new terminal; third, the elevated driveway carried on an arch bridge over Forty-Second Street connecting with Park Avenue south to the street; fourth, north of the terminal from Forty-Fifth to Forty-Eighth Streets, over the underground train yard, provision made for a "grand court or park" over the train yard and for future development of revenue-producing buildings; fifth, a new hotel on Madison Avenue between Forty-Third and Forty-Fourth Streets, to be "run on first class lines, similar to the Waldorf-Astoria"; sixth, a waiting room eighty feet in width extending across the entire station; seventh, the main concourse, sixty feet in width, with direct connections to Vanderbilt Avenue on the west and Depew Place on the east; eighth, from the concourse, ramps leading down to the long-haul train platforms; ninth, ramps from the concourse, along with stairs and elevators, to the lower concourse, where ramps would lead to the suburban train platforms; tenth, a direct connection with the IRT (Interborough Rapid Transit) subway at the suburban level; eleventh, north of the station between Forty-Fifth and Forty-Eighth Streets, construction of a separate baggage facility connected to the tracks below by elevators and "endless belts"; twelfth, changing from steam to electric power, which would make possible "all of these improvements, which otherwise would be impracticable owing to smoke, cinders and gas"; and thirteenth, separation of the suburban service from the through-train service.

Ramps were used generously, not only to get passengers to and from the platforms but also to get them in and out of the station. One ramp from the main Forty-Second Street entrance was a 205-by-65-foot main waiting room. A second ramp led passengers into the new terminal's centerpiece, the 120-by-287-foot, 125-foot-high main concourse. The reliance on multiple levels to handle the complex circulation problems was carried further than in any other station. All of this was achieved without forcing passengers to walk excessive distances between destinations underground. The engineers, "not satisfied with theoretical calculations, built experimental ramps at various slopes and studied thereon the gait and gasping limit of lean men with heavy suitcases, fat men without other burdens than their flesh, women with babies, school children with books, and all other types of travelers," according to a *New York Tribune* article published on December 15, 1912. Their work, it is said, has given rise to a popular expression on Broadway, "Well, I'll be ramping."

Electrification permitted real estate–conserving bi-level construction, allowed the terminal tracks to be entirely covered, and simplified operations by allowing trains to be bidirectional. Thus, when a train arrived at the terminal, there was no locomotive that needed to be taken off the train, turned, and serviced. To reverse the multiple unit out of the station, the engineer simply had to change ends; even that was not necessary if the train arrived at a loop track. The flow would now empty from thirty-two upper-level and seventeen lower-level platforms. This all fed from as many as sixty-six and fifty-seven tracks, respectively, still the largest in any station in the world.

The grand, and very photogenetic, concourse contained ticket windows for both the Central and New Haven Railroads, and had at its center an octagonal information booth. The spherical four-faced brass clock above promptly became one of the terminal's most recognizable symbols and a meeting place for travelers. The main concourse was 275 feet long, 120 feet wide, and 125 feet high (spreading nearly 38,000 square feet) and was flanked by 90-foot-high transparent walls punctuated by glass walkways connecting the terminal's corner offices. The colossal scale of the concourse was a deliberate choice, a successful attempt to match a grand space to a great city's transportation needs.

If anyone was centrally responsible for these choices, it was Whitney Warren. His focus on the "main element," the space at the heart of the terminal, manifested itself in design and detail. The ceiling of the main concourse was decorated with an adaptation of the night sky, mostly depicted accidentally in reverse, with more than 2,500 bulbs representing stars. Along the walls, soaring arched windows admitted natural light; the image of sunbeams streaming through this glazing is a meme of Grand Central Terminal. Wilgus's dismay with the decision to abandon the high-rise office building was mitigated by the laying of a structural foundation for a revenue-producing tower that might someday be built over the building.

The new design called for a Beaux-Arts jewel to be placed in the center of New York's Park Avenue, diverting the street around the building's perimeter. The completion of the road's viaduct suddenly changed Park Avenue from an inconvenient local street to the most modern highway in New York. Indeed, the viaduct, which was built without sidewalks, may be the earliest thoroughfare in New York designed solely for vehicles, without any accommodation for pedestrians. The viaduct is three arches in length, and all were originally open. An ornamental iron railing with shell medallions runs along most of the roadway; elaborate bronze streetlights originally stood atop granite piers.

By any measure, the new terminal would be grand. Once the design was agreed upon, building Grand Central was a gargantuan undertaking. Ground had been broken in June 1903. Gasping steam shovels excavated nearly 3.2 million cubic yards of earth and rock to an average depth of forty-five feet to accommodate the subterranean train yards, bi-level platforms, and utilities—some as deep as ten stories. The daily detritus, coupled with debris from the demolition of the old station, amounted to a thousand cubic yards and filled nearly three hundred railway dump cars. At peak construction periods, ten thousand workers were assigned to the site, and work progressed around the clock. Construction would take ten years and impacted an area bounded by Forty-Second Street on the south, Fiftieth Street on the north, Lexington Avenue on the east, and Vanderbilt Avenue on the west.

According to a 1919 issue of *Architecture Magazine*, "esthetic considerations called for arches" in spanning the three openings, but the spaces were too cramped to allow footings for true arch construction.

So the architects and Olaf Hoff, the engineer, designed great steel girders, curved as if built as arches but actually cantilevered out from the opposing piers. The steel members were up to 136 feet long and were pulled by a fifty-two-horse team from Nineteenth Street and the East River to the site.

An essential element of Beaux-Arts design is that the outside of a building reveals what is within. Charles Garnier, one of the first employers of Beaux-Arts style, explained that Beaux-Arts had "a great first principle, a principle of reason and truth. It is the requisite: the exterior mass, the composition of the outside, indicate the interior plane, the composition of the inside." The Beaux-Arts facade incorporated a monumental statuary group of Mercury, Hercules, and Minerva ranged around the exterior clock on the Forty-Second Street side of the terminal.

The sculptor chosen to execute the statues for the south facade, Jules Alexis Coulan of Paris, held the coveted position of professor at the École des Beaux-Arts. Whitney Warren had studied with Coulan while in Paris. William K. Vanderbilt played a role in selecting Mercury as the personage to crown the building's south facade. He knew his mythology; after all, he had directed Richard Morris Hunt to adorn the doors of his Newport mansion with Apollo. One cannot mistake these Beaux-Arts buildings for anything else; their exterior language speaks clearly. The railroad described Transportation, the sixty-foot-wide, fifty-foot-tall sculpture, considered at the time the world's largest sculptured group, as representing "Progress, Mental and Physical Force," with Hercules embodying physical strength, the reclining Minerva wisdom and the arts, and Mercury, wearing a winged helmet and protected by a vigilant American eagle, science and commerce as the messenger of the gods.

Warren's monumental treatment, with its triumphal arches facing south down Park Avenue, created the grand entryway that, he wrote, every great city deserved. His original elevation for Grand Central includes three grand arches flanked by paired columns, suggesting the arched gateways to the city of Paris, topped by a large sculpture consisting of figures from the ancient myths. Warren continued, in a 1913 *New York Sun* interview, "It is expected that the exterior shell Façade and sectional views of the 42nd Street side of Warren's building appeal to the average citizen, that in its shape and in the composition of lights and shadows which give it its character—lights and shadows formed by cornices and pilasters, not to mention windows and doors—there shall be something that will have that quality which the public understands as architectural beauty."

Grand Central was finished in Belstone and Stoney Creek granite. If one can delineate a "front" to this complex and multifaceted structure, it would have to be the magnificent Forty-Second Street facade where three arched windows, sixty feet tall and thirty-three feet wide, faced south to take in the sun most of the day. Mimicking monumental porticos in classical architecture, these windows were bracketed by enormous Ionic pilasters. The exterior exhibited restrained ornamentation and the minimal use of sculpture. However, an enormous statuary and giant, ornate clock—thirteen feet in diameter—sat above the central portico window. As the Roman god of travel, commerce, and eloquence, and a conductor of travelers, Mercury was a particularly appropriate choice to preside over Grand Central Terminal and its patrons.

Revenue and Reputation

Wilgus had assumed that the income from the trains would be insufficient to finance the new terminal. What he proposed was dramatic and had never been done before. He stated somewhat dramatically: "Thus from the air would be taken wealth with which to finance obligatory vast changes otherwise nonproductive. Obviously it was the right thing to do." The "air rights" were the proposed fifteen-story office building over the 200,000 square feet of surface area then occupied by the old terminal building and train shed. Wilgus projected rental income of $1,350,000 a year, representing a 3.5 percent return on "all of the Grand Central Station terminal changes, including those for depression of the tracks, yard improvements, etc.," including electrification.

The lower cost of Wilgus's and Reed & Stem's design was one of its appeals to the New Haven Railroad. The joint committee estimated that with its twelve-story revenue-generating building (constructed north of the terminal), it would cost $36,194,000, leaving the New Haven's share of the financing at $281,170 per year. By comparison, Warren's monumental building, estimated to cost $42 million to build, would require the New Haven to contribute $382,042 a year. Warren's plan increased the New

Haven's share by $100,000 a year, an increase of 36 percent over the Reed & Stem plan. For Grand Central, yearly costs equaled 80 percent of the New York Central and New Haven Railroads' combined gross from passenger revenue to and from New York. Building and operating these monumental terminals strained even the wealth of the mighty Central and Pennsylvania systems.

At the time, *Munsey's Magazine* recognized the new Grand Central as

> The Greatest Railroad Terminal in the World.... similar enterprise was ever undertaken on so gigantic a scale, or in the face of such conditions.... On the site of the old terminal, which could not be abandoned... promises to be the most successful combination of the esthetic and the practical in city building yet planned in America. ... You will find that it is much more than a railroad station. It will be a new city center; a vast theater of great events; another triumph of constructive American achievement.

Contemplating a plaster model of the sculpture in his office, Warren was later quoted in the *New York Sun*, on February 2, 1913: "While the ancients entered cities through triumphal gates that punctuated mighty fortifications, in New York and other cities of to-day has no wall surrounding that may serve by elaboration as a pretext to such glorification, but none the less the gateway must exist, and in the case of New York and other cities it is through a tunnel which discharges the human flow into the very center of the town. Such is the Grand Central Terminal."

Later observers were just as effusive. Anthony W. Robins, whose podcast on New York life is widely heard, concluded, "Its monumental proportions, sublime style, and clever architectural plan were an immediate sensation. It was the latest shining jewel in New York's gilded crown, symbolizing the optimism and progressive attitude of the time. Grand Central was truly electrifying and it satisfied the need for a glamorous gateway to America's foremost metropolis." John Droege, an expert on trains and terminals, praised the new Grand Central as a great civic center: "The Grand Central Terminal is not only a station; it is a monument, a civic center or, if one will, a city. Without exception, that part of it which is the station is not only the greatest head station in the United States but the greatest station of any type not only on this continent but in the world." The architectural historian Francis Morrone wrote, "As the historian Paul Johnson reminds us . . . so-called robber barons such as the Vanderbilts, ruthless though they undoubtedly were, not only left magnificent monuments in their wake but also created the vast national enterprises into which the teeming multitudes of immigrants were absorbed and uplifted by the engine of prosperity. To deny that this is what New York, in its essence, is about is to posit a fantasy city."

Was the beauty and the convenience worth the cost? An article in *Railway Age Gazette* in 1913 pointed to the extraordinary capital costs of both Grand Central Terminal and Pennsylvania Station: "The new passenger terminal facilities of the New York Central in New York City will probably cost $200,000,000 when completed. This sum would build 2,000 miles of double track road at $100,000 a mile. The fixed charges, taxes and depreciation will amount to nearly $20,000,000 per annum." Robert A. M. Stem, Gregory Gilmartin, and John Massengale observed that the effort to establish a New York civic identity akin to that of Paris or Vienna failed because it materialized both too early and too late: "Too late, because by 1907 the great urban set pieces were in place or well under way: the public library, Grand Central and Pennsylvania stations, and the development of an 'acropolis of learning' on Morningside Heights. Too early, because the grand scale of the parks, parkways and boulevards would not seem urgently needed until the automobile became an everyday thing 30 years later."

The First Grand Central Terminal Lawsuit

The terminal was completed in 1913, but the viaduct was not finished until 1919, and the elevated structure was then credited in the architectural press solely to Warren & Wetmore. Indeed, the quasi-partnership of the two firms would be fraught with dissension, design changes, and acrimony and would climax two decades later in a spectacular lawsuit and an appropriately monumental settlement. In 1921 a referee appointed by the New York Supreme Court found that Warren's accounting was "improper and erroneous" and awarded Stem, the surviving partner, the fantastic sum of $223,891.16—in effect validating Warren's maxim that "the standard of success in this country is the making of money, therefore, the architect should make money and be considered successful."

According to Kurt C. Schlichting, who studied the case, Whitney Warren was referring to a slight of hand by the railroad company, adding a clause to the original contract that allowed the Central to cancel the contract with Reed & Stem should one of them die. Charles Reed died in 1911, and the railroad contracted with Warren & Wetmore to complete all design work solely. Charles Wetmore, Warren's partner, engineered the underhanded deal with New York Central's president William H. Newman as they returned to New York in Newman's private railroad car after attending Reed's funeral in Scarsdale, New York. In effect, Warren & Wetmore, with Reed hardly cold in his grave, conspired with the railroad to take over all design work for the Grand Central project.

Penn Station

As its terminal's construction progressed, the New York Central was keeping one very wary eye on what was happening across town. Its archrival, the Pennsylvania Railroad, was challenging the Central's monopoly by finally providing direct service to Manhattan. In the nineteenth century, the PRR was an also-ran in New York City, although it was the wealthiest American corporation. At its peak the railroad operated more than ten thousand route miles, with total track miles at a staggering twenty-eight thousand, and was described by *Fortune* magazine as "a nation unto itself." The Pennsylvania Railroad billed itself, without much hyperbole, as "The Standard Railroad of the World." From its four-track "Broad Way," through Pennsylvania, main line to its hundreds of standardized, home-built steam locomotives and monumental 1930s electrification, the Pennsy was, for decades, America's largest railroad, and the Pennsy, consequently, did things in a big way.

To reach New York, Pennsylvania Railroad passengers rode to a large terminal on the New Jersey shore called Exchange Place and then transferred to ferries, which brought them across the river. The ferry ride was anything but glamorous, and in the winter it was downright unpleasant. In addition to its vast rail yards in New Jersey, the Pennsylvania had to lease eight piers on the Hudson River and one on the East River. The railroad operated a virtual navy to provide freight service around the port of New York: 27 passenger and freight steamboats,

55 tugboats, 124 car floats, 226 barges, and a motley collection of other barges and scows.

All of this maritime equipment cost a small fortune to acquire and operate. The Baltimore & Ohio (B&O), Erie, Lehigh Valley, Philadelphia & Reading (Reading), and Delaware, Lackawanna & Western (DL&W) maintained similar facilities and equipment at the western shore of the Hudson, although not on the same scale as the Pennsylvania Railroad. In addition to their fleets of ferries, tugboats, car floats, and barges they employed a small army of railroad workers to operate the maritime equipment day and night throughout the year, adding to the overall cost of handling freight. These costs only magnified the advantage enjoyed by the New York Central & Hudson River Railroad because of its direct freight service onto Manhattan Island.

In 1899 Alexander Cassatt, brother of the painter Mary Cassett, became president of the PRR and quickly exerted his new authority toward realizing his goal of a terminal in New York City. It was his dream to build a new railroad structure that would dwarf any terminal that had been constructed in the United States. But the problem of how to get his trains to Manhattan still had to be solved. The Hudson River was a mile wide from the various railroad terminals in New Jersey, and it was one of the busiest waterways in the world. No bridge or tunnel had ever been conceived on such a large scale. A Union Bridge idea was floated by the Pennsy, but the other railroads did not want to pay for a joint line and station.

In 1901 Cassatt was in Paris visiting his sister Mary, and went to the recently opened Gare d'Orsay. There he witnessed firsthand the advantages of using electric locomotives rather than steam, while experiencing the splendor of one of Europe's finest railway stations. The French had electrified a short section of railroad, allowing trains to pass through a tunnel directly into the station. There was no separate shed; the station and platforms were a single, integrated facility. These electric trains were notably quieter and cleaner than steam-powered trains. Much later, the train station would be home to an art museum that featured many of his sister's paintings.

Cassatt saw the Gare d'Orsay as the prototype for a New York Pennsylvania Station and a possible tunnel route under the Hudson. He hired his friend Charles McKim, one of America's foremost architects of the French Beaux-Arts school, to design the station, and he set

Pennsylvania Railroad's engineers to work on a complex network of tunnels that would connect New Jersey, Manhattan, and Long Island, and on a bridge from Manhattan to the Bronx on the mainland, which would allow service to New England. Pennsylvania Station was not to be a stub-end terminal like Grand Central, but a magnificent through station. To this end, in 1900 the PRR acquired the Long Island Rail Road (LIRR) for $6 million, part of Cassatt's long-range plan to provide efficient commuter service throughout New York and to connect Manhattan with Long Island and New England.

Technical considerations forced the company to build the station away from the center of activity in midtown Manhattan. Cassatt originally wanted the massive terminal on the east side of Fourth Avenue in the heart of the city, right on the first subway route—for what more suitable place could there be for a civic vestibule to the world metropolis? But when Cassatt sought advice on the location of the station from local experts Charles M. Jacobs and John V. Davies (the two had previously investigated the possibility of an LIRR tunnel under the East River into Manhattan), he discovered that grades for tunnel approaches to Manhattan would not permit a station anywhere except west of Broadway. This meant that the company would have to locate the station in the Tenderloin district, bounded by Seventh Avenue on the east, Tenth Avenue on the west, West Thirty-Third Street to the north, and West Thirty-First Street to the south. It removed the PRR's great public building from the heart of Manhattan—where it would have awaited the construction of a new subway to link it with the rest of the city. "While Grand Central was intricately interwoven into the city around it, Penn Station stood apart," the urban historian James Sanders has written.

McKim also convinced Cassatt that a skyscraper could never serve as a grand civic structure. As a result, Penn Station included almost no rental space to generate revenue directly; instead, the magnificent station would improve business for the company generally, serving as an appropriate monument to the greatness of both the city and the railroad. Despite its stark grandeur of girders and glass, Penn Station would never become the catalyst for planned development that Grand Central became, and unfortunately, neither Cassatt nor McKim lived to see the palace they had long dreamed of. Cassatt died in 1906, and McKim passed away two years later.

The station would, with the expense of the two sets of tunnels, cost $114 million, or about $2.7 billion in today's dollars. The architects' Beaux-Arts temple conception was inspired in part by public baths built in Rome between AD 212 and 216 by Emperor Caracalla. McKim used the same variety of stone as the Romans had: travertine marble. Enormous Corinthian columns, more than sixty feet high, supported the vaulted ceiling that rose to a height of 150 feet. The critics' attack on such halls is typified by Harvard School of Design dean Joseph Hudnuf's comment: "Architecture at the time existed 'for its own sake' or at the most as an ornament applied to civilization.... So judicious a creature as the Pennsylvania Railroad could heavily increase its corporate debt in order to hide the steel roofs of its stations under the vaults of Caracalla."

The Seventh Avenue facade featured a row of immense Doric columns, and sculpted beautiful maidens representing day and night decorated the main waiting room. The building was designed with multiple entrances and large, wide corridors to allow for a smooth flow of traffic. In the Beaux-Arts tradition, McKim built the great station to be functional as well as beautiful. Penn Station would in turn influence railroad terminal architecture across the United States and Canada for more than two decades. "The breathtaking pink-granite-colonnaded station—a great Doric temple to transportation," as historian Jill Jonnes called it, featured a thirty-five-foot-tall main entrance colonnade facing Seventh Avenue.

Passengers entering there traversed a 225-foot-long retail arcade before arriving at the station's main waiting room, a cavernous 277-by-103-foot, 150-foot high space touted at its debut, true or not, as the world's largest room. In the event that this area was not large enough, additional men's and women's waiting rooms—each measuring 100 by 58 feet—were located just beyond. A similarly sized restaurant and lunchroom were to be found on the opposite side of the main waiting room. Ticketing and baggage-checking facilities were also located in the main waiting room. As was the case with the rest of the structure, Pennsylvania Station's concourse was built directly over the tracks—a circumstance made possible by the trains' state-mandated electrification.

Contemporary newspaper reports marveled that the concourse could comfortably hold ten thousand people. This glass-roofed, two-level steel lattice-and-stone enclosure measured 341 feet wide and 210 feet long, and provided stairway access to the twenty-one platform tracks below. Architecture historian Fiske Kimball would later describe the practical functions of the "soaring, musical spaces" of the station's waiting room as insignificant": "It is conceived, rather," he affirmed, "in accordance with its higher, ideal function—as a civic vestibule to the world metropolis."

New York's Pennsylvania Station could not compare to Grand Central in magnitude, however. Penn Station and its yards spanned twenty-eight acres. Grand Central covered seventy. Penn Station had sixteen miles of rails that converged into twenty-one tracks serving eleven platforms. The comparable figures for Grand Central originally were thirty-two miles, forty-six tracks, and thirty platforms. Between 1898 and 1906, the PRR invested nearly $400 million in its various projects, including $180 million in new stocks, $104 million in long-term borrowing, and $92 million of retained earnings (capital remaining after paying fixed charges and stock dividends). Still, by drawing on the financial strength of the entire PRR system, company officials carried out their mammoth plans for Greater New York. Penn Central would become one of the city's most influential private corporate agencies in New York City.

More Politics as Usual

For the city's political leaders, franchises and licenses were long objects of intense lobbying. In addition, there were legitimate local issues that could have been raised about massive corporate projects like Penn Station and the Hudson River tunnels. Nevertheless, even the most partisan city political institutions would have to find ways to cooperate with private companies to address the multilayered transportation planning challenges facing the consolidated city after 1898. Although PRR officials worked out much of their New York improvements scheme privately, the success of their plans rested heavily on the cooperation of city officials.

Equally telling for the PRR's prospects were issues not raised in the partisan arena. Creating the monumental Penn Station involved the same sort of urban redevelopment that would draw such criticism in the post-1950s urban renewal era. Construction began with "house-wrecking on a grand scale": "Tenements four and five stories high densely inhabited with Italians covered the property chosen as the station site." Between

Ninth and Tenth Avenues, ninety-four buildings stood in the way of the proposed terminal.

In the case of the Church of Saint Michael at Ninth and Thirty-First Street, the PRR agreed to build a new church, rectory, convent, and school at another location. Often times, however, the company encountered recalcitrant owners whom it did not treat as generously as Saint Michael's. In such cases, the PRR instituted "condemnation proceedings," and the city marshal forcibly removed the tenants. The neighborhood was notably Black, and many moved north to Harlem in the years after construction. Fortunately for Cassatt's plans, public debate never focused on the issue of the location of the station or any other specific feature of the PRR's plans for building in the city.

Finally the PRR network of tunnels, stations, bridges, and rail lines through New Jersey, Manhattan, Brooklyn, Queens, and the Bronx could begin. Many "firsts" in tunnel construction for the PRR were a source of both amusement and prestige in the engineering community. Engineers at the PRR even went to the trouble of lowering an automobile into their tunnels in order to be the first group to motor under the Hudson, nearly twenty years before the Holland Tunnel opened to cars. The tunnels extended five and one-half miles, through solid rock at Bergen Hill, through sand, rock, and gravel in New Jersey, and through Hudson River silt, underneath Manhattan Island and the East River, to Queens. These massive tunnels could move up to 144 trains per hour from the mainline of the PRR in New Jersey through Penn Station in Midtown to Long Island.

The Reimagined Cityscape

The architects of the two terminals changed the railroad's place in the city. The horizontal landscape around the terminals reimagined stations as grand monuments at the heart of a new metropolitan civic center. The resulting complex—huge construction projects that took decades to complete—brought the city not just the terminal, but an entire new neighborhood. In particular, Grand Central emerged as the transportation hub for fashionable Midtown: numerous streetcar lines converged at Forty-Second Street, and the IRT, the city's subway, built a major station underground adjacent to the terminal. Adding to the transportation mix, the Third Avenue elevated railway's spur above Forty-Second Street stopped at Grand Central's front door.

The reimagined cityscape was vertical as well as horizontal. Wilgus and Cassatt recognized the magnitude of the building costs and proposed that the space above these yards, once they had been completed—the air rights—be sold to developers. Wilgus insisted that Grand Central's footprint allow for an office building atop the terminal. Space could then be rented out to pay for its capital outlay for electrification and construction. For the 1901–1902 fiscal year, revenue of the New York Central, from all its vast railroad operations stretching from New York to Chicago and St. Louis, totaled $61 million. By developing just a small portion of the railroad's vertical acreage in the city, the railroad stood to gain almost $1.3 million in additional profit (for just one potential office building).

Potentially, the New York Central's property at Forty-Second Street represented a tremendous real estate asset, once the air rights development got underway. In a lengthy article published in *Transactions*, the journal of the American Society of Civil Engineers, in 1940, Wilgus recalled, "I had sketched one day in 1902 an annex of office buildings." It explained his "concept of an Entirely New Terminal Utilizing Air Rights." He described how, dissatisfied with the other proposals for expansion, he had wondered if the best solution might not be to "tear down the old building and train shed and in their place, and in the yard on the north, create a double-level, under-surface terminal on which to superimpose office quarters and revenue producing structures made possible by the intended use of electric power. . . . Thus from the air would be taken wealth." An article in *Railway Age* observed that the Grand Central project "introduced in our system of railroad economics the conception of a new value of railroad property; namely, that of air rights over railroad tracks and new facilities."

Hugh Thompson, writing in *Munsey's Magazine*, defined precisely what air rights involved and explained their potential value: "Air rights simply mean the right to build over ground you own. Most people do not stop to consider that ordinarily there are three rights in the ownership of property—the ground right, giving possession of the surface; the lower right, giving power to excavate or mine; and the upper right or air right. . . . The air rights will doubtless prove immensely valuable." Indeed, as time proved, much of the city's commercial enterprises moved north to be in close proximity to the terminal.

In this era of railroading, no one expected the real estate revenues to surpass the railroad income. As Joshua D'Esposito, writing a *Railway Age* article on air rights, explained, real estate development should remain a sideline for railroads: "It is important to keep in mind one cardinal principle: that the railroad needs are always paramount, and the air rights incidentals. After all, the principal duty of a railroad is to manufacture and sell transportation, and every other activity should be subordinated to this primary requirement." Nevertheless, *The New York Times* reminded its readers that the new depot would always be "more than a gateway, more than a terminal. The terminal proper, the great head house, and its accompanying buildings, are simply the heart and the cause of a group of buildings that has best been described as a terminal city."

In December 1912, a month before the new terminal opened, the first solid hint that a tower might be in the future appeared. *Outlook* magazine printed a revised rendering of the concourse interior, without any east stairway. But no journal reported directly on the failure to build the tower. Wilgus's 1940 memoir said only that it "fell by the wayside" and might still be built. Perhaps the railroad was preoccupied with the continued stream of new hotels, apartment houses, and office buildings that went up in the 1910s and 1920s north of the terminal on Park Avenue. By 1914 the assessed valuation of properties bounded by Forty-First and Fifty-Seventh Streets and Lexington and Madison Avenues had more than doubled, from $55 million when construction on Grand Central began, to $117 million. A decade later, it would more than double again. By 1946, a peak year for long-haul passenger train traffic, the New York Central had a stake in twenty-one buildings, whose assessed value was more than $121 million.

The "Terminal City" that resulted from the air rights plan was destined to be transformed within a decade into some of the most valuable real estate in the world. As well, it was an unlikely showcase for the flourishing City Beautiful movement that had remade Philadelphia, Washington, DC, and other urban centers. Wilgus envisioned a civic center, opera house, hotels, and office buildings lining a grand boulevard—a planned, harmonious city to replace the obstructive terminal and the chasm occupied by tracks and trains that were the logical extensions of an architecturally illogical city. "The changes which are to come about within a comparatively short time will entirely alter the complexion of the city," Mayor Seth Low said in 1903. The architects even envisioned an extraordinary "Court of Honor"—a fantasy of columned palaces flanking a broad central plaza and ceremonial roadway approaching the terminal—reminiscent of the Court of Honor at the World's Columbian Exposition in Chicago that had given birth to the City Beautiful movement ten years earlier.

By the 1920s the terminal city was becoming a reality, just not on top of either station. World-class hotels—the Biltmore, the Commodore, the Roosevelt—and office buildings—the Graybar and the New York Central building—rose around the terminal. In addition, the air rights included special-purpose buildings—Grand Central Palace, the Yale Club, and the US Post Office—and stately rows of apartment buildings of the highest class along Park and Lexington Avenues as far north as Fiftieth Street and along Madison Avenue and Vanderbilt Avenue as far north as Forty-Eighth Street and Forty-Ninth Street, respectively. Wilgus concluded, "The Grand Central Zone has become a self-contained city clearly evident to the casual onlooker."

The 1920s were good years for Manhattan real estate. Office space was in demand, and accessibility to a work force was crucial. Businesses long identified with downtown were moving north, particularly to the area increasingly referred to as the Grand Central Zone. In September 1920, *The New York Times* announced, "One of the outstanding features of the real estate market has been the pronounced buying and leasing movement in the Forty-second Street section, which has resulted in a new banking center, a 'Little Wall Street.'" So desirable was a midtown location among bankers that the Manhattan Hotel of 1896 on Madison at Forty-Second Street was converted into the uptown branch offices of National City Bank in 1921. *Buildings and Building Management* magazine reported in 1920 that a hundred millionaires lived at 270 Park Avenue. Named for the founders of the Western Electric Company, designed like a Jazz Age ziggurat and home to corporate giants like Remington Rand and Conde Nast, the Graybar Building over Grand Central Terminal was once the largest office tower in the world. The Chrysler Building provided another example of Grand Central's stimulus. Designed by William Van Alen, a graduate of the École des Beaux-Arts, and built on the east side of Lexington Avenue at Forty-Second Street directly across from Grand Central, the Chrysler Building stood as the tallest building in the world until the completion of the Empire State Building in 1931. The Chrysler Building dramatically increased the commercial space available at Forty-Second Street and added thousands of jobs—and commuters—to the Grand Central district.

Because of the real estate activity around its base, atop the terminal's forty-eight acres sat some of the richest real estate and the most prestigious addresses in the world. Its construction established the legal principle of air rights, which created an ephemeral commodity worth billions of dollars today. Together, the total investment in the first two phases of the air rights development around Grand Central reached nearly $85 million. Never before in the history of New York had a single development led to the investment of such enormous sums in such a brief period of time, representing a massive commitment to the future of the midtown business and residential district.

It was this idea—the use of air rights above the terminal—that would infuse Penn Central's plans for high-rise office buildings. In turn, its plans would directly confront a new movement in city planning: preservation.

CHAPTER THREE

The Terminal in Post–World War II New York City

Fifty years after the Grand Central Terminal's construction, railroad historian Carol L. V. Meeks found it still an amazing structure, but "the situation has changed, and today operating costs are proving a heavy burden. As a result, the great concourse may soon be torn down to make way for more profitable office buildings, thus destroying one of the finest interior spaces ever erected." The dramatic reversal of fortunes for Grand Central Terminal and the New York Central Railroad in the post–World War II era could be a book in itself. On the one hand, "Terminal City" and the Midtown East office market had become extremely popular and valuable due to the presence of the still-useful suburban commuter rail lines and the new zoning code that enabled more development. On the other hand, formerly lucrative long-distance rail traffic, both passenger and freight, faced increasing competition from trucks, cars, and airplanes.

With competition from automotive travel diminishing passenger revenue, in 1938 the New York Central and Pennsylvania Railroads each introduced new streamliners. Rather than relegate their once-premier trains to secondary status in favor of all-new, flashy streamlined trains, as had the Union Pacific, Burlington, and other western lines, the NYCRR and Pennsy worked with Pullman to design Twentieth Century Limited and Broadway Limited cars. During the era of the streamliner, the New York Central referred to its parade of intercity passenger trains—most of which operated between Grand Central and the Midwest—as the "Great Steel Fleet." The line also served numerous suburban schedules and a raft of intercity runs belonging to the New Haven Railroad.

But the automobile and the highways' supremacy over passenger rail lines could not be sidelined by the introduction of the new passenger fleet. What had begun as a local recreational auto and parkway boom in the 1920s had morphed in the 1930s into a free federal highway system. After World War II the government-subsidized road system was hurting the private railroads. By the early 1950s, as urban growth spawned the suburbs and exurbs, the NYCRR claimed that it cost $24 million more to maintain Grand Central Terminal than it realized in income. The Eisenhower administration made things worse for the railroads in 1956, when the president signed the Interstate Highway Act. A vast limited-access highway system, funded initially on the premise that it was a necessary component of national defense, crisscrossed the country. The aircraft industry, using the research and production resources it had developed during the war, grew at a rate that eclipsed even the auto and truck industry.

The birth of suburban America was not a spontaneous occurrence but rather the result of deliberate federal government policies. G.I. loans and mortgages, unavailable for apartments, fueled the postwar suburban housing boom. Low-density suburbs rapidly took shape on the outskirts of older cities, beyond the reach of the prewar suburban rail systems. The railroads were unable to provide the same regular, affordable, and convenient service to these far-flung, sprawling bedroom communities without massive infusions of new capital—which the railroad companies did not possess and the government was not about to provide. Government had chosen instead to support the newer forms of transportation: automobiles, trucks, and airplanes.

Air Rights and Wrongs

In New York City's first zoning law of 1916, based on a projected ultimate urban population of sixty-six million people, no limit had been set on building heights on many properties in business districts, only on wedding-cake-like setbacks, basically taller narrower buildings to allow light and air to reach the street level. The original air rights buildings along Park Avenue, from Forty-Fifth to Fifty-Second Streets, stood only eight or nine stories. With the lack of office space following the war, the Central quickly realized that the construction of new, taller buildings would generate significant additional revenue. The first came in 1947, when an office building was completed at Fifty-Seventh Street and Park

Avenue. The typical height of towers built in the 1950s was then thirty to forty stories. The character of Park Avenue just north of Forty-Fifth Street changed from residential to commercial. A number of commercial buildings had been constructed as part of Terminal City, but on Park Avenue from Forty-Fifth to Fifty-First Streets, the original air rights buildings consisted largely of hotels and apartments. Meanwhile, the Grand Central Palace on Lexington Avenue between Forty-Sixth and Forty-Seventh Streets, the city's premier exhibition hall, was razed, to be replaced by a forty-seven-story office building.

The keys to redevelopment were all available: single owners or lessees, obviating costly and time-consuming negotiations to assemble sites; sufficiently large properties, affording ready development; and, usually, land owned by the railroad, whose cooperation would be needed in those cases where the new giants were to be built while trains continued to operate. The result of all this was an almost complete remake of Park Avenue from Forty-Sixth to Fifty-Ninth Streets. For example, in 1957 the Montana Apartments, at twelve stories, became Seagram's House, at forty stories. The "C and T" in the name engraved on the thirty-four-story New York Central Building at 230 Park Avenue, the railroad's sublime and historic gem of a headquarters since 1929, were ignominiously chiseled into a "G and E" when the building was sold to General Tire & Rubber.

In 1951, despite its elegance and popularity, the Hotel Belmont came down. Its owners decided that its site alongside the new Lincoln Building, the latter assessed at over $20 million, was simply too valuable to use for a hotel. Historian Allen Nevins commented in 1957 that "the fame of Park Avenue is so great that it has generally been forgotten how recent it is." Neither the quality of the architecture, the prestige addresses, nor public opposition stopped developers from removing from Park Avenue's frontages the refined structures that the electrification of Grand Central Terminal had made possible only twenty years earlier.

A new zoning law in 1960 was devised to serve a smaller conceptual population of 12.3 million; nonetheless, it made the conflict between low landmarks and high development still worse. Not only was it no longer required that tall structures adhere to the street walls of the city's rectangular grid, but the new regulations encouraged such deviations. In fact, they made it more profitable to build skyscrapers that were set back in plazas, inside property lines, and at greater average height and bulk, removing them from street life. After the change in zoning, buildings of fifty to sixty stories proliferated. The abandoning compliance with the street wall, the simple system of architectural organization that had aesthetically married the buildings of cities for more than a thousand years, was eliminated.

At the same time, the increased interior construction costs and new minimal aesthetics of modernism led to less investment by builders in the exteriors of contemporary buildings. In 1960 the Hotel Marguery, at twelve stories (on land owned by the New York Central), became the Union Carbide Building, at fifty-two. In 1964 the apartments at 277 Park, at twelve stories, became Chemical Bank, at fifty stories. And so on, until the fashionable residential enclave in the heart of midtown Manhattan's business district itself became Midtown's fashionable business district. "Extensive amounts of tin can architecture became the norm in a cityscape randomly fractured by large structures that ignored the existing urban geometry," later argued the P. W. Grosser Consulting firm, in its engineering report on the site.

By the end of the 1960s, new construction replaced almost all of the original Beaux-Arts and Art Deco–style structures of Terminal City. All of the new office towers built over New York Central's air rights were blockish and bland. "Modern glass-curtain skyscrapers replaced the classical facades' harmony of design. An air of inevitability accompanied the change, which encountered only modest public opposition from architectural traditionalists and preservationists and from those alarmed by the heedless pace of the change," historian Kurt C. Schlichting would write.

The only significant remnant of the pre-1950s era was the New York Central's own office building, dating from 1929, which spanned Park Avenue between Forty-Fifth and Forty-Sixth Streets and contained the portals to the circumferential drive around the terminal. But gradually Park Avenue became one road among many, and the viaduct's prominence diminished. A gritty sameness settled over Midtown, especially as International-style architecture seemed to force all older structures into one undifferentiated lump. The Central building's distinctive silhouette gave Park Avenue what little composure remained. That composure was not to last for long.

From Railroad to Real Estate Company

By the 1950s the glory days of the passenger train were gone. Grand Central Terminal no longer had sixty-three million people passing through its doors as it did throughout the 1940s. The decline was irreversible. As Robert R. Young, the Central's chairman, observed, "Pigs huddled in the bowels of freight cars could cross the country without changing trains, but passengers could not." By 1954 the Central was sending only eighteen long-distance trains weekdays from Grand Central to upstate and the West, compared with thirty-two in 1947.

The train passenger could not miss the declining prestige of long-distance rail travel. Lee Stringer, the author of *Grand Central Winter: Stories from the Street*, wrote in 1998 that the porters, with their "Red Caps," and conductors had "all treated us like first class passengers, though we were traveling the equivalent of steerage." But facts were facts: the Central's passenger revenues plummeted from $135.5 million in 1948 to $106.5 million in 1954 and a mere $55 million a decade later. "I live in the twilight of railroading, the going down of its sun," E. B. White wrote in 1960. "For the past few months I've been well aware that I am the Unwanted Passenger, one of the last survivors." Then, the famed Central Twentieth Century Limited made its final run, a graceful descent of threadbare elegance. It was slower and nearly as expensive as an airplane (one-way by coach, the cheapest ticket, cost $43.26, compared to $43.70 by plane), and sleeping accommodations were costlier. On some nights, the eighty-man train crew outnumbered the passengers. On December 2, 1967, just a month after the *Queen Mary*'s final voyage, the Century left Grand Central for the last time. It departed precisely on time, at 6 p.m., from Track 34; the train was only half-full, carrying 104 passengers.

Based on its continued loss of income, the New York Central Railroad concluded that Grand Central Terminal was a waste of space and that modern skyscrapers should be built over the site. NYCRR's president, Alfred E. Perlman, threatened to shutter Grand Central altogether and leave passengers to fend for themselves on public transportation from the Bronx or Westchester.

The Central was not alone in this predicament. The Pennsylvania Railroad was in a similarly dire situation. Real estate ventures like Penn

Plaza bought time for the railroad, but they were insufficient to cover mounting costs and diminishing revenue. In the 1960s the Long Island Rail Road, which the Pennsylvania had controlled since 1900, was sold for $65 million. New York State, the new owner, would buy or lease Penn Station's tracks and pay them to operate its commuter trains. A similar arrangement would produce Metro-North for Grand Central Terminal. Such retrenchment seemed financially inevitable. The railroad recommended the cancellation of all nine predawn passenger trains (only a decade before, in 1950, there were thirty), sending musicians, bartenders, printers, and other graveyard-shift workers scurrying to find alternative routes home. *The New York Times* recalled, "Overnight, the Gateway to a Continent devolved into a gateway to six counties in two states."

A station for commuter trains was not the same as a terminal for long-distance Limiteds. Station space needs were different, and people using the terminal behaved differently. Commuters rush though stations on their way elsewhere and just need direct access to trains. Commuter travel is a burden at best and agony at worst when expeditious travel within the station is most important. By contrast, passengers who traveled long distances arrived at the terminal with baggage and had looked forward to their experience in the terminal as part of their travel, appreciating the grand waiting rooms, restaurants, and baggage areas. Grand Central was designed to handle as many as a hundred million such passengers per year. With the dying of the long-distance passenger trains, the terminal seemed weary and dilapidated.

Penn Central's management was watching. So were other eyes. "We carefully weighed our own pride in the present building," wrote Alfred Fellheimer, a New York City architect, in defense of replacing Grand Central Terminal, finances trumping whatever its emotional and esthetic significance might be. "Our reluctant but firm conclusion is that neither pride nor reverence should be permitted to clot the vitality of a great metropolis. In turn, that very vitality may guarantee that if one expression of human aspiration must be destroyed in the process of growth, it will be replaced by an even greater one."

Where once the limited passenger rails were paragons of comfort, progress, and profit, the leaders of the Grand Central concluded that Americans of the next generation would only move around in cars and planes. The terminal looked as if it agreed. "The Grand Central

Terminal," reported *The New York Times* in 1954, "looks as though it were built for the ages, but people probably felt the same way about the Grand Central Depot that it replaced. Apparently, we begin to get restless about these buildings every forty years or so."

Advertisements

Still, hungry advertisers and developers had long wanted a piece of the terminal. In response, the railroad commercialized the terminal by monetizing every space it could. In 1949 the railroad experimented with daily canned broadcasts from more than forty loudspeakers accompanied by 240 commercials over seventeen hours. These netted the railroad $1,800 a week, against what it said was then an $11 million annual deficit to operate the terminal. In 1950 Grand Central leased the grand concourse's east balcony to Eastman Kodak. Kodak installed a mock photo lab. "We've had our eyes on this balcony for some time," a Kodak exec said gleefully at the time. A thirteen-and-a-half-foot-diameter replica of the Westclox Big Ben clock over the south concourse was another money maker. A thirty-foot-diameter clock advertising *Newsweek* was suspended above the ramp linking the waiting room and the main concourse, just a few short steps from the jewel-like clock atop the information booth. Merrill Lynch erected an informational booth with a large ticker-tape display in the middle of the public circulation space of the main concourse. The Chrysler Corporation rented space to display its latest automobiles. Fiscal necessity was the mother of these interventions. The grand concourse, though not designed as a giant billboard, was soon draped with billboard displays, second only to Times Square in the mammoth scale of their commercial messages.

Harold Ross, the editor of *The New Yorker*, lampooned the piped-in advertisements in his magazine, and James L. Fly, a former chairman of the Federal Communications Commission, declared that "the forced feeding of advertising" destroyed a listener's right not to listen. Harold J. Harris, a psychiatrist, cautioned that the noise pollution could unleash behavior triggered by "suppressed rage." Passenger Virginia L. Rowland warned of even more dire consequences. "It is not too fantastic," she testified, "that one of those employed in the terminal might go berserk and start shooting up the customers." A month later, the Central gave up and halted the "broadcasts" without apology. The company's advertising displays did not go far enough toward upkeep of the terminal.

Anthony Robins of the New York Transit Museum took a longer view. "What is it that Grand Central, in particular, does for people? It's a question I've been trying to get to the heart of during several decades of writing about the city." He thought about people and spaces, and how they interacted. "In the 1970s, I noticed that when you come up out of the subway and along a low passageway and then into the huge Main Concourse with the painting of the night sky in cerulean blue high above it, your breath stops for an instant. It's like having been preoccupied with your own affairs and suddenly remembering the vast and populous and beautiful world around you." After that he made a point of walking through Grand Central at lunchtime, "since it was a couple of blocks from where I worked. Millions of eyes and every variety of deficient sight had their weight in deciding just what size and what shape letters to use over the train gates." He concluded that "the essence of this, the shining message that Grand Central broadcasts to humanity, is that each moment can be refreshing, fulfilling, inspirational, worthwhile; that even getting to work and going home is something that can add to life's rewards and be looked forward to."

Plainly, Robins had come to love the terminal as a special place, special to him and to New York City. "When you love a building, you come up with very different ideas for it than if you hate it." Case in point: Vanderbilt Hall, a towering, ballroom-size space adjacent to the main concourse, and originally the terminal's main waiting room. In 1960 the New York Central hoped to hasten the terminal's demolition by trivializing this room, inserting Grand Central Bowl, a three-story bowling alley, into the top forty-seven feet between floor and ceiling. The bottom eleven feet, cramped and harshly lighted, would still have been available for travelers. Shoehorned into the 210- by 60-foot space would be a bowling center with forty-four lanes, arena seating for competitions, and a restaurant and bar. Noting the "serious annual deficit" of the terminal, its manager pointed out that in addition to the economic benefit of the proposal, "The entire area will be brightened and air-conditioned. These innovations will indeed add to the comfort of our passengers while providing them with a recreational outlet." The plan was rejected by the city's Board of Standards and Appeals. Because it was located in a restricted retail area, a bowling alley would violate zoning regulations. The railroad's justification (forget the railroaders' love of the sport) was financial. The NYCRR claimed that it faced a $6.75 million deficit to operate the terminal and without income it would grow to $13.5 million in 1959.

Among those who joined in the battle against the proposed bowling alley was Robert Weinberg. Reminding the readers of *The New York Times* that the "misguided" bowling alley proposal would require government approval since such a use was not authorized under the zoning ordinance, he correctly predicted that if the railroad sought such permission, "every civic organization, from the Municipal Art Society to the local taxpayers' groups, will be out in force to argue against it."

Joining Weinberg would be Harmon Goldstone and the Municipal Art Society, the distinguished architect Victor Gruen and the New York Chapter of the American Institute of Architects, the Citizens Union, the Fine Arts Federation, the National Trust for Historic Preservation and other voices decrying the "desecration of a nationally renowned classical building." The controversy also triggered a passionate editorial in *The New York Times*. Characterizing the proposal as "one more step in the disastrous erosion of architectural values that is reducing the heart of this city to a shambles of mediocrity," it marked the editorial debut of the renowned architecture critic Ada Louise Huxtable. Her presence at *The New York Times* would become a deciding factor in helping shift the balance of power in favor of preservation in the public debate over landmark protection.

In January 1961 the Board of Standards and Appeals, the government agency empowered to grant the required zoning variance, denied the application for the bowling alley in a unanimous vote. The vote underlined the dire situation of the terminal as well as other important buildings in the city. Grand Central's waiting room was spared only because the proposed use, bowling, required a variance. Gruen, a leader in the opposition to the bowling center, realized this had only been a "skirmish, not the main battle." Recognizing this, the American Institute of Architects created a special subcommittee, chaired by Gruen, to keep its eye on the vulnerable terminal.

The Skyscraper Terminal

Saying no to bowling did not say yes to preservation. Indeed, the great concourse was starting to look like a shabby suburban mall on the way to desertion. The concourse was saved in 1954, but architecture historian John Belle reported that its "cannibalization" was well underway already. Douglas Haskell, writing in *Progressive Architecture*, was even more suspicious that "filling its once magnificent space with turntables, land-boom selling booths, oversized clocks, and other gimmicks to turn a quick buck, is all meant to offset declining railroad revenues because the owners are railroads." In fact, demolition was visible on the horizon. Hidden behind this woeful declension narrative, however, were various tax benefits (offsetting profits) for obsolescence, a benefit to the owners that was never far from their calculations. Finance, rather than function, had become the driving force behind the company's planning.

In 1954, after many years of his persistence, a stockbroker from Texas named Robert R. Young gained a controlling interest in the New York Central Railroad. Having little success in merging the Central with other railroads due to burdensome regulations, he began to look to the railroad's real estate assets as another source of revenue. New York City's desirable office market seemed attractive, especially since Grand Central Terminal was running a $24 million annual deficit.

Young, now chairman of the board of the NYCRR, working with William Zeckendorf, president of Webb & Knapp, a real estate development company, and renowned architect I. M. Pei, proposed an eighty-story tower to replace Grand Central Terminal. The slick, angular tower had "a circular footprint and, thanks to a taper halfway up the shaft, an hourglass profile." Pei's design included a 2,400-car garage, a heliport, restaurants, and retail—which would keep as many office workers as possible inside, spending as much money as possible. The proposal also included extensive changes to the street patterns, including rebuilding the curving Park Avenue overpass into a straight line. It would be the largest commercial office space in the world. In addition, it would be topped by an observation tower that would boost its height to 1,600 feet, well beyond the (then) record-holding 1,250-foot Empire State Building.

In the eyes of its co-owner, the New York Central Railroad, Grand

Central Terminal had become "a very costly luxury." "World's Loftiest Tower May Rise on Site of Grand Central Terminal," announced a 1954 page-one headline in *The New York Times*. "Blueprints," the accompanying article explained, "call for a structure that would tower over the 102 stories and the television tower of the Empire State Building, the tallest edifice ever built by man." Pei at the time "would fly from city to city persuading mayors to apply for federal funds for slum clearance 'healing the wounds of the city,' in Pei's telling phrase." Pei later admitted that his first priority was to design a modern icon rather than retain the historic terminal.

No plans for this tower were published, and Pei insisted that he had no recollection of the design. This is especially intriguing given the renderings that can be found online. Grand Central's other co-owner at the time, the New Haven Railroad, effectively doomed the idea of the hyperboloid—"Pei's dream," as it's now called—by producing a more modest plan to obliterate the station with something un-grand but cheaper to build: a conventional fifty-story office tower. No crusade sprang forward on behalf of New Yorkers' good fortune, but the proposal, and a subsequent alternative (ironically by a successor firm to the terminal's original architects), generated an outcry among architects. *Architectural Forum* published a letter signed by 220 architects pleading that the terminal's main concourse be spared. Young architect John Belle, Welsh born but already a leader in New York City restoration projects, was one of the first soldiers in the trenches to lead the crusade to save Grand Central.

Despite the negative reception of Pei's tower plan, similar proposals were waiting in the wings. For example, in 1955 Emery Roth & Sons published a design for a tower that did not encroach on the station. Schemes like Roth's and Pei's brought into question whether a monument should be destroyed simply because its owners' tax and revenue problems demanded it. A *New York Times* editorial declared that the terminal "belongs to all America," whatever that meant, and a commuter from South Orange, New Jersey, wrote a letter to the paper "to urge that a real crusade be started to insure the perpetuation of this landmark. Truly the main waiting room is a magnificent one—one that is unique and a source of artistic pleasure to those whose good fortune it is to walk through it."

Preservation Planning

Part of the reason for the public outcry over Pei's tower was that the danger to the terminal was one of an increasing number of threats to prominent and beloved New York City buildings. In the mid-1950s Grand Central Terminal was in immediate peril, but it was not alone. Storm clouds were gathering over Pennsylvania Station, Carnegie Hall, and the Jefferson Market Courthouse. These had a cumulative effect.

The architects who protested against the towers agreed that the central concourse "is probably the finest big room in New York." Responding to the *Architectural Forum*'s plea, the Municipal Art Society decided to take action to publicize the cause. The new co-owners were not moved by these aesthetic arguments. *Harper's Magazine* lamented the general state of affairs: "And now the boys with the sledge hammers and crowbars have a new target; the next proposal is to tear down Grand Central Station, on the grounds that it is uneconomical."

A month before his death in 1963, President John F. Kennedy spoke of the importance of heritage conservation in the United States: "I look forward to an America which will not be afraid of grace and beauty, which will preserve the great old American houses and squares and parks of our national past, and which will build handsome and balanced cities for our future." This collision of competing values—passive vs. active use, aesthetic value vs. economic worth, private benefit vs. public enjoyment—was as fierce then as it can be, at times, today, and nowhere was it fiercer than in New York City.

The outcry against the office building plans rested on the theory that the city's architectural treasures belonged to everyone who visited the city, including those who came through the terminal. For a democratic society whose culture, including most of the television programming of the 1950s, catered to the lowest common denominator, the concourse seemed to inspire something higher. The room was "noble in its proportions, alive in the way the various levels and passages work in and out of it, sturdy and reassuring in its construction, splendid in its materials—but that is just the beginning. Its appeal recognizes no top limit of sophistication, no bottom limit. The most exacting architectural critic agrees in essentials with the newsboy at the door." *The New York Times* added tentatively that "before the plans reach rigid crystallization, there is a chance that public opinion can persuade the heads of these railroads to consider some scheme whereby, without arresting the desirable progress implicit in their project."

Over the years, Grand Central's main concourse had become a kind of public assembly room for the people of New York City. National officials weighed in as well: President Harry S. Truman in 1952 said, "Grand Central is monumental architecture in the very best sense. It is not a huge, forbidding object, awesome but distant. It is deeply connected with the life of the city." "Like other great works of monumental architecture—the Brooklyn Bridge, the New York Public Library, Rockefeller Center—it unites the noble and the ordinary, the sublime and the mundane." Or so *The New York Times* would write decades later.

The editorials, the letters, and the public outcry still did not dissuade the officials of the railroad from seeking to maximize the real estate value of the terminal space. Alfred E. Perlman, chief executive of the New York Central, was upset that the Central was unable to achieve its real estate plans. Neither of the two skyscraper schemes came to fruition. Perlman threatened to end all commuter service into Grand Central and abandon the terminal completely unless New York City mayor Robert Wagner and the state helped him subsidize the rail service.

Within a few weeks, the beleaguered New York Central was again inviting architects to submit plans for a two-million-square-foot building as tall as forty-five stories atop Grand Central's main waiting room. From 1954 to 1958 the New York Central and New Haven Railroads' plans remained just that—plans—as the railroads labored to sustain their operations with no ability to work together on real estate development. In order for a building project of this scale to begin, the two corporate giants had to join forces; they did so in 1958 with an agreement made by Young and McGinnis to use Erwin Wolfson as their developer in the creation of the office space.

Wolfson added famed Bauhaus architect Walter Gropius and Pietro Bellusch, the dean of the MIT architecture and planning school, to his team. Their collaborative design, initially proposed on February 18, 1959, was called Grand Central City: a complex of buildings that would not necessitate the destruction of the terminal. Wolfson quickly expanded the team to include Emery Roth & Sons and made whatever changes were necessary to succeed with the project. In fact the resulting work, completed in 1963 as a fifty-nine-story, 2.4 million-square-foot building (known today as the MetLife Building), did not eliminate the terminal. The concrete-and-glass structure, with its trademark logo and faceted facade, was built against the terminal's northern flank. Gropius brutally welded the tower to the back of the terminal, with four escalators clumsily piercing the concourse. The building was monolithic and stark, an imposition rather than an improvement.

When it opened, the structure was the largest commercial building in the world. More of a sky blocker than a skyscraper, with massive, precast concrete walls of a bland gray that loomed up and down Park Avenue and along Forty-Fourth Street, the tower blocked the sky and overfilled the space. It was never popular. "Gigantically second-rate," judged *The New York Times*. As if to add insult to injury (to the railroad company) the skyscraper became the headquarters of Pan Am Airways. With the airline's gigantic logo on the top of the structure almost mocking train travel below it, the terminal looked even sadder. Ironically the interior of Grand Central Terminal remained intact not because of any design conviction or public pressure, but because James O. Bolisi, vice president of real estate for New York Central, failed to include the terminal building in the air-rights package awarded to Wolfson for development.

Though the facade and the concourse were saved, the once-dramatic Park Avenue vista framed by the three arched windows of the terminal and the delicate Grand Central tower behind was gone. It was now clear that the threat to Grand Central's survival came from what was to be built around and on top of it. The Central owners hoped that an anticipated $1 million in rentals would help stanch its bleeding debt. Instead, the new building touched off a simmering dispute with the New Haven Railroad over who owned the terminal and adjacent property. It also whetted the deficit-ridden Central's appetite to develop even more real estate.

A City in Decline

New York City was declining alongside the terminal, despite the mass construction of office buildings. "The cautious 1950s, the decade of the 'lonely crowd' when people conformed to get ahead, was also the decade when New Yorkers started to fear the once vibrant downtown," Robins would write. The lack of investment outside of Midtown following the Great Depression and war years led to seedy and worn-down businesses filtering into the center of the city. Sex shops and hotels for the homeless appeared among the theaters and restaurants of Midtown. Crime also increased in postwar New York. From a low of 240 murders in the city in 1943, the number had doubled to 482 in 1960 and ballooned over the course of the 1960s to more than 1,100 murders annually—without much of an increase in population. Demolition of neighborhoods for the interstate highways and high-rise low-income housing projects, as well as flight from the city to the suburbs, was diminishing the tax base and leaving behind a city increasingly and visibly poorer.

As Grand Central and the city were struggling, so was public life in America. The demonstration for civil rights in Washington, DC, featuring Martin Luther King Jr.'s "I Have a Dream" speech, was followed by the assassination of President Kennedy. The long-awaited Civil Rights Act of 1964 was followed by rioting by Black citizens against police brutality in major cities. "Long, hot summers" became part of urban life, making worse the decay that had begun to form. Increased racial tensions were one element of the country's social and political climate. The war in Vietnam reached its height between 1966 and 1969; in 1968 domestic opposition to the war reached a new level.

New York City was not immune to the crises. On July 18, 1964, riots broke out in Harlem in protest over the killing of a fifteen-year-old Black male by a white NYPD officer. One person died and a hundred others were injured in the violence. On February 21, 1965, Black Nationalist leader Malcolm X was assassinated in the Audubon Ballroom in Harlem by a member of the Nation of Islam. Part of the crisis the city faced lay in its relationship to municipal union contracts. The municipal workers were unionized, with good middle-class pay and employment in the notoriously expensive city. Relations between union leaders and the city's mayors were not always cordial. For example, on New Year's Eve 1966, the Transport Workers Union of America (TWU), led by Mike Quill, shut down the city—with a complete halt of subway and bus services—over contract negotiations. As New Yorkers endured the transit strike, Mayor John V. Lindsay remarked, "I still think it's a fun city," and walked four miles from his hotel room to City Hall in a publicity stunt. Dick Schaap, then a columnist for the *New York Herald Tribune*, coined and mocked the term in an article titled "Fun City." In the piece, Schaap sardonically pointed out that life in the city was anything but fun. The transit strike was the first of many labor struggles, with unions winning major victories in salaries and benefits that the city could not afford to pay. Other unions took notice, including those for teachers and sanitation workers, both of which took to the picket lines in 1968. The quality of life in New York reached a nadir during the sanitation strike, as mounds of garbage caught fire and strong winds made the stench unbearable. The police engaged in a slowdown, firefighters threatened job actions, and with the city awash in garbage, racial and religious tensions bubbled to the surface. Lindsay later called the last six months of 1968 "the worst of my public life."

The terminal was not spared the protests and crime. One evening in March 1968, a so-called Yip-In was held to promote the Yippies' Festival of Life. "Come to Grand Central at Midnight," the flyers read. When the organizers were asked what the political or tactical reason was for choosing Grand Central, the response was simple: "It's Central, man." An estimated six thousand people filled the main concourse with chants like "Long, Hot Summer" and "Burn, Baby, Burn." Just before 1:00 a.m. some of the crowd began to climb onto the roof of the information booth, striking a "workers arise" fist-in-the-air pose. Two cherry bombs exploded, and someone grabbed the hands off the information clock. "I was standing on the balcony looking down," remembers Clark Whelcon, a former reporter for the *Village Voice*. "When I looked down, I saw this guy holding the hands from the clock and I saw a police officer take a nightstick and knock it on the marble balustrade. You could hear that sound reverberate through the crowd. Suddenly a flying wedge of cops charged into the Concourse. The crowd and the cops went wild. Most of the people being arrested were automatically beaten with nightsticks."

Architect John Belle remembered that the historic preservationists were still determined to save a building that had once been a jewel of city life. It was an uphill battle. A terminal that had not closed its doors in over sixty years was now locked up each night for several hours. The growing population of the homeless, with increasingly fewer options, looked at Grand Central as a refuge. "One day I saw a girl and a fella run in through the entrance near the Waiting Room as if they had entered the front door of their own home," recounted assistant stationmaster Robert L. Smith. "There was something so private about this public display. They were arguing and she kept yelling, get out of my house, this is my house, why don't you go over to Penn Station and live." Decades later *The New York Times* took a long view of the crisis. It was "painfully clear that urban centers [were] not well served by the cultural dichotomy between city and suburb. Their economic viability depends in part on healing that split: on the reintegration of cities with their surrounding regions."

The graying and emptying terminal still retained a hint of its former nobility. Belle recalled: "To step from a train platform into Grand Central's extraordinary concourse, one of the greatest interior spaces of the 20th century, is to feel in every fiber that you have arrived someplace important, to know that you have come into a great city and that that great city has greeted you properly. There may be disappointment ahead, but between the train track and the street there was only glory."

But Belle was philosophical about the prospects for preservation. "Nothing ever gets old around here," he observed. If the political climate of shunning the past prevailed, and the great architectural monuments of previous eras continued to be destroyed, Grand Central would end as a pile of rubble in New Jersey's meadowlands. Kenneth Jackson, Columbia University's prize-winning urban historian, was not hopeful. But in a city that never valued its history as much as Boston or Philadelphia, where relatively sparse prime space is periodically recycled to produce bulkier and taller buildings, there was nevertheless still hope. That hope lay in the framing of a landmark law and giving that law teeth.

CHAPTER FOUR

Landmark Law

The origins of the New York State Landmarks Preservation Law, the creation of the city's Landmarks Preservation Commission, and the drama played out over several decades with a cast of well-known names—Robert Moses, Jane Jacobs, Mayor Robert Wagner, and Jacqueline Kennedy Onassis among them—one individual stands out. He was lawyer and preservationist Albert Bard. Bard's commitment was unshakeable and his efforts were indefatigable, but given how many preservation-worthy buildings there were in New York City, one has to wonder, why did it take New Yorkers so long to win the right to protect their landmarks? The answer takes us to the story before Bard came to rewrite it.

The start of the landmark preservation movement in the United States is thought to have been in 1850 when General George Washington's headquarters at Newburgh-on-Hudson was bought by private donors, restored, and opened to the public as a historic site. The protection of sites of historic value, particularly patriotic sites linked to the origins of the country, was a keen motivating force behind early preservation efforts in New York City, which had been the first capital of the United States and had hosted many famous politicians and Revolutionary War battlefields. Like the preservation of Mount Vernon and Monticello in Virginia, these were private ventures, however, and rested on the mythos of the founding generation after they had all passed away. Yet a century later, while other states and municipalities were doing something to preserve their best old buildings—New Orleans its Vieux Carré, Boston its Beacon Hill, Washington, DC, its Georgetown, and Providence its College Hill—New York State did nothing. The reason lay in the very success of the city as a commercial and financial venue.

On April 7, 1845, Philip Hone, merchant, canal owner, former mayor, and friend of the rich and famous in New York City, wrote in his diary: "Overturn! Overturn! Overturn! is the maxim of New York. . . . One generation of men seem studious to remove all relics of those which preceded them." Walt Whitman identified the same force for change in an 1845 essay as the city's "Pull-down-and-build-over again spirit." More recently, former landmarks commissioner Barbaralee Diamonstein-Spielvogel eloquently summed it up: "New York's quintessential characteristic is its quicksilver quality, its ability to transform itself not just from year to year, but almost from day to day." In short, real estate in the city was so valuable and limited that developers had an irresistible urge to build taller, and business demanded more and more retail, warehouse, and office space. Older structures must give way to bigger and higher replacements.

In Manhattan, the few who cared most about remedying the excesses of the developers were assembled together in the Municipal Art Society. Founded in 1892, this society is, "by New York standards, a venerable institution—though a mere upstart when compared to others," preservationist Harmon Goldstone would later recall. Its members recognized the threat that the physical and aesthetic embodiment of the nation's history could be sacrificed to commercial demands. Luckily, many of the historic buildings initially considered as worthy of preservation were then in the hands of the federal, state, or local governments. Still others, Grand Central Terminal being a prime example, were privately owned. The members had studied New Orleans's preservation efforts. In these, exteriors were more important than interior spaces, but the society was also concerned with the latter. The key may have been the invitation to the public to enter. This and other concepts became backbones of preservation of private structures.

Still, the movement was small, almost a clique, and weak. As Landmarks Commission founder Goldstone recalled, "A handful of people—ladies with floppy hats and tennis shoes joined by a few crackpots (I was one of them)—began to be seriously alarmed at the rate at which our architectural heritage was disappearing." A 1941 survey across the United States had listed some 6,400 structures as worth saving; by 1963, 2,560 or 40 percent of them, were gone. But as the buildings were being torn down, a nationwide effort to stem the tide was swelling. In 1945 only two US cities had any sort of legal protection for landmarks; twenty years later, there were sixty-four.

Serious work toward preservation goals began in 1951 when Edward

Stecse, chairman of the society's Committee on Historic Architecture, submitted for the Board of Estimate's consideration a list of buildings worth saving in New York City. The idea for an inventory is generally ascribed to Talbot Hamlin, who was for many years director of the famous Avery Architectural Library at Columbia University. The proposal garnered a lot of attention but went nowhere.

The story next moved to the courts. The Committee on Historic Architecture submitted a friend of the court (amicus curiae) brief in the landmark case *Berman v. Parker*, 348 U.S. 26 (1954). *Berman v. Parker* was argued before the US Supreme Court on October 19, 1954, and the Court issued its decision a month later. The decision upheld the constitutionality of the District of Columbia's Redevelopment Act of 1945 and, in so doing, affirmed the government's right to acquire private property—in this case, a department store—as part of its efforts to redevelop a blighted neighborhood. On its face, the decision did not appear to be a boon to historic preservation, but indeed it was. In upholding the District of Columbia's right to redevelop 712 Fourth Street SW, Washington, DC, the Court also affirmed the power of municipalities to prevent the redevelopment of thousands of other structures. The language of the Court's decision, crafted by Justice William O. Douglas, helped preservationists understand the wider implications of the ruling.

The District of Columbia's actions provided for the clearance of blighted areas and their redevelopment, with the new construction fulfilling optimal planning standards. The plaintiff, an owner of a thriving business in a redevelopment project area, sought an injunction against the application of the statute to him and against the condemnation of his property. In an article that would become the basis for a renewed effort at preservation, Albert Bard wrote that the Supreme Court held that "a project for the replanning and redevelopment of a large section of the city is entirely constitutional and that all property within the area is subject to condemnation in order to compel its participation in and contribution to the new development." Key to the decision was the Court's view that the redevelopment plan itself served a public purpose. He had been waiting for that moment to finally put his historic preservation plans into action.

Albert Bard

Bard was born on December 19, 1866, in Norwich, Connecticut. He attended Harvard Law School, Class of 1892. In 1901 he launched his own firm and was an enthusiastic and vigorous participant in civic and urban affairs in varying areas such as city planning, good government, billboard advertising, and ballot reform. He joined numerous civic and professional organizations, to which he contributed his legal expertise, either formally as legal counsel, or as officer, board, or committee member. Bard's influence extended through his work on committees of the Bar Association of New York City, the Citizen's Union, and the City Club of New York.

Bard was what historians call a Progressive. He thought that honest city governance and civic virtue went hand in hand, and that lawyers owed time and energy to reform causes. Thus other organizations of which he was a board member or officer included the Honest Ballot Association, Proportional Representation Committee, the National Roadside Council, Fine Arts Federation of New York, and, not least, the Municipal Art Society. Bard was a progressive Republican, whose anti–Tammany Hall stance on issues was felt through the combined weight of the influence that several organizations could bring to bear on a single issue or piece of legislation. His party affiliation would not line up with today's political parties because a hundred years ago politics were more local and identification was more regional and fluid.

Bard understood the importance of local political power. In 1897 he helped found the Citizen's Union. In 1909 he coauthored a revised consolidated election law for New York City. In 1912 he helped found the Honest Ballot Association. His interests were, however, eclectic rather than consistently political. Bard joined the Municipal Arts Society Board in 1911, chaired its committee on charter revisions starting in 1912, and had taken on the role as president of the organization by 1917. He also became an officer of the Fine Arts Federation.

In 1921 he began serving on the Advisory Council to the New York Port Authority. In 1926 Bard became involved with the Central Park Association. He developed a particular interest in the protection of city streets and rural landscapes from the proliferation of advertisements and billboards. From 1912 to 1914 Bard served as secretary and legal counsel to the Mayor's Billboard Advertising Commission, and he was the author of its final report.

While politics might always be local, Bard was aware that reform must be national as well as local. On the national scene, Bard undertook investigation of the conduct of corporations such as Standard Oil and lobbies including the Outdoor Advertising Association of America. As legal counsel to the National Roadside Council from 1924 to 1955, Bard lobbied for the regulation of outdoor advertising, and, in the absence of legislation, put consumer pressure on corporations to reduce offensive advertising. This gave him an impressive résumé sixty years later.

Bard's 1955 essay in *American City* entitled "Esthetics and the Police Power" summarized his views and plans on the importance of aesthetic regulation to the public. Bard, among other preservationists, heeded the implications of the growing popularity of glass, steel, and skyscraper structures. His was a turn-of-the-century "green cities" esthetics. He deemed Midcentury Modern and International designs "the enemies of civic beauty." Bard wrote: "Not until Courts recognize community beauty as a ground for the exercise of police power by the state or community upon the same basis and as fully as they recognize health, safety, morality, and good order as grounds for such exercise, and as an equal partner with those factors in the term 'community welfare,' will planning and the law of planning come full circle." His papers reveal that as early as 1946, he was in correspondence with the secretary of the Vieux Carré Commission of New Orleans, inquiring about the legal methods used in New Orleans to preserve its historic French Quarter. Bard had realized that the courts were the place where landmarking would be vindicated.

In 1955, at eighty-eight years of age, Albert Bard retained his feisty spirit and temperament, commenting some years later on his strategy of advocacy: "I have another theory which I have found works. Have a bad temper. Disguise it in some form of humor, but don't forget the bad temper. I have a bad temper." Goldstone recalled Bard's personality at one meeting of the Board of Estimate. "Why don't you let me have your statement. I will read it on your behalf, as well as my own statement," Goldstone told Bard. "No, no! I can attend to my own statement," Bard said. "He wouldn't leave! So finally, everybody else had left, and it must have been about nine o'clock at night, and he got up and made a most impassioned speech, strong voice and everything else." Goldstone, a cooler head, was nevertheless impressed:

> Then the Board of Estimate went into executive session right then and there, and came back in fifteen minutes, and they turned us down. And I thought, well now he's going to collapse, after sitting there for twelve hours.... And then I said, "Can't I see you home?" He lived somewhere in New Jersey, in the suburbs, and he was almost blind. "No, you can see me to the head of the stairs of the Hudson Tube; I'm perfectly capable of going home by myself." But that was what made him what he was.

In the 1950s Bard continued his campaign for aesthetic causes. In 1953 he served as volunteer legal counsel to the Joint Committee on Design Control of the New York chapter of the American Institute of Architects and the New York regional chapter of the American Institute of Planners.

The Bard Act

In 1954 Bard drafted an act for New York State to recognize landmarks. It was only the first step toward enabling New York City to pass landmark protection legislation, however. Bard had drafted a version of his act prior to the decision in *Berman*, but the case altered the legal environment for such legislation. In a December 27, 1954, letter to Simon E. Sobeloff, the US solicitor general who argued *Berman*, Bard wrote: "For more than 40 years I have been interested in the legal question to what extent aesthetic considerations may constitutionally be made the basis of the regulation of private property. The development of planning in late years and the decisions on the subject indicate a marked trend in judicial decisions in support of aesthetics as the basis of the exercise of the police power." In a reply written the following day, the solicitor general responded: "I think that Justice [William O.] Douglas' opinion, not only because of its authority, but because of its sweep, will be as great a landmark in the law as the old *Euclid v. Ambler*, the case that established the legitimacy of urban zoning." After *Berman*, no longer would Bard and a band of ill-assorted planners, architects, and lawyers stand alone in asserting that aesthetics was an appropriate realm for legislative authority. In sum, *Berman* supported what Bard had already proposed. At the October 26, 1954, Municipal Art Society board meeting, he presented his work as a rallying cry for action, and with the hope it would provide the legal underpinning for New York City's own landmarks law. Bard noted that while this had not yet taken place, "the law is on its way and the recent case of *Berman v. Parker* . . . helps close that gap."

Bard's labors coincided with the breaking preservation story of the day: the threatened demolition of Grand Central Terminal. His own words suggested the impact of this pending threat on his thinking and activity. In a letter dated November 24, 1954, he wrote to Lawson Purdy, a noted expert on tax law: "At the City Club, the Citizen's Union, the Municipal Art Society and elsewhere we are now puzzling our noodles over a method of saving from destruction important buildings that are an asset to the city. The problem arises particularly because of the proposal of the New York Central Railroad to tear down Grand Central Station [*sic*] and build a skyscraper in its place." Bard ended his letter seeking advice on a possible tax solution to the problem of saving the terminal, with typical droll Bard commentary: "An autocratic government could quickly dispose of the whole problem by doing as it pleased. But other methods are necessary here." It was this conviction, not the Supreme Court decision, that initially prompted him to draft legislation to advance aesthetic tools.

Bard's reputation as a national expert on the subject of aesthetic regulation made him the logical choice for legal counsel to Robert Weinberg's Committee on Landmarks of the City Planning Board. Weinberg was no shrinking violet. A respected planner, he had worked in New York City and Chicago, and battled with Robert Moses over preservation of parks in the face of Moses's plans for highways. As the committee began its work, it had to grapple with the issue of the legality of "planning for community appearance." Bard advised: "Proceed on the assumption that esthetic control of private property in the interest of the community is a legal exercise of the police power."

The threat to Grand Central Terminal gave growing urgency to Bard's efforts, and his work with the Weinberg Committee offered the perfect institutional setting to nurture them. On November 18, 1954, before the Supreme Court had announced the *Berman* decision, Bard again presented his proposed legislation. After discussion and with some minor modifications, Weinberg was asked to "pass the proposal on to the proper authorities so as to get it 'into the hopper' for the coming session of the State Legislature's December session."

New York State's Historic Preservation Enabling Act, as the Bard draft was labeled, granted municipalities authority to provide for the protection and preservation of buildings and places of "special historical or aesthetic interest or value." In 1955 state senator MacNeil Mitchell introduced the bill, which was passed in Albany, only to be vetoed by the governor, Averell Harriman. But Bard did not accept setbacks. He was behind the Committee on City Development of the Fine Arts Federation report for its annual meeting on April 28, 1955, that bore a not incidental resemblance to Bard's article in *The American City*. Commenting on *Berman v. Parker*, the authors of the report noted that "the decision itself does not expressly state that esthetic considerations alone—the making of a pleasanter and more sightly city—will support such legislation, nor that esthetic considerations by themselves will support the regulation of land uses, but the language of the opinion by Mr. Justice Douglas may be claimed to go so far as to support such a case." Bard and architect Geoffrey Platt, who later played a significant role as a leader in New York City's preservation community, were the two signatories on the report. The report underscored the fact that the opinion of Justice Douglas constituted the "opinion of the court," and no dissent was filed. The report stated: "His language is broad enough to support legislation which replans a city area upon new standards of appearance and beauty."

From 1947 to 1964 Bard represented State Assembly District 20. In the state house, he found an invaluable ally in senator MacNeil Mitchell. Mitchell was also well known to the civic community and represented Greenwich Village in Bard's district. As chair of the state senate Committee on Affairs of the City of New York and of the Joint Legislative Committee on Housing and Multiple Dwellings, he was an important player and well positioned to be the champion for Bard's proposed legislation. Anthony C. Wood, in his book *Preserving New York*, attests that "Bard is not only the uncontested author of the Bard Act; he is truly its father." But Mitchell introduced and succeeded in securing the passage of the Bard Act in 1956 and would later help deliver the legislation needed to save Carnegie Hall.

In 1956 the Bard bill was reintroduced and, again, passed by the legislature. It was signed into law on April 2, 1956, as new subd. 25-a of the General City Law, § 20. It read:

> To provide, for places, buildings, structures, works of art, and other objects having a special character or special historical or aesthetic interest or value, special conditions or regulations for their protection, enhancement, perpetuation or use, including appropriate control of the use or appearance of neighboring private property within public view, or both. In any such instance such measures, if adopted in the exercise of the police power, shall be reasonable and appropriate to the purpose, or if constituting a taking of private property shall provide for due compensation, which may include the limitation or remission of taxes.

As a result, in 1956 New York became the first state to authorize its municipalities to enact "landmark" ordinances designed to protect individual buildings, as opposed to historic districts. The Bard Act provided localities across New York State the authority they needed to pass local laws to protect landmarks, and it was the state legislation that enabled the creation of the New York City Landmarks Law.

Preservation activists in Greenwich Village and Brooklyn Heights rallied behind the banner of the Bard Act. But the law did not mention districts. In 1968 the law was amended to more specifically define the types of places for which the legislation provided protection under the law. The word "districts" was added to the list including "places, buildings, structures, works of art and other objects." Lawyer and city planner Frank Gilbert recalled,

> Albert Bard's law did not include the word "district," and so we went to a great deal of trouble in the late '60s to get the word "district" added to the state enabling legislation. The important thing was we added the word "district" and then the legislative note, and this note was important to convey the original understanding when the law was passed in the 1950s because people were questioning whether or not you can have historic districts under the state enabling legislation.

That was all solved, and it's a bit of a story how it was done, but in sequence that came at the end of the '60s.

This new law became General City Law, § 20, new subd. 26-a, which reads:

> Protection of historic places, buildings and works of art. In addition to any power or authority of a municipal corporation to regulate by planning or zoning laws and regulations or by local laws and regulations, the governing board or local legislative body of any country, city, town, or village is empowered to provide by regulation, special conditions and restrictions for the protection, enhancement, perpetuation and use of places, districts, sites, buildings, structures, works of art, and other objects having a special character or special historic or aesthetic interest or value. Such regulations, special conditions and restrictions may include appropriate and reasonable control of the use or appearance of neighboring private property within public view, or both. In any such instance such measures, if adopted in the exercises of the police power, shall be reasonable and appropriate to the purpose, or if constituting a taking of private property shall provide for due compensation, which may include the limitation or remission of taxes.

A week later, after the passage of the original act, Bard introduced a resolution that was passed by the Board of Directors of the Municipal Art Society of New York. It deplored "the absence of adequate consideration of the factor of appearance in the planning and zoning of the city." It is telling that many close observers of the preservation and professional planning scene in New York City today, over half a century later, believe that the same situation exists. Albert Bard would not live to see his namesake law utilized. He died in East Orange, New Jersey, on March 25, 1963, at the age of ninety-six.

Putting Teeth in the Bard Act

The Bard Act was not exactly stealth legislation, but only a few really grasped its full possibilities. Even so, the nine-year gap between the historic preservation authorization act and the passage of the New York City Landmarks Law proves that enabling legislation and using it are two very different animals. The City of Syracuse would go forward to utilize the Bard Act before New York City did. Perhaps the threat the act posed to real estate interests in New York City seemed too distant and theoretical to have stirred up a defensive response at the time it was introduced. Then again, those interests may have been focused elsewhere. Soon they saw the threat the act posed to unregulated real estate ventures, however.

The act did not directly counter the threat. Real estate developers in the city still had the upper hand. As long as he lived, Bard continued to push the city council for landmark protection, sending his articles to a wider and wider circle of potential allies. One recipient, architecture critic Henry Hope Reed, wrote to Bard that the article was "one of the most encouraging statements for the future of municipal art that I have seen." Reed went on to indicate that he was having copies sent to friends who are "very much interested in the problem of community beauty in Charleston, Germantown (Philadelphia), San Francisco and New Orleans." Bard's article helped educate people to "the revolution that has taken place in fifty years with respect to the legal power of the community to deal with the individual landowner in his dealing with his own land, including, what, in response to individual taste, whim ambition, or cupidity, the owner plans to make his property look like to the public."

Owen Grundy of *The Villager*, someone who had been in correspondence with Bard on the general subject of preservation and the effort to preserve the character of Greenwich Village since the early 1950s, wrote to him in June 1959. (At the time the Village neighborhood was under siege from Robert Moses and his allies in highway development.) Grundy's letter framed what would be a key strategic question for those seeking protection for New York's landmarks: "My own feeling is that now is the time to put on a grand push for historic and aesthetic zoning or some similar protection in the City of New York. There are those who feel that we should get behind the proposed Zoning Resolution and get it passed and then discuss historic and aesthetic zoning. But I fear that if we wait, we may never get historic and aesthetic protection in the City of New York." He deferred to Bard's expertise, however. "That is a matter of strategy which should be decided upon by you and the wiser heads who have been through these things over the years."

However, Grundy was confident that if the decision was to go forward to seek such protection, "we should organize for it on a city-wide basis." In offering to help in such a campaign, he suggested, "We should bring in Brooklyn Heights Assn, Greenwich Village organizations, American Scenic & Historic Preservation Society, Fine Arts Federation, Municipal Art Society, Citizens Union, NYC chapter of the AIA, Staten Island Historical Society and other interested organizations." Though Grundy was uncertain as to the correct timing of such a push for preservation, he was prescient in recognizing the type of coalition ultimately needed to achieve it. Bard responded that because of the 1956 law, the city "now has the legal right to do practically anything in the way of planning it wants to do," and suggested that the first step was to produce a draft that should go into the new zoning resolution.

Limitations of the Bard Act

Bard wanted to live long enough to see his act gain traction. Goldstone took note: "I didn't know him well till much later. And it was a wonderful experience to meet this old man. He was tiny, very frail and absolutely indomitable. Now, I can tell you a couple of stories about Albert Bard." Goldstone admired Bard. "He was on the side of the angels, always, with the good government people."

The Bard Act was the beginning of landmark legislation in New York. Even as the act passed through the assembly, there were indications that "the boys with the sledge hammers" were still going to have a bright future. In 1955 another Zeckendorf project was unveiled. The site on the west side of Midtown would become home of the Palace of Progress, the "world's largest building" and a "permanent World's Fair and Merchandise Mart." As the media would report, Mr. Zeckendorf, "a fabulous figure in real estate circles because of the magnitude of his deals," added more luster to the deal by enlisting "as his lieutenant to help realize his vision the impresario Billy Rose, who, with Maj. Gen. William J. Donovan, will go on the road in a world tour to enlist interest, exhibitors and tenants." The site, once the jewel of McKim, Mead & White, was the now dilapidated Penn Station.

Goldstone was worried that the Municipal Art Society literally had no teeth against such ferocious enemies. "This bunch of idealistic old fogies," Goldstone called the society. He was buoyed when Mrs. Richard Henry Dana brought some new young faces onto the society's board. He was one, along with L. Bancel LaFarge, and both would later become presidents of the society. Other newcomers were Geoffrey Platt and William Jayme. Coming aboard at that time was future society president, architect Giorgio Cavaglieri. *New Yorker* columnist Brendan Gill credited attorney Whitney North Seymour Sr. with the effort to revive the society. Seymour particularly appreciated the need to build membership to increase the appearance of the organization having some real power. But old and new members were not comforted by developments like the proposals for demolition of Penn Station.

Revived, the Municipal Art Society went to work drumming up support for landmarks with exhibits, radio shows, walking tours, publications, and plaques. It prepared a list of "New York Landmarks: An Index of Architecturally Notable Structures in New York City." The list, unlike its earlier incarnation, did not stop at buildings constructed before World War I, but included those built up to 1930. Shortly after the list's publication, the New York Community Trust publicly unveiled its plaque program. Twenty plaques were dedicated in 1957, with more promised. The press release for the program noted: "Buildings of architectural distinction with historical associations are among those being identified." Grand Central Terminal was among the first named.

The press release continued, "Millions of our fellow Americans say they like to visit New York but wouldn't want to live here. For all of these, the plaques will help to explain why so many of us prefer to visit elsewhere and live here." The unveiling of the plaque program triggered a *New York Times* editorial, which referenced both the recent publication of the "book listing the landmarks of New York City" and Seymour's remarks at the unveiling when he said it is "high time that New Yorkers and visitors have some way to identify our historical and architectural treasures." From 1955, when the Bard Act went to the state legislature, until 1965, when the ugly truth loomed that Bard's efforts seemed to have borne little effect, New York City still did not have an effective mechanism for preserving landmarks.

The razing of Penn Station is the most often cited reason for the turnaround in the fortunes of preservation. But it was not yet a reality when a resolution passed at the meeting of the Municipal Art Society called for the exploration of the creation of a permanent board to seek "means to prevent demolition" in the future. The likely trigger for that meeting was the threat to historic Castle Clinton in Manhattan's Battery Park. The man behind that threat was Robert Moses.

Robert Moses

Robert Moses (1888–1981), known as the "master builder" of mid-century New York, favored highways over public transit and helped create the modern suburbs of New York. Although he was not a trained civil engineer, his achievements in the most influential city in the country inspired a generation of engineers, architects, and urban planners. Moses held up to twelve official titles simultaneously, including parks commissioner, but was never elected to any public office. Nevertheless, he created and led numerous semiautonomous public authorities, through which he controlled millions of dollars in toll revenues and directly issued bonds to fund new ventures with little or no input or oversight from outside sources.

Moses's projects were considered economically necessary by many contemporaries after the Great Depression. He led the construction of a varied list of projects, including New York campuses for the 1939 and 1964 World's Fairs and large hydroelectric dams at Niagara Falls, and helped persuade the United Nations to locate its headquarters in Manhattan instead of Philadelphia. His reputation for efficiency and nonpartisan leadership was later damaged by Robert Caro's Pulitzer-winning biography *The Power Broker* (1974), which accused Moses of lusting for power, questionable ethics, vindictiveness, and racism.

With one eye on the imperial plans and imperious methods of Moses, residents of neighborhoods like the West Village in Manhattan and Brooklyn Heights began to organize to preserve their buildings from destructive freeways. Moses was a feared man with an amazing amount of power and the ability to accomplish his goals, so community leaders had to act fast and forcefully. According to Brooklyn Heights preservation leader Otis Pratt Pearsall's recollection of the events, "The Municipal Art Society [had] started the ball rolling in 1954 with a forty-page mimeographed list of noteworthy buildings in New York City." What was the motivation behind this and related society actions leading up to the law? Not the fear that any particular historic structure would fall. According to Pearsall, it "was Robert Moses, really, who had more effect than anybody else."

Pearsall's recollection suggests that the conventional explanation of the rise of the landmark movement—the outcry over the destruction of Penn Station in the opening year of the next decade—was incorrect. By 1958 the city was already what *The New York Times*, in a page-one story, called "a battleground of opposing philosophies of what American cities of the future should be like." Whole neighborhoods like Greenwich Village on Manhattan's lower west side and Brooklyn Heights faced plans to demolish old housing and run highways through the rubble. Slum clearance became the war cry of so-called urban reformers, Like Moses, they attacked brownstones throughout the city as being too old and outdated. Moses even wanted roads through Central Park's open space.

By 1958, 10 percent of the buildings on the Municipal Art Society's highly selective list had already been torn down because of decay, the need for more car storage, and new development. Constantly recurring and only occasionally successful battles to save buildings and districts of historic value convinced many in the preservation movement that there ought to be some more orderly and efficient way of saving the city's architectural heritage than intermittent guerrilla warfare.

Then there was a Moses plan to run a 120-foot-wide highway through the middle of Washington Square Park in Greenwich Village as a way of connecting Fifth Avenue to a swanky new address on the south side of the park—Fifth Avenue South (West Broadway renamed)—and then down to an intersection with a Robert Moses–planned elevated river-to-river elevated expressway along Broome Street named LoMAX. In the neighborhood, Washington Square was everyone's favorite little park, celebrated by one 1950s writer as "the kindest enclave I know, an island of no pressure," and the new highway, it was said, "would turn it into a mere grassy roadside plot."

It turned out to be a highway too far even for Moses. Greenwich Village activists like bestselling author Jane Jacobs were unmatched in their creativity and activism. For example, the closing of Washington Square Park to traffic was celebrated with the ceremonial driving of the "Last Car through Washington Square" on November 1, 1958. At the subsequent gala "Community Masquerade Celebration" of the closing, over one thousand Villagers gathered and a car was burned in effigy to mark the elimination of the automobile from the park. Ten thousand Villagers wrote postcards to the mayor protesting the new road, and Washington Square was permanently closed to traffic.

The next year was again a time of trial for preservationists. On April 21, 1959, over four hundred residents of Brooklyn Heights attended a town meeting in the Bossert Hotel ballroom. The headline announcing the meeting in that morning's *New York Times* read, "Brooklynites Set Action on Heights; Residents Meet Tonight to Discuss How to Preserve Community's Charm; Seek to Use State Law; Ask City to Invoke Measure to Protect Area's Historic and Esthetic Values." The villain of the piece was again Robert Moses, who wanted to drive a highway through the middle of the neighborhood.

Battles like these kept coming, and the Action Group for Better Architecture in New York (AGBANY) began recruiting establishment voices for preservation. Charitable fund manager Ray Rubinow of Greenwich Village and Carnegie Hall fame joined its board of directors, bringing along his organizational and political experience and recruiting others to the cause. Also lending their names to AGBANY's cause were long-time preservation supporters Eleanor Roosevelt and Fannie Hurst.

Looking back, lawyer James Felt, whose interests lay both in real estate development and urban planning, judged that the ad hoc campaigns and the work of AGBANY and the Municipal Art Society gave organizational impetus to the Bard Act: "The Bard Act did not stand alone." A less well-known event came in January 1956, when Felt was sworn in as chairman of the New York City Planning Commission. According to observers, "in the light of the enormous changes that have taken place in the last few years, his sights were set on tackling the city's zoning resolution." In July he announced plans for a major study of the city's zoning, which led to a two-and-a-half-year effort to change the planned development of the city. Preservationists were hopeful. The commission arranged for a series of public hearings. At these, the planning commission voices were joined by an informed and passionate chorus from two of New York's most historic and preservation-conscious neighborhoods, Greenwich Village and Brooklyn Heights. Both neighborhoods saw the need to include preservation in the new zoning resolution.

Felt and Wagner

All of these efforts delivered the message that New York City needed a legal mechanism to protect its threatened landmarks. Neither Mayor Robert Wagner nor James Felt was openly a champion of a preservation agenda. Nor were the protests, meetings, and celebrations part of a coordinated effort. But together they brought New York City tantalizingly closer to the day when it would have the ability to protect its landmarks.

As a third-generation real estate man specializing in "assembling land for big private developments" and as a governor of the Real Estate Board of New York, Felt seemed an unlikely candidate for a hero of the preservation movement. Yet the critical role he played in advancing the Landmarks Law would lead two people intimately involved in the law's history, Geoffrey Platt and Harmon Goldstone, to see him in this light. The first and second chairs respectively of the Landmarks Preservation Commission used identical words when talking about Felt's singular role in the efforts that led to the creation of the Landmarks Law: "We couldn't have done it without him."

More easily understood than Felt's support of preservation is Wagner's selection of Felt for the role of chair of the City Planning Commission. Felt was acclaimed "an almost ideal appointment." Having been immensely successful in business, "reputedly a millionaire," when he entered public service he "cut all private business ties." Prior to being sworn in as chair of the City Planning Commission in January in 1956, he had held a variety of appointed positions. He was highly respected within and outside of the public weal. Known for his personal integrity, as a child Felt had planned to become a rabbi. His appointment was greeted positively by several government organizations, including the Municipal Art Society.

In addition to prodigious energy, wide knowledge, and a deep love of the city, he brought to the chairmanship just the right personality needed to address the challenges facing his agency. Described as having both "inner toughness and outer mildness," his style was not to "hammer down opposition"; instead, he was "both persistent and ingratiating, achieving goals by indirection." Blessed with "great personal charm and persuasiveness," he would need all these traits to energize the City Planning Commission.

Felt inherited an agency in which public confidence "was so low that its very survival was in question." Years later, *The New York Times* described his appointment as getting "the unenviable job of pulling the City Planning Commission out of the doldrums in which it had languished much of the time since its creation in 1938." The agency had been thwarted in its efforts at zoning reform and, daunted by the task of master planning and mastering the city's capital budget, "it was having difficulty keeping the thin shreds of prestige that remained to it." It was an agency on life support. Felt knew he had to demonstrate that the agency could play a vital role in the affairs of the city. Fortunately, Felt had an ally in the mayor. Having himself briefly held the chairmanship of the City Planning Commission, Robert Wagner appreciated the Municipal Art Society original "docket; and that he believed the Commission would be extremely interested in having some suggestions along these lines." This approach led to the society's participation at the April Zoning Board's hearings. Everyone took away something from the hearing. The Art Society saw it as a stepping-stone for landmark zoning; the Villagers, as another battle to be fought with hope for a resolution. All left united in their quest for historic preservation.

By the end of its round of informal hearings, the City Planning Commission had heard a lot about a subject not even on its agenda: historic and aesthetic zoning. The coming together of the citywide civic organizations, Brooklyn Heights, Greenwich Village, and anticipated support from Staten Island, led *The Villager* to recognize that this chorus crying out for historic and aesthetic zoning was actually a "growing city-wide movement." In August, *The Villager* recognized the addition to this chorus of voices from Gramercy Park, Riverdale, and Richmondtown, noting that "civic organizations in all these areas are actively campaigning for such protection."

But when New York City's major zoning changes were complete, they conspicuously lacked any acknowledgment of historic preservation needs or goals. Felt's concern was that adding the subject of historic preservation to an already politically charged proposed new zoning system could keep him from achieving his primary goal. "Aesthetic zoning was only one of a number of reforms that would be left behind on the road to the resolutions approval." As part of the compromise that Felt reached with leading preservationists, Mayor Wagner established a "Committee for the Preservation of Structures of Historic and Esthetic Importance." At its third meeting, on September 12, 1961, minutes reveal that a question was raised whether the master list of New York City landmarks "should be made part of the Zoning Resolution. It was felt that this could best be resolved in conference with the City Planning Commission."

The chair of the committee was Harmon Goldstone, president of the Municipal Art Society, named by Mayor Wagner to the Committee for the Preservation of Structures of Historic and Aesthetic Importance, a forerunner of the Landmarks Preservation Commission. That year, Goldstone was also named to the City Planning Commission. He was the first architect to serve on the commission in a long while, and *The New York Times* hailed his appointment, saying he had "demonstrated his devotion to preservation of the aesthetic, historic and recreational values." In effect, the baton had been passed from Bard to Goldstone, and from general legislation to a commission style of administration. Felt's position was suspect, for, at least according to the recollections of other members of the City Planning Commission, he and his family were deeply involved in real estate renewal, and that included Penn Plaza.

But the committee had its eye instead on Grand Central Terminal, and with victories in Central Park and Carnegie Hall, and with the support of the mayor, there seemed some light at the end of the tunnel. Goldstone admitted that a "cliff-hanging operation that only just rescued Carnegie Hall from destruction . . . shocked the Municipal Art Society Board into full awareness of the crisis." So Goldstone sat down to lunch with Felt, and that May 9, 1961, "wonderful lunch" with Felt—and Platt—led to a letter to Mayor Wagner. "I think also, you see, there was a second coincidence: we had watched what Felt was doing in regard to other things in the city, and the Municipal Art Society had decided to give him a medal or award at our annual meeting; that was the first time I'd met him. And the award was the day before our luncheon." Felt was persuaded to join the campaign for a landmarks law, a commission to name sites, and a process to enforce the landmark designation on the owners. "Felt was the catalyst; we couldn't have done it without him. And he became a great friend," Goldstone recalled.

Goldstone did not reveal what everyone in the movement knew—he was now its central figure. He was born on May 4, 1911, in New York City and raised in the city. In 1932 he graduated from Harvard, with a major in fine arts. He then went on to get his architecture degree from Columbia University's School of Architecture. He was noted for the work he did there in helping to develop the "World of Tomorrow" piece for the 1939 New York World's Fair. He then served in the US Army as a statistician and economist for three years. In 1952 he established the architecture firm Goldstone & Dearborn. Goldstone's role in preservation was pivotal in the formation of the New York City Landmarks Preservation Commission (LPC). In 1960 he became president of the Municipal Art Society. A year later, Mayor Wagner appointed him to the Committee for the Preservation of Structures of Historic and Esthetic Importance (an early incarnation of the LPC).

Wagner set up the committee under the influence of Felt, to serve as a study body and ensure the protection of important historic buildings and landmarks. The mayor first appointed Geoffrey Platt to head the committee. During his subsequent term, Goldstone observed that "by 1958, even prior to the informal hearings on the new zoning resolution, 10 percent of the buildings on the Municipal Art Society's highly selective list had already been torn down." It was clear to Goldstone that the Municipal Art Society alone did not possess the influence necessary to prevent the demolition of the buildings on its list. The recommendations made to Mayor Wagner included setting up a permanent Landmarks Preservation Commission that would designate buildings, landmarks, and districts of historic and architectural worth, and legislative measures that would enforce these regulations. Just as Goldstone was the influence on Felt, Platt was the shaker and mover at Wagner's side. Platt, an architect by trade, a member of the Art Society, and a nationally famous landscape designer, understood the importance of planned spaces, and he impressed this on Wagner. So here was the preservation troika: Felt, Goldstone, and Platt, pulling Mayor Wagner into the fray.

Everyone among the preservationists realized that some kind of legal mechanism was needed to put teeth in the Bard Act, in effect, to identify quasi-public and historic buildings and protect them against architectural changes that would detract from their distinction. This, of course, was part and parcel of what the American Institute of Architects and its civic partners had unsuccessfully tried to advance during the zoning revision process. One critical element was now different. Only a month earlier, Felt's hard-won but flawed zoning resolution had been approved by the Board of Estimate. Now it was time to draw his attention to an important piece of unfinished business. In a January 24, 1961, letter to Felt, Michael Gruen, another member of the circle whose particular interest was historic districts, reminded Felt of his request to the Municipal Art Society and the American Institute of Architects to "wait" on advancing their agenda to protect "historic buildings and other buildings of public importance—as well as of public spaces, until after the new zoning resolution was passed."

In his acceptance remarks for the medal awarded him by the Municipal Art Society, Felt thanked the members for their "recommendations and suggestions" and then went on to address the subject near and dear to the society's heart. Noting an "emerging awareness on the part of the general public," he cited the irony that in World War II, efforts had been made to spare art treasures from destruction, but "we have no plan to protect our architectural and historic landmarks from becoming casualties of a peacetime real estate market." Stating his belief that New York City was now ready to "seriously consider a program of saving some of the city's most important structures," he announced: "Very soon, I hope to call a meeting with representatives of your Society and related organizations to work out a plan for insuring the preservation of these landmarks."

Perhaps realizing that this audience might mistake his remarks as a manifesto for nostalgic preservationism, Felt followed with cautionary language. He stressed the need to distinguish between structures of "nostalgia or special group interest" and those of "true value to society." He pointed out that "New York, unlike Venice, cannot afford to offer antiquity as one of its major products. The genius and strength of New York lies in its dynamic vitality and its continuing self-regeneration. To be sure we must cherish our past but we must not let it lure us to looking backwards instead of looking ahead." Noting that there "will be difficulties—legal and economic problems are intertwined," Felt observed that "other cities have worked out some of these problems, and I feel that we can do the same." Comments coming from such a prominent government official, even with the caveats, were revolutionary. It appears that Felt had been prepared to make an even stronger statement. According to Robert Weinberg, a city planner whose role in saving Greenwich Village had shown him as a central player in the group, Felt had told him in a "long conversation" that he had planned to announce something more concrete at the society's event.

The mayor accepted his committee's report with record speed, but the formal wheels of government turned more slowly. In its March 10, 1962, editorial, "Farewell to Landmarks," *The New York Times* commented on the delay. "By action of the Board of Estimate, New York City now has a Landmarks Preservation Commission and a budget of $50,000 to help it carry out its function. The Fine Arts Federation is busy making up a list of potential commission members to be submitted to the Mayor for appointment. While this due process plods on, the bulldozers have been busy." The editorial examined the workload confronting the new commission, including the drafting of a law and compilation of lists of buildings and areas to be protected, and lamented: "If we are slow enough—and we have set an ignoble precedent on this score—most of New York's architectural heritage and almost all of the city's remaining early nineteenth century structures of historical interest will be gone. We can then point to our documents, plans, reports and excellent intentions, and say that no one was really to blame."

If *The New York Times* thought that things were moving slowly, it is easy to understand the frustration Francis Keally felt. It had been twelve years since Keally, as president of the Municipal Art Society, had issued his early call for a landmarks law. But the seeds of Keally's labors were blossoming. On April 21, 1962, Mayor Wagner appointed the first Landmarks Preservation Commission. "Its membership was to include at all times an architect, a realtor, an historian qualified in the field, a practitioner of the fine arts, a landscape architect or city planner, and a representative of the public at large—one of whom shall be a member of the Art Commission."

It was no coincidence that the people working on the issues the past decade were on the commission. They were members of the Municipal

Art Society (Platt), the Society of Architectural Historians (Russell Lynes), the American Institute of Architects (Frederick F. Woodbridge, its president at the time), and the American Scenic and Historic Preservation Society (Loring McMillen). Also included on the commission were articulate voices from two geographic hotbeds of preservation: Greenwich Village's Stanley Tankel, and Brooklyn Heights's William Fisher. Goldstone was not on the panel. While Platt's mayoral study committee was still at work, a vacancy had opened up on the City Planning Commission. There was public clamor that the new appointee should be an architect: "Surprisingly, although it deals with many architectural matters, the commission has long lacked an architect member. . . . An architect is the obvious and proper choice for the commission's vacancy." By this time, because of their conversations about landmarks, Felt had developed a close and trusting relationship with Platt and Goldstone, both architects. Felt approached them regarding their possible interest in filling the vacancy. Goldstone was appointed.

Goldstone's new position was a boon to the cause of preservation. As a planning commissioner he was able to facilitate a smooth working relationship with the other key groups. Goldstone got Platt to appoint as executive director of the commission James Van Derpool. Van Derpool was a professor of architectural history, an Avery Librarian, and was acting associate dean of Columbia's School of Architecture. When consulted about the opening, Van Derpool delighted Platt and "dumbfounded" Goldstone, by offering to fill the position himself: "This is my dream all my life." With a former president of both the local chapter and the national Society of Architectural Historians, a trustee of the American Scenic and Historic Preservation Society, and a nationally recognized expert in the field at its head, the commission's staff would be led by a high-profile, respected professional.

At last, the personnel of the Landmarks Preservation Commission was set. Its charge was clear: identify and designate landmarks, draft a law, and receive and answer preservation questions from other city agencies. Goldstone understood his task. Platt "and I discussed our problem with James Felt, then chairman of the City Planning Commission. To our surprise, he was sympathetic to our objective and, more important, had the knowledge, which none of us amateurs did, of how to achieve it. He enlisted Mayor Wagner's support, got him to appoint a policy advisory committee, which led to an official commission which guided the long and intricate process of legislative drafting which eventually produced the enactment of Local Law 45 of 1965 amending Chapter 8A of New York City's Charter and Administrative Code."

The city government was a labyrinth, however, and Goldstone could have used a guide through it. For example, when Frank Blaustein, a lawyer serving as the vice chairman of the City Planning Commission, saw a draft of the proposed landmarks law and tore it apart, Goldstone was very upset. What Blaustein was actually doing was making an important partition between the powers of the LPC and the powers of City Planning. A new draft that went back to the city's Corporate Counsel was very clear and had the desired separation that some other cities' landmark laws miss.

This all helped in the long run, for when the first landmarked building proposal went to the Landmarks Planning Commission for review, it did not have much trouble with overlapping jurisdictions. Goldstone recalled:

> "I can remember distinctly: the first designation came.... And the members of the Commission—all of whom were fine people and good friends—they started saying, "Well, you know, this building realty isn't that good or that important."... And I said, "Now look. This is not our job: it has been decided by the Landmarks Commission. All our job is, is to determine if it interferes with any public improvement that we know of? Have we got a school going on that site? Have we got a highway going through it that will cause a problem? Or is it free and clear of our jurisdiction? And it was. So I said, "O.K. Whatever we think of what those long-haired lunatics decide to designate, that is their responsibility." And thank heavens I was there at that moment, because that kind of overlapping jurisdiction never came up again. We were just lucky that when that first one came down the line.

The commission, which existed at the pleasure of the mayor, needed permanent status as a part of the city government to have real power. Thus the enabling legislation was very important. The LPC had twelve nonsalaried members, with the research work done by a salaried staff headed by Van Derpool, and consisting of John Barrington Bayley, an architect and preservation specialist; Mrs. Agnes Addison Gilchrist, former president of the Society of Architectural Historians; and Henry Hope Reed, an architectural historian specializing in old New York. In addition, two unsalaried volunteers initially participated in the research work—Justin O'Brien Haynes and Regina Kellerman. The researchers got most of their information from city tax and property deed records, and historical documents of the New-York Historical Society, the New York Public Library's Local History Room, and the Museum of the City of New York. Mayor Wagner formally endorsed the commission's recommendations.

Felt urged Platt to proceed cautiously: "Take this time that you've got." In Platt's mind, that time was a three-year window. Felt also advised, "Don't surprise anybody in government." Most prophetically, he advised Platt to keep his eye on the prize. "You're going to lose some buildings during this period and don't let it bother you. You just—you're going to lose 'em." Platt did not realize he was talking about the magnificent Pennsylvania Station. Still, the loss of Penn Station prompted the sense that time was of the essence if further demolition was to be prevented. While the narrative of the demolition of Pennsylvania Station spurred New Yorkers to demand preservation, the movement was older, at least as old as Bard, and thus had a foundation of people and ideas. The Penn Station myth being recognized as a type of historic "shorthand," it has been mistaken as the entire story. As such, it denies New Yorkers and preservationists in particular their full legacy.

Losing Penn Station

By 1960, disguised and disfigured by poor maintenance and cheap and garish modifications, the attractiveness and value of Pennsylvania Station had almost become invisible to the stream of countless commuters flowing through it every day. When the impending demolition of the station finally penetrated the public consciousness, only several hundred New Yorkers were moved to action.

The railroad had pushed hard for demolition. By the 1950s, Pennsylvania Railroad was no longer the most valuable corporation in the nation, nor was it the "Standard Railroad of the World." The Depression and World War II put off years of needed investment. The symbol of the system, Pennsylvania Station—a steel-and-glass evocation of the vaulted public monuments of ancient Rome, once one of the city's finest individual works of architecture—had fallen into disorder. It simply cost too much to maintain, and major systems needed replacing. The railroad could not see a future in which the building could be profitable. In 1961 the president of the Pennsylvania Railroad, Jim Symes, decided to raze the building and sell the air rights to build a new Madison Square Garden arena, an exhibition hall, bowling alleys, and a thirty-three-story office tower while keeping a much-diminished station below. Company executives insisted that the company was in business to make money, not lose revenues maintaining a public monument—unlike previous generations' public mindedness.

Supporters of the proposed new Madison Square Garden included unions and business associations. Local 32B of the Janitorial Workers added its voice and the clout of its forty-two thousand members to "the many farseeing groups who put the interests of the city ahead of any artificial self-aggrandizement." Further attacking the defenders of the station, the union's president continued: "It should be noted that Pennsylvania Station has no city, state or federal historical significance.... It is designed as a copy of an original building in Europe and its removal would in no way affect the historical significance of the original." The Real Estate Board of New York, the New York Board of Trade, and even the station's famously competitive neighboring department stores, Macy's and Gimbel's, were united in their support of the new project to rise in the place of Penn Station, assuming that the project would bring in more customers than long-distance train travelers. The statements sounded in the prevailing attitude of the time: the "responsible position" for those with "the interests of the city at heart" was to support the new Madison Square Garden. With the granting of the permit, the station's fate was sealed.

The New York Times front-page story on Sunday, April 22, 1962, "City Acts to Save Historical Sites," was followed by the prominent subhead, "Wagner Names 12 to New Agency—Architects Decry Razing of Pennsylvania Station." The Landmarks Preservation Commission mobilized to prevent the demolition of Pennsylvania Station. From the moment the prospect of the station's imminent demise had become news the previous summer, opponents of the demolition warned what its loss would mean to the landmarks movement. The April 22 *Times* article noted the New York chapter of the American Institute of Architects' opposition to demolition. They were joined by the Municipal Art Society and the National Trust for Historic Preservation.

Objecting to the demolition of the station was one thing; preventing it was something else. What actually could be done? To be sure, this was not just another threatened building. Pennsylvania Station occupied nine acres of exceptionally valuable real estate in New York, and that was what made the issue so fraught. For the American Institute of Architects membership, the threat to Pennsylvania Station was "the first straw," not the last, as many of New York City's historical structures stood on valuable real estate. Years later, one of the key instigators of AGBANY, Diana Goldstein (Kirsch), would recall, "We knew that we would lose, but we wanted to protest, which was why we had the pickets; and we wanted to change the climate.... We felt a moral obligation to protest the tearing down of a great building."

AGBANY succeeded in capturing the public eye with its picketing of Pennsylvania Station. Until AGBANY's efforts, the Wagner administration and the new Landmarks Preservation Commission had sidestepped the issue of Pennsylvania Station. In the press story announcing the creation of the commission, Platt staked out its initial position: "He personally regretted that his commission had come into being too late to try to save the terminal." At the end of July 1962, with press interest growing in AGBANY's activities, Platt told the press that he "personally 'deplored the doom of the station," but reasserted "that the commission has no legal powers available now to prevent demolition. It must await instructions from Mayor Wagner even to take a public interest in the issue." Wagner had been in Europe on vacation and returned the evening of AGBANY's protest at the station. Perhaps it was Platt's comment that led defenders of the station to greet him with their pleas. *The New York Times* joined in: "Something should be done, and it can be done, in certain areas. The newly appointed Landmarks Preservation Commission must take clear and immediate positions on threatened buildings of historic or artistic value."

City Council member Edward Sadowsky, at AGBANY's request, proposed a resolution in the New York City Council "urging the mayor of the city of New York to request the landmarks preservation commission for an opinion on the desirability of preserving Pennsylvania Station." One of AGBANY's strategies, as proclaimed in an ad it purchased in *The New York Times*, was to make "the preservation of our heritage an issue in the forthcoming campaign." Alice Sachs, Democratic-Liberal candidate for the East Side state senate district, "called on the city ... to consider setting up a museum of science, technology and industry in Pennsylvania Station." Ironically, Sachs was running against a proven friend of preservation, the man who had introduced the Bard Act in Albany: MacNeil Mitchell.

The protest drew the attention of Congressman John V. Lindsay, a liberal Republican with an upper-class background and great appeal to the ordinary New Yorker, who publicly pushed for the preservation of Pennsylvania Station during his reelection campaign. Lindsay formally called on the City Planning Commission to do something. Felt made it clear that "the city could not block demolition," but that the new Madison Square Garden would require a permit, which would require City Planning Commission approval—a delaying action that bespoke Felt's cautious approach to preservation. In the future, Lindsay would replace Wagner in the mayor's office. "I remember when he swore me into the Landmarks Chairmanship," Goldstone recalled. Lindsay said, 'If you need my help, yell!'"

AGBANY finally got a meeting with Mayor Wagner in September. Among those joining Norval White were Ray Rubinow; L. Bancel LaFarge; Morris Ketchum Jr., president of the Municipal Art Society; and Frederick J. Woodbridge, president of the New York chapter of the American Institute of Architects. Felt had already made it clear that the City Planning Commission could not deal with the proposed demolition of the station, however. Its sole focus would be on the permit required for the construction of the new complex. "With these ground rules, the outcome of their hearing was predetermined." Despite a robust showing by the station's defenders and a serious effort on their part to fight the permit on planning grounds, they could not win. As was aptly reported in *Architectural Forum*, "To the surprise of few people (but the disappointment of many) the New York City Planning Commission ... issued the permit."

In February 1962, assuming the building was already a lost cause, parks commissioner Newbold Morris advanced the notion of saving and relocating eighty-four of the station's columns to create a "classical landscape in Flushing Meadow Park." This idea was greeted with the following response from *The New York Times*: "Among the saddest words of tongue or pen—at least from a civic point of view—was Park Commissioner Newbold Morris' recent epitaph for the doomed Pennsylvania Station.... 'Pennsylvania Station is one of the city's great buildings. I'm working on a plan to save the columns.'"

The most visible protest, the picketing of the station, was famously described as one of the city's strangest and most heartening picket lines, a legend in the annals of preservation, with men in suits and women with white gloves marching from 5 to 7 p.m. on August 2, 1962, in front of the station. Today, those few who marched that August day in 1962 are saluted as preservation heroes, losing the battle to win the war.

In the end there was not enough support for the station. Forty years after the demolition began, one of the protesters recalled: "What I remember about that day is the indifference of people on the street to the message that we were trying to communicate." Robert Weinberg would later write, "Except for that memorable picketing event some of us participated in ... there was not a scream of protest, nor any real struggle." Years after the effort to save the station, Giorgio Cavaglieri would tell Charles Hosmer, "It was not a mass movement. The architects paraded back and forth. And the fact that some of them (like Philip Johnson) were very well known, made the parade a curiosity for the public.... It was not the subject-matter that was their concern. Even applying the most creative math, the number of people who did anything to try and save the station—picketed, testified, wrote a letter, signed a petition—was tiny and inadequate to the task. It was too little, too late." Mayor Wagner dismissed AGBANYs pleas, petitions, and demonstrations. The City Planning Commission under Wagner's leadership had allowed the special permit and thus enabled the Madison Square Garden Corporation to destroy Penn Station.

On October 28, 1963, "with great fanfare and extensive press attention," demolition began. The day scheduled for demolition, a forlorn band of six architects picketed, wearing black armbands and carrying signs that read "Shame." Demolition began with the staccato sound of jackhammers tearing into the station's granite skin and the lowering of

{ *Landmark Law* }

the first of eight stone eagles. "Just another job," said John Rezin, foreman of the wrecking crew. His assessment was echoed by Morris Lipsett, president of the demolition company: "If anybody seriously considered it art, they would have put up some money to save it." Then the eight two-ton stone eagles were carefully removed from the atop the building. The eagles' removal marked the symbolic commencement of the station's demolition. The rubble of the station was dumped in the Secaucus, New Jersey, Meadows as landfill for what would become the Meadowlands. Pennsylvania Station was razed in progressive phases over a three-year period, keeping pace with construction of the $70 million sports and entertainment facility that replaced it. "The message was terribly clear," the *Times*'s Ada Louise Huxtable wrote. "Tossed into that Secaucus graveyard were about 25 centuries of classical culture and the standards of style, elegance and grandeur that it gave to the dreams and constructions of Western man."

The New York Times had an appropriate epitaph two days later: "Until the first blows fell, no one was convinced that New York would permit this monumental act of vandalism. Even when we had Penn Station we couldn't afford to keep it clean. We want and deserve tincan architecture in a tinhorn culture. A city gets what it admires, will pay for, and ultimately deserves." The prophecy was fulfilled. "Once leveled, the magnificent Roman Revival train station was replaced by a modern office and sports complex of pedestrian architectural quality. A building that complied with the grid was replaced by a building that violated the grid. A beautiful dialogue between two important structures [Penn Station and Grand Central Terminal] was ended. Greatness has been traded for the mundane."

Lost landmarks usually fade from public consciousness. Pennsylvania Station would be different. According to an editorial in *Fortune* a year after the demolition, "The city regards the past with contempt and hastens to obliterate its heritage. Symbolic of New York's self-destructive frenzy is the destruction of Pennsylvania Station. . . . This will be the fourth Madison Square Garden in eighty-five years. There will never be another Penn Station." Penn Station's post-1963 address was the basement of the new Madison Square Garden complex, where it offered a total of six street entrances and the addition of a to-and-from track level. Inadequate and cramped facilities placed commuters into a maze of corridors. A subterranean squalor prevailed. Would-be passengers needed a sharp eye to find their tracks, or even information about trains' coming and going. A banal office building and the fourth incarnation of Madison Square Garden rose in its place. Indeed, if Pennsy passengers and Long Island Rail Road commuters felt claustrophobic, they were justified. The ceiling of the old station's awesome main waiting room was 150 feet high. In the new one, it would barely reach 25 feet.

Vincent Scully memorably summed up what had been lost. Then, "One entered the city like a god," he wrote. "One scuttles in now like a rat." The New York chapter of the Architects Institute joined in the lament: "Like ancient Rome, New York seems bent on tearing down its finest buildings. In Rome, demolition was a piecemeal process which took over 1,000 years; in New York demolition is absolute and complete in a matter of months. The rise of modern archaeology put an end to this kind of vandalism in Rome, but in our city no such deterrent exists." The last touch was in some ways the most galling to the architects. The new Madison Square Garden was deemed a visual monstrosity by most critics. Below it, Amtrak, NJ Transit, and Long Island Rail Road trains still roll. But they serve an unimpressive facility not very different from an enlarged bus station. One unanswerable question remains: Did the project also have a highly placed friend in city government?

James Felt, the chair of the City Planning Commission, was the brother of one of the two "prime movers" of the Madison Square Garden project, Irving Mitchell Felt. Actually, it was not James Felt's position as chair of the City Planning Commission that raises eyebrows as much as his leadership role on Wagner's team. For all practical purposes, he was the master strategist behind the Wagner administration's embrace of preservation. He had arranged for the creation of the mayor's Committee for the Preservation of Structures of Historic and Esthetic Importance and handpicked its membership. He had become the political mentor of Geoffrey Platt and Harmon Goldstone. He met with them regularly as the committee did its work, coaching them on the intricacies of government, and he followed the drafting process of the law. His old real estate ties and deep roots in that community certainly would have made him privy to inside information on a major project like Madison Square Garden before it became public. Could he have done more to block the demolition of Pennsylvania Station and impede his brother's project?

{ *Landmark Law* }

Both Platt and Goldstone had only the highest opinion of James Felt. They appreciated that his brother's project put Felt in an awkward spot but felt that "he had very different values and interests than his brother." Even the fiery Otis Pearsall had only praise for Felt's support of preservation. "I don't think it would ever have gotten across the goal line had it not been for Felt. He was the true friend of preservation that Goldstone held him to be." Nevertheless, the loss of Penn Station reminded everyone in the preservation movement that the notion of advancing preservation through public policy was far from accepted.

In addition, the Landmarks Preservation Commission was not ready for the fight to save Penn Station. Trying to do battle against those supporting the project would have been suicidal for a neophyte mayoral agency that functioned without statutory power. Working to block the demolition of Pennsylvania Station would have demonstrated that such an agency could be a major threat to real estate interests and would have unleashed the full might and wrath of that industry on the commission and its efforts to secure legal power to protect landmarks. Moderation was the wiser course. To sequence events so that the new commission would avoid a head-on clash with the Madison Square Garden juggernaut was the type of strategic thinking that came naturally to James Felt. As was noted at the time, "Only extraordinary political action could 'save' Penn Station now; and only extraordinary evidence of extraordinary public interest could spur such action." If so, it had already been being spent in the effort to physically transform its sister building, the James A. Farley Post Office—McKim, Mead & White's old general post office—into the latest incarnation of Pennsylvania Station.

Yet, even compared to earlier preservation efforts in Brooklyn Heights and Greenwich Village, "support for Pennsylvania Station was disappointing. Pennsylvania Station was in nobody's backyard. It didn't have a resident constituency." It was mainly used by people from New Jersey and Long Island. Because of the enormity of the project, made even more daunting by the need to continue train service during the demolition, the destruction of Pennsylvania Station was spread out over three years. Instead of receiving one burst of publicity, the long, agonizing dissection of the monument took place publicly for years. It was etched into the collective consciousness of the city. This meant that even with the end result foretold, there were endless opportunities to revisit the issue and countless chances for more and more New Yorkers to confront the loss. Reports such as "the commission's race against extinction is dramatized by the current demolition work at Pennsylvania Station" would keep the civic wound open and inextricably link the demolition of the station to the landmarks cause.

Personal feelings were another matter. For example, the newspapers reported that "James Van Derpool, executive director of the city's Landmarks Preservation Commission, hasn't recovered yet. He considers Penn Station the 'most monumental on the face of the earth and its destruction a tragic loss.' Van Derpool says he has no doubt that 'in the years to come we will be consumed with regret for allowing this supreme example of the architecture of the period to be destroyed.'" In fact, regret redoubled the determination of the preservationists to fight "renewal."

CHAPTER FIVE

Landmark Status for Grand Central Terminal

On April 19, 1965, Mayor Wagner signed the New York City Landmarks Preservation Law, and the city became the largest jurisdiction to pass a landmarks law with any substantial protection for individual buildings. "The Landmarks Law contradicts one of the city's most chronic characteristic traits: its bullish pride in the new. How the city tempered its raging lust for the new, traditionally at the expense of the old, is an amazing yet largely unappreciated story," wrote Anthony C. Wood. "It will take imagination, dedication, concern, citizen action, private financing and public cooperation to effect preservation under the new law.... The past is yet to be secured for the future. Celebration is premature until we can point to a safe and substantial legacy. New York is still the city that marks its history with gaping holes in the ground." The law created a permanent commission that could designate a building to be a "Landmark" or a district to be a historic district. The structure had to be at least thirty years old and exhibit either historical or architectural merit. The power to label was delegated to the commission. The city's Board of Estimate could modify or overturn a designation. The legal owner could seek judicial review of the designation but, in the interim, had to keep the building in good repair and gain commission approval for any alterations.

Wood would later state that "the passage of the Landmarks Law did not end the battle to save the city's past; it just shaped the battlefield and defined the rules of engagement.... It sounds backward-looking, but the Commission's most significant responsibility is to safeguard the future. It sends forward the best achievements of our age and those of earlier ones—parks, a great concert hall, a super train station—so they can enrich and transform the lives of people we'll never meet."

The City Council acknowledged in its enactment of the law the importance to the "health, prosperity, safety and welfare" of the people of New York of the preservation of these buildings, paying particular attention to the cultural and economic harm that would follow if they were unnecessarily destroyed. The law created a process that would be fair and balanced to create landmarks and yet not harm the property rights of owners.

The Landmarks Preservation Commission's eleven members, including at least three architects, one historian qualified in the field, one city planner or landscape architect, and one realtor, also included one resident of each of the five boroughs. The members were appointed by the mayor for three-year overlapping terms. Part of the reason why it was organized in this fashion was so that the elected officials, who had other things on their minds, could delegate historic preservation to a commission rather than having to be involved in the day-to-day future of valuable buildings. But elected officials gave their support, and that made all the difference in New York City and elsewhere. The Board of Estimate then approved, disapproved, or modified the commission's landmark designations after it received a report from the City Planning Commission. Frank Gilbert recalled those early days: "Geoff Platt and Harmon Goldstone were close friends and collaborators in developing the program. Geoff Platt started the program. His involvement in the program was from his office in the Grand Central area about Fortieth Street and Park Avenue, whereas Harmon Goldstone actually had an office at the commission. Geoff Platt was unpaid, and Harmon Goldstone got a modest salary, so that Harmon Goldstone was there every day."

J. Clarence Davies, another early commissioner, was a leader in the real estate industry and remained a good bridge to it during his term. He knew what was on the minds of real estate people's minds, and he could also explain what the Landmarks Preservation Commission was doing. Capable of dealing with tough characters, he had been the director of the Housing and Development Board that had taken over the urban renewal program from the influence of Robert Moses. He also had been real estate commissioner for the City of New York. Gilbert was excited but nervous to be working with men like Davies. "We were in a new area. Speaking personally, there was a lot of tension because there were people objecting and lawyers objecting. I think one or two of us felt most of that pressure working with Alan Burnham and, before him, with

James Van Derpool. I think we felt the pressure of the opposition. I think the other people worked quite hard on the research, the photography, the writing of reports. It was a happy place to work and an exciting place to work."

The commission designated landmarks when buildings were found to be significant examples of one or more of the following: architectural style, such as a particularly beautiful Greek Revival house, an Italianate factory, or a Beaux-Arts museum; architectural type, perhaps a singular example of a schoolhouse, department store, or office building; a specific method of construction, such as an early cast iron, or one of the first noteworthy curtain-wall buildings; or the work of a master, like Stanford White or Cass Gilbert. Also included were structures with high artistic value, such as the US Customs House, with its large exterior sculptures by Daniel Chester French (who also carved the giant statue in the Lincoln Memorial in Washington, DC), and unique historic aspects of the nation or city, like the Statue of Liberty and the Brooklyn Bridge. The only limitation was that a landmark had to be at least thirty years old, so, at first, nothing built after 1935 was considered.

Several reasons for safeguarding buildings and places were cited in the Landmarks Preservation Law. They included stabilizing and improving property values, fostering civic pride, protecting and enhancing the city's attractions for tourists, strengthening the economy of the city, and promoting the use of such sites for the education, pleasure, and welfare of the people of the city. Under New York City's law, the Landmarks Preservation Commission identified and, after public hearings, designated as landmarks and historic districts those properties and areas having "special character or special historical or aesthetic interest or value as a part of the development, heritage or cultural characteristics of the city, state or nation." This ensured that the designation was not arbitrary or capricious.

Landmark districts across New York City varied in size from a dozen to more than three thousand buildings. Obviously, some of these were exceptionally large districts. The Greenwich Village Historic District, for example, is now comparable in size to the Altstadt of Vienna; the Upper East Side Historic District to the historic Old and New Towns of Warsaw; the Upper West Side Historic District to the Old City of Jerusalem; and the Brooklyn Heights Historic District to the Old Town of Edinburgh. Frank Gilbert explained that "the people in Brooklyn Heights liked what we were doing, and after its designation, people in Greenwich Village liked what we were doing. There was a lot of support there. It's just that some people were vehement, and typically it was the lawyers—and I'm a lawyer—typically it was the lawyers who said eventually this won't last." After an area was named a historic district, all new construction and exterior modifications to buildings were regulated by the Landmarks Preservation Commission. Significant modifications required a public hearing, just like individual buildings' landmarks.

To participate fully, community groups quickly became knowledgeable in issues of historic architectural aesthetics and urban design. They often sent representatives to the public hearings unrelated to their communities simply to learn the process. Subsequently, they used concepts talked about by commissioners and professional staff members to argue on behalf of their own neighborhoods. The advocacy and knowledge of preservation groups made it increasingly difficult for politicians to intercede on behalf of narrowly focused private interests. As public testimony became substantive and probing, the level of analysis among commissioners was also raised. Open debate on the future of the cityscape attracted the press. Newspaper coverage gave exposure to the arguments of all parties, providing yet another counterbalance to narrowly oriented political influence.

In historic neighborhoods across the city, restoration of old buildings became a broad cultural phenomenon, although the process was barely noticeable in the United States in the 1950s and 1960s. When undertaken en masse, whole areas were physically and economically revived, an evolution now synonymous with "gentrification." This process often has negative connotations in the United States because in many places the majority of Black Americans are poor and cannot afford to live in wealthy neighborhoods. Gentrification was a code word for driving out poorer residents. To ameliorate the negative social repercussions, European cities commonly offer rent subsidies to preserve the mix of social classes and economic uses—a balance of social equity rarely practiced in the United States.

After the prescribed public hearing, the commission proposed to the Board of Estimate the designation of landmark properties and historic districts. The Board of Estimate, at the time the city's legislative body, could modify or overturn the historic district designation after it considered a report from the City Planning Commission on the relationship of the designated property "to the master plan, the Zoning Resolution, projected public improvements, and any plans for the renewal of the area involved." Frank Gilbert recalled, "I went on behalf of the commission to every executive session of the Board of Estimate. That would be on Wednesday afternoon, a meeting to get an idea what was on the calendar for the next day and how people were going to be acting the next day. So we were very conscious of the Borough Presidents, there are a number of stories reflecting that; you wanted their affirmative vote to confirm the designation. You spend a lot of time being in touch with the Borough Presidents' offices and the City Council president and the comptroller's office."

For political reasons, the Landmarks Preservation Commission could not have designated these areas if their inhabitants were opposed—because the elected officials of the Board of Estimate (including the borough presidents) would not have confirmed such wide restrictions of property against the will of their constituents. Contrariwise, when organizations of conservation activists sought designation of their communities, the task of convincing reluctant property owners of the benefits of preservation status was undertaken by their neighbors.

Once a landmark building or district was designated, the ordinance required that those in charge of it keep it "in good repair." The LPC was authorized to regulate construction, reconstruction, alteration, and demolition on a landmark site. Comprehensive procedures were provided when an owner wished to make such changes. A landmark owner could seek a "certificate of no exterior effect" or, if there would be exterior effect, a permit for minor work or a "certificate of appropriateness." There was also a procedure for seeking a certificate of appropriateness on the ground of insufficient return in the case of taxpaying commercial properties; and a similar procedure, but a different form of relief, for certain tax-exempt properties used for charitable purposes. There were also certain amendments to the New York City Zoning Resolution related to the Landmarks Preservation Law that permitted the transfer of unused development rights over landmark properties located in certain high-density areas of the city to other nearby sites. Denial of the certificate was subject to judicial review.

New York City's landmarks legislation defined a "reasonable return" on investment as when the property in its existing condition is unable to earn 6 percent profit per year on its assessed value. If a property owner challenged the Landmarks Preservation Commission, the owner had sixty days to develop a plan that would provide the owner with a reasonable return. The obvious method of achieving this was a partial or full abatement of real estate taxes. Such a plan needed approval by the City Council. If this tax relief offer was rejected by the owner, the commission could continue denying permission to alter the site sought by the owner. The owner was left to seek relief in court. New York City's legislation on these matters was similar to that of other cities.

The transfer of development rights did not exist in the original legislation but was added in May 1968. Only 20 percent of total unused development rights could be transferred. Common ownership was not necessary. In December 1969, the Zoning Resolution was amended to expand the availability of transfers of development rights from landmark properties. In central business districts, the 20 percent limitation as to the recipient lots was removed. In addition, the definition of "adjacent lot" was expanded to include lots across the street from the landmark site. John Costonis stated in his book, "The plan assumes that most sites occupied by landmarks are zoned for significantly greater bulk and density, that these sites are 'concentrated into reasonably compact areas of the city, usually downtown,' or in areas that are about to undergo intensive development, and that the sites which will receive additional development are located where there are plentiful public services and facilities to 'absorb large numbers of people with greater efficiency.'"

The bonus for an owner to adopt preservation plans was that it would negate the possible threat of a "taking" action or an inverse condemnation. In the former, the entire property is taken, with compensation. In the latter, the property is condemned and razed, with no compensation to the owner. There's interplay in these scenarios, and either could lead to legal issues. Still, attorney Michael Gruen, who sat on the Historic District Commission, created in 1971, argued, "I don't have ideas on how it would be improved. It always seemed to me to be a quite well conceived and written law. And the people who originally wrote it did a good job and the people who did the amendment did a good job."

Mayor Wagner's temporary Landmarks Commission had already

recognized seven hundred possible landmarks for preservation, including Grand Central Terminal, when Pennsylvania Station was demolished. The commission then reported, "Just as the designation of medieval monuments embodied the roots of cultural identity in France in 1840, in New York in 1965 many of the first buildings to be officially protected were those from the era of the founding of the United States." The comparison to France was apt, given the influence of its Beaux-Arts style on much of later nineteenth- and early twentieth-century New York architecture. "Such structures were historic house museums whose preservation was already ensured, churches, or structures located at the city's outer perimeter, where property was less valuable, and their designation was popularly, legally, and politically incontestable,"

Some important buildings were not so easily accorded landmark status. For example, Frank Gilbert, secretary of the Landmarks Preservation Commission, remembered working out the landmarking process with Trinity Church on Wall Street. "They [the owners] originally objected to the designation of Trinity Church and their related properties such as St. Paul's Chapel, and we spent a lot of time with them, we listened to them. In the end, they did not object to the designation of their property; that was the type of thing. Each situation was different; we spent a lot of time with property owners, and we were not in a big hurry."

The landmarks movement received a significant boost when the National Historic Preservation Act of 1966 (NHPA) was passed in Congress. It became the most important of the historic preservation laws to date. During the debate on July 11, 1966, Senator Ralph Yarborough of Texas said, "Anyone who has seen some of our modern urban renewal projects ... knows that we have not discovered how to build variety into a planned project. There is a depressing sameness about it all. We must not allow ourselves to be victimized by monolithic exteriors."

Landmark Status for Grand Central Terminal

Although Congress had seen the value of certain older buildings, Community Planning Board No. 5 in midtown Manhattan did not; it voted overwhelmingly against landmark status for Grand Central Terminal. Luckily for the terminal, the ruling was overruled by the LPC and the terminal was proposed for landmark status. The chairman of the Landmarks Commission told Frank Gilbert, "What happened to Penn Station must not happen to Grand Central." Gilbert's job from the very beginning was to make sure that "we follow due process," but he recognized how serious the situation was. "I think my primary thought was really to be very careful and be prepared for a very challenging situation."

As secretary, it was Gilbert's task to send out the certified letters to property owners as they appeared on the tax rolls, the first step in landmarking a building. In 1966 he sent a letter to the New York Central Railroad, the owners of Grand Central Terminal. "We had been very conscious, as I've indicated, of the importance of Grand Central, the city having lost Pennsylvania Station just a few months before the Landmarks Commission began its work," Gilbert later recalled. The commission thought the floor area ratio—all the buildable floor space for the Grand Central site—had been used up by the very large Pan Am Building (today the MetLife Building), which was over two million square feet. "They informed us that there was still potential to build another two million square foot office building. That came as quite a surprise to us. . . . So in the back of my mind was the idea that there could be objections from the railroad, but there was no potential to build a large building on that site." As events proved, Gilbert was "certainly wrong in that regard."

The Real Estate Board closely followed the activities of the Landmarks Preservation Commission. On May 10, 1966, the LPC held a public hearing on the proposed designation of Grand Central Terminal as a landmark. Three people spoke in favor of the designation. A representative of the owner also spoke in opposition. The public hearing on Grand Central Terminal closed on January 31, 1967. On August 7, 1967, the Grand Central Terminal landmark designation became official, along with nine other buildings and structures, including the Metropolitan Museum of Art and Carnegie Hall. *The New York Times* made little fuss over the designation. The "Paper of Record" only had a short article on the list, mainly focusing on the designation of a water tower in upper Manhattan. "Obviously at that time we didn't know what building would really test the law, but surely we were concerned about Grand Central," Gilbert later remembered. The committee prepared a short designation report, similar to designation reports on other buildings, and spoke in very strong terms in favor of Grand Central Terminal as a New York City landmark.

The Description and Analysis section of the Landmark Commission's report identified Grand Central Terminal as "one of the great buildings of America. . . . [Its] spirit is unique." The terminal featured "distinguished architecture with a brilliant engineering solution" and "the most fabulous railroad terminal. . . . Monumental . . . best of French Beaux Arts," with "handsome sculpted details . . . in its timeless grandeur." The Findings and Designation final portion of the report stated that the terminal "has a special character, special historical and aesthetic interest and value as part of the development, heritage and cultural characteristics of New York City." The Designation paragraph described its "artistic splendor" and asserted that it was "one of the great buildings of America." The Board of Estimate confirmed the commission's action on September 21, 1967.

The Railroad Crash

On February 1, 1968, shortly after the landmarking of the terminal, a worst-case scenario loomed for long-distance passenger rail traffic in the Northeast. Revenues had fallen far short of costs for many years. The only remaining option for the survival of the railroads was a merger. The New York Central and the Pennsylvania Railroad joined forces to form Penn Central. The combination became the country's biggest real estate company and the owner, through Madison Square Garden, of the New York Knicks and the New York Rangers franchises. Railroad leaders hoped that the consolidated lines could better compete with the trucking and airline industries. But, almost from the start, the merger proved unsuccessful. The new Penn Central was poorly run and quickly began to disintegrate. There was a clash of business cultures and responsibilities, and the new company hemorrhaged money.

While the merger drama was being played out in both the legal and the public arenas, New York City's real estate economy was also spiraling downward. Optimists argued that in the existing business climate, a new skyscraper atop Grand Central Terminal was not economically feasible; hence Grand Central Terminal was not realistically in any imminent danger. From Penn Central's viewpoint, however, making more money from its vast real estate holdings became imperative. Grand Central's available sellable air rights appeared to be an attractive development opportunity. Less than a year after the New York Landmarks Commission protected the facade of the terminal, its new owner, Penn Central Railroad, came out with a series of plans to demolish it.

Even as the New York Central Railroad turned into Penn Central, change also came to the Landmarks Preservation Commission. Geoffrey Platt, the first chair of the LPC, stepped down, and Harmon Goldstone was named his replacement. Goldstone was a natural pick for the post. He had helped form the committee, had the ear of the mayor, and as head of the Planning Commission had pushed for historic preservation. "He was there at the birth," recalled Kent L. Barwick, who would succeed Goldstone both as the commission's chairman and as president of the Municipal Art Society.

Goldstone concluded that any landmarks that were lost before a "workable" law could be achieved for the entire city was a price worth paying to avoid the chaos of having standalone districts. He grew to dislike the theatrics that certain organizations employed for publicity, such as "organized torch lit processions." He believed those days were over and that the Landmarks Law was well written, based on sound jurisprudence, and the weight of the law would prove sufficient to protect New York City's most beloved historic structures. Goldstone saw the preservation of historic and architectural landmarks as "an enormously stabilizing force in a city set in a society that's increasingly rootless and in a state of flux," according to a report in *The New York Times*. But would this approach save the terminal?

Air Rights and Wrongs

There was a repeat player in the next series of events: air rights. William Wilgus and the New Haven Railroad had conceived of air rights as a source of revenue. As the terminal's chief engineer in 1903 Wilgus had recognized the intangible legal principle of air rights, taking value from the air above the land owned by New York Central's partner railroad, the New Haven and Hartford, to monetize the terminal's excellent location.

Selling air rights by building a tower above the terminal would defray construction expenses.

It is disputed whether the Penn Central Railroad intentionally blindsided the Landmarks Preservation Commission and the City Planning Commission by revealing its full plans for this tower to the news media in the summer of 1968 instead of going to the LPC. According to *The New York Times*, the commission "expressed annoyance at not having been given notice of the design [for an office building above the terminal]." Alternatively, the railroad may simply have decided, after consulting the commission, to get the ball rolling on the public approval process to monetize the terminal. But at the time, Glenn Fowler of the *Times* stated that "the Landmarks Preservation Commission . . . has not yet seen the plans, although the commission was consulted by the railroad before it invited bids for the space over the waiting room." Either way, the railroad appeared confident in the press, while the commission privately was shocked and had very deep misgivings about the entire tower scheme.

The scheme was a real estate venture in partnership with Union General Properties (UGP) Ltd. Morris Saddy was president of UGP, a London development company that built office buildings and hotels in England and Switzerland. In 1968 he was serving as a director of the New York's famed Plaza Hotel on Central Park South. "He said he plans to supply the initial money for development of the Grand Central structure—which will be known as 175 Park Avenue—from funds of his own company, and then to seek permanent financing in the United States." According to the New York Central, UGP promised to pay Penn Central $1 million annually during construction and at least $3 million annually for fifty years. The money would offset the loss of some $700,000 to $1 million in income received from concessionaires displaced by the new building, for a total profit of $2 million a year for Penn Central.

The proposed tower would actually be the second built above the terminal. It would be four stories shorter than the Pan Am Building, but would rise about 150 feet higher because the new structure's first real floor would begin 188 feet above street level—just above the roof of the present waiting room of the railroad terminal. "A spokesman for the Pan Am Building's owners declined comment yesterday on the plans for the Pan Am's new neighbor. The older skyscraper, completed five years ago in spite of protests that it would despoil the terminal, contains

2.4 million square feet more than the new building will have," *The New York Times* revealed.

Like the New York Central's earlier plan for the Pan Am Building, the new Penn Central Railroad management wanted a bold modern design from a famous architect. They found their man in Marcel Breuer, according to Paul Goldberger's *New York Times* obituary of Breuer. Breuer was a Hungarian national born on May 21, 1902. He went to art school in Vienna in 1920, but left the Academy of Fine Arts after only five weeks. He craved a more modern style and traveled to the new Bauhaus school in Weimar Germany. He enrolled there that same year, and by 1924 was himself a Bauhaus master in charge of the carpentry and furniture department. His fame originally came from the famous desk chairs he designed, which were revolutionarily simple and tensile, light structures of wood and metal. In the 1930s he moved to England to escape Nazi Germany's Jewish persecutions. After World War II Breuer came to the United States and built a reputation as a daring, unabashedly modernist architect.

Breuer designed a number of buildings in the 1960s, including the headquarters of the Housing and Urban Development (HUD) Department in Washington, DC, which consisted of highly textured prefabricated concrete panels, each containing a window set deeply into the panel to create shadow and a sense of depth. Buildings with these prefabricated concrete panel facades were generally rather massive—although many, like the HUD Building and the IBM research facility in Boca Raton, Florida, were set on concrete legs to lighten their visual appearance.

Penn Central had found a winning architect at the height of his career, one well respected within the profession. In fact, the timing could not have been better for the scheme's public unveiling, for Breuer was to receive the prestigious Gold Medal of the American Institute of Architects for 1968, "the highest honor the architectural profession can bestow on one of its own." In an interview reported in *The New York Times* at the time of the award, Breuer said that "his prime concern in designing the new skyscraper was to provide a 'calm background' for the landmark façade of the terminal." The *Times* article went on to say that the "66-year-old Hungarian-born architect [who] has built one of the most prestigious international design practices, was given a free hand in planning the building atop the railroad terminal. His solution to the central problem of putting a modern skyscraper behind a façade designed in 1912 was to attempt a visual separation of the two elements." Clearly Breuer thought there was no aesthetic conflict when he took on the commission.

Breuer proposed to place a black box tower encased in concrete and granite on a square above the facade of the terminal. The skyscraper's bulk would extend the full width of the terminal waiting room, 309 feet from Vanderbilt Avenue eastward to the roadway between the terminal and the Commodore Hotel. The building would be 152 feet deep, and the distance between the new slab and the octagonal tower would be 221 feet—a little more than the length of a city block. Breuer said at the time that "floating of the new tower over the old waiting room" would solve the visual discord of the skyscraper dominating over the terminal.

The building would be supported by a central core that would be anchored in bedrock and run upward through the waiting room space, costing more than using traditional high-rise construction techniques. To accomplish this, four huge trusses would be cantilevered from the core to the first-floor level of the new structure, just above the present waiting-room roof. This process could eliminate column supports at the ground level. The present waiting room would be transformed into a vaulting lobby that would incorporate the building access with a pedestrian walkway leading to the main concourse, thus eliminating use of the Vanderbilt waiting rooms permanently.

Breuer promised that the concourse itself north of the waiting room leading to the train gates would not be directly affected by construction of the new building. The railroad offered a carrot to officials: to "'clean up' the concourse . . . the clutter of advertising signs, photo displays, commercial exhibits and the like will be banished." Many preservationists, design groups, and architects looked forward to this, but they had had no means of forcing the railroad to comply. Also, the city's landmarks law did not protect buildings' interiors, and many worried that the railroad would cut corners or break its word.

Goldstone, the LPC chair, knew Marcel Breuer well and later said he "had a very amicable relationship . . . knew his wife, and I knew him, and we were very good friends." The so-called Breuer Plan was one of the first issues to arise after Goldstone assumed the chairmanship. He recalled telling Breuer, "I think this is going to be big, a lot of issues... and I just think we better not meet any more; we better not have any discussions; we better do all the discussing through the lawyers, because I don't want any personal involvement." But, Goldstone conceded, "it was a difficult step to take, at the very beginning."

The City Planning Commission was very concerned about the pedestrian and automobile congestion that would come from putting two million square feet of office space on top of a major transit facility that already experienced strain from nearby office development. But Breuer claimed that the new design he envisioned would provide four additional passageways from the terminal and the office building into the subways, "without loading the surrounding streets with pedestrians." Breuer's design called for a covered plaza off Forty-Second Street with a taxi driveway for off-street loading. Pedestrian traffic would flow through a broad lobby at street level that would lead up to elevator lobbies for the new building and down to the terminal concourse. Two new subway entrances would be built, and pedestrian traffic from the three lines that serviced the station—the Lexington Avenue, Forty-Second Street shuttle, and the crosstown line to Queens—would be rerouted, but Breuer provided no further public details. The Forty-Second Street sidewalk would be widened from twenty-three feet to seventy-three feet, and the row of stores on the Forty-Second Street side of the terminal would be removed and replaced with expanded space for shops inside the terminal. Breuer said that restaurants at all price levels would be incorporated into the new building and would be capable of serving several thousand lunchtime customers.

UGP and the railroad hired the consulting engineering firm of Wilbur Smith and Associates to make an extensive study of pedestrian use of the terminal and the probable impact of the twelve thousand additional people that the planned skyscraper would bring into the area. The study concluded that the proposed corridor system would provide a more even distribution of people over a greater number of passageways than existed at present, and that it would eliminate overloading during rush hours—a finding that strongly supported Breuer's design.

Despite Penn Central's well-orchestrated and publicized plan, there were more critics of it than just those who admired the great vaulted waiting room. City planners, the public, and even some architects spoke angrily about Breuer's proposed tower. "It's the wrong building, in the wrong place, at the wrong time," Donald K. Elliott, chairman of the City Planning Commission, said the day after the tower scheme was unveiled to the public. He had already seen the preliminary plans. The Planning Commission was upset but had few regulatory tools at its disposal to stop the proposed construction. "Mr. Breuer's plans require no variance from the zoning rules, commission members concede," *The New York Times* reported. Though the City Planning Commission and development authorities had no formal power, they did raise an argument that would be successful against the project at the Landmark Commission. Jaquelin T. Robertson, one of the city's leading architects, claimed that the space above the terminal, south of the Pan Am Building, is "a sort of air park," opening to the south and the sunlight. "It is in fact the area's only window to the sun," journalist David K. Shipler wrote. Battles over air rights were old, for "ancient lights," the doctrine of access to sun and air, was as old as the first skyscrapers. This one would be a doozy.

After the initial reports went public, *Time* magazine called the scheme "Breuer's Blockbuster," adding, "The American Institute of Architects is presenting its Gold Medal to Breuer this week. It may be a good thing that this is happening in Portland, Ore., 2,445 miles away from Manhattan, where such an award ceremony right now would be sure to bring out pickets." *The New York Times*'s Huxtable called the plan "a truly remarkable shotgun wedding between sentiment and speculative economics." She wryly observed that "the trick is pulled off with striking technical elan. Mr. Breuer has done an excellent job with a dubious undertaking, which is like saying it would be great if it weren't so awful."

Less admiring opinion pieces with headlines like "Jumbo Atop Grand Central" and "The City, Dear Brutus" called the tower's impact "devastating" on Grand Central and proclaimed that "the new tower soaring from the classical Beaux Arts terminal like a skyscraper on a base of French pastry has the bizarre quality of a nightmare." Others were still less equivocal: the "Pan Am Building, balanced on the back of Grand Central Terminal north of the great room is, I believe, one of the few structures which New Yorkers really do resent, overbearing as it is to Park Avenue... this proposal as architecture. It is dental work. They will drill out to the outer walls of a building which many people are actively fond of, an authentic New York landmark, and make it the quaintly phony base of an immense skyscraper"; and "The proposed new structure is represented to be modeled on that effort, but its bulk will make it a mockery."

Architects were split on the Breuer Plan. Richard Roth, who was the primary architect of the Pan Am Building, called it "Horrible—terrible. . . . We put the Pan Am Building way back from the main part of the terminal, replacing an ugly structure over the train shed. It formed a gracious backdrop for the terminal itself." The widely respected architect Philip Johnson's comments on the Breuer Plan were especially sharp, calling it an "outrage. . . . It's wrong in every possible way. . . . Hiring a very great architect to design that building isn't enough justification to build it in the first place."

While many architects grumbled on and off the record, a few broke ranks to praise the proposal openly. Walter F. Wagner Jr., editor of *Architectural Record*, said that the building would "make a powerful contribution to the overcrowded hub of New York City's transportation system." Peter Blake, in a Cityscape piece in *New York Magazine*, shot down the critics of Breuer and Penn Central. "To sum up: there is no City Plan to which Breuer or anyone else could have conformed and so the villain in this case is a City Planning Commission too spineless in the past to have fought for tough zoning laws and too unconcerned to have developed a master plan for the city as a whole. As for Penn Central, the 'villain' is not the Penn Central Railroad, but a society that permits and encourages wild and unrestricted speculation with the price of land."

The public give-and-take was a backdrop to the public hearing process at the LPC that began in the fall of 1968. The first step was for the developer and railroad to apply for a certificate of "no exterior effect." Frank Gilbert later recounted, "They wanted to test whether or not we would give permission at that point, and we were a little surprised that a two million square foot office building on top of Grand Central would qualify for a certificate of no exterior effect." Marcel Breuer came to the public hearing at the Landmarks Preservation Commission, to explain that he thought that because the development was something positive it would have "no adverse exterior effect." He also felt that the way it was designed, it actually did not touch the exterior fabric of Grand Central.

There was some trepidation at the Landmarks Preservation Commission. Goldstone remembered one of his key people saying, "We can never stand up to this power; we're all going to have to knuckle under this one." To which Goldstone responded, "We may well be torpedoed, but let's go down with all flags flying." On September 20, 1968, the commission rejected Breuer's initial proposal. John Belle, later lead architect on Grand Central Terminal's restoration, celebrated this decision in his book about the struggle to preserve the station.

After the LPC's decision, Penn Central and Marcel Breuer came out with a new plan known as Breuer II. It obliterated the exterior of the terminal but restored the entire main concourse. This was no longer a case of a blocky clash of styles, bulk, or air rights but of destroying the south facade of Grand Central Terminal. It was as if Breuer, Penn Central, and Union General Properties were doubling down on the critics by saying that if the modern mixed poorly with the old, then it would be better to destroy the old and make everything modern. Belle said it clearly: "The design of Breuer II Revised upped the ante. Not only was it three stories taller than Breuer I but it also required the demolition of much of the Terminal building."

Penn Central replied that the concourse interior was the only part of the building worth saving, that the exterior had not been worth designating in the first place, and that it was the smarter choice to replace the current building with a good building by a famous architect than to risk, in the future, one being built by a lesser talent. Many in the modernist architectural community still supported Breuer's architectural design. "There has been some question in the minds of informed people," Breuer said to *The New York Times*, "as to whether the exterior of Grand Central Terminal is worth preserving." "The best part of the present station," he said, is the main concourse—"the last one of New York's great interior spaces."

A new application, this time for a certificate of appropriateness, together with the Breuer II proposal, was submitted by UGP on January 20, 1969, to the Landmark Preservation Commission. There was a significant public hearing in April 1969 with more than seventy speakers standing against the proposal. Belle recalled "that so many well-respected professionals could have voted in favor of proposals that prophesied Grand Central's demise is indicative of a time in our history when people believed that preserving the old kept us trapped in the clutches of the past." But they had not.

Those speaking against both Breuer proposals included then congressman Edward Koch; Jean Paul Carlhian, representing the American Institute of Architects; Giorgio Cavaglieri, New York State preservation coordinator for the American Institute of Architects; Charles Hughes and Frederick Williams, from the Municipal Art Society; Margo Gayle, of the Victorian Society and the Village Neighborhood Committee; architects David Todd and George Lewis, from the New York chapter of the American Institute of Architects; Professor James Marston Fitch of the Graduate School of Architecture, Planning and Preservation at Columbia University (who later became the chair of historic preservation at Beyer Blinder Belle); Arthur Rosenblatt, administrator for planning at the Metropolitan Museum of Art; John Baur, director of the Whitney Museum; and other prominent New Yorkers and professionals. The vast majority of local and national architectural organizations spoke against the demolition or defacement of Grand Central, despite their respect for Breuer as one of their own. Chiming in were the president of the City Council, the editor of *Architectural Forum*, and representatives of the American Institute of Architects. Goldstone judged, "It was very impressive, people who spoke up and spoke up strongly against the proposal."

The Planning Commission's Samuel Roberts presented a map highlighting the land that Penn Central owned near Grand Central from Forty-Second Street to Fiftieth Street. The presentation implied that another office building was not needed. Remember, New York City was in the midst of its financial doldrums, and office space was then going begging. The land in question contained a substantial number of buildings and properties including the Waldorf-Astoria, Biltmore, Roosevelt, and Commodore Hotels. Samuel Hellenbrand, representing the railroad, responded by pointing out that those properties were tangled up in long-term leases too complicated to break, with terms ending from 1987 to 2062. Roberts replied that the leases could have been bought out, as was common "all over New York."

A considerably smaller number of people spoke in favor of the proposal, including renowned modernist architect I. M. Pei (whose own proposal was still AWOL); John I. H. Bauer, the director of the Whitney Museum; and several other architects. Commissioner Gilbert recollected, "Listening to their testimony, I think these architects felt that something was going to happen at Grand Central, and the city was better off with an architect of Marcel Breuer's quality rather than some other architect who might be drafted to design a building."

Concurrent with these hearings, Penn Central and UGP realized Breuer II was to be built on land that extended over a city-held easement that was outside the private developers' control. The Breuer II proposal was withdrawn and later resubmitted as Breuer II Revised, which was restricted to land controlled by Union General Properties. Public hearings reopened in August 1969 on both Breuer I and Breuer II Revised.

Before it ruled on the certificate of appropriateness, the Landmarks Preservation Commission found out that the application from the developers also included plans for a site that they did not own: a fast-food restaurant called Cobb's Corner. The railroad explained to the commission that it was about to buy the site including Cobb's Corner. "This raised in their minds the thought that they might have an invalid application and that the commission might turn them down without ever getting to the merits, turn them down on a mere technicality," Frank Gilbert, then a member of the commission, feared. At that point, they would have a choice of appealing the LPC's rejection or starting all over again. Neither of these alternatives looked attractive to them, and so UGP wrote to the Landmarks Commission, which was then considering the application, the public hearing having been closed and completed, and asked for some additional information on what grounds it would reach a decision. The applicants wanted to avoid this problem, and they wanted to avoid losing on a mere technicality.

Gilbert recalled what followed:

> In any event, the railroad's and developer's thinking was such that they wrote this letter about on what basis will the commission reach its decision. The chairman and I went over to see a good friend, the corporation counsel, Lee Rankin.... Lee Rankin's letter or draft was quite simple. It said, ... I urge you to do whatever you think best under the circumstances. That passed the ball back to the developers and the railroad, and they sent Marcel Breuer back to the drawing boards, and he came up with Breuer 2 revised. There were two alternate designs; Breuer two revised only involved property they already owned, and in the years since then, I've gotten a number of phone calls asking what is this Breuer two revised? They understood Breuer

one, but they didn't quite understand Breuer two revised. It all went back to Cobb's Corner, this property they did not own.

The developers never did acquire Cobb's Corner. They obviously invested quite a bit of money in payments to the railroad and also in the legal fees. At the end of August 1969, the Landmarks Preservation Commission presented its opinion on the application for a certificate of appropriateness. The commission noted it was not the place where the public should go with comments and concerns about the interiors of Grand Central, the vehicular and pedestrian traffic, and the air rights issues. These things fell within the purview of the City Planning Commission. The decision had and was to be made based only on the architectural and historical merits of Grand Central Terminal.

The LPC rejected both the resubmission of Breuer I and the initial submission of Breuer II Revised. In its written opinion the commission noted that the Pan Am Building was set back 375 feet from the terminal's south facade whereas the proposed Breuer I tower was only thirty feet away. "The softening effects of distance (atmospheric perspective) and all the present sense of separation would be lost. The full play of sunlight and shadow on the Breuer façade would be in direct competition with the richly modelled design of the Terminal below it and nearly in the same plane." The commission's report strongly warned, "To balance a 55-story office tower above a flamboyant Beaux-Arts façade seems nothing more than an aesthetic joke. Quite simply, the tower would overwhelm the terminal by its sheer mass. The 'addition' would be four times as high as the existing structure and would reduce the landmark itself to the status of a curiosity."

The report went on to say that "to protect a landmark one does not tear it down. To perpetuate its architectural features one does not strip them off." It affirmed the majesty of the terminal after calling it "one of the great buildings of America." In its report, the commission compared New York unfavorably with Paris and other cities that it said were "rich in dramatically terminated vistas." New York, it observed, had "Trinity Church at the end of Wall Street, Washington Arch at the foot of Fifth Avenue and the RCA Building at the end of the Rockefeller Center gardens." "Yet none of these," the report continued, "have the sweep that Park Avenue still proved for Grand Central Terminal from the south."

The air above Grand Central Terminal was sacred space to the commission and not to be given away lightly. The report also judged that "landmarks cannot be divorced from their settings—particularly when the setting is a dramatic and integral part of the original concept. The Terminal, in its setting, is a great example of urban design. Such examples are not so plentiful in New York City that we can afford to lose any of the few we have. And we must preserve them in a meaningful way—with alterations and additions of such character, scale, materials and mass as will protect, enhance and perpetuate the original design rather than overwhelm it." Granting permission to construct the giant tower would have memorialized in the cityscape a failure of moral authority.

It was this certificate of no exterior effect that the commission unanimously denied on August 26, 1969, with three of its eleven members absent. By a unanimous vote in 1969, the commission rejected two plans, one for a fifty-five-story tower that would have preserved the Forty-Second Street facade of the terminal and one for a fifty-six-story tower that would have demolished the facade. The LPC also noted that it thought it did not have authority to judge Penn Central's application for relief based on economic hardship.

The Real Estate Board of New York would later question the ruling. In its amicus brief in support of Penn Central before the US Supreme Court in 1977, it would argue that

> there is nothing on the face of the designs for the proposed Breuer buildings that could be regarded as a community nuisance. There is certainly nothing inappropriate about the existence of a modern, high-rise office building in a section of the City which is zoned for, and indeed now contains a cluster of such buildings which may well be the most concentrated in the world. It was a reasonable position that the status quo of tearing down or altering older structures and building up Midtown East to its fullest zoned potential . . . was natural and legal.

Going to(o) FAR

Despite the support he and the Landmarks Preservation Commission had gained to reject the application, Goldstone worried about "ending up in court and losing the landmarks law," Kent Barwick recalled. "That made his sure-handedness in the matter of Grand Central all the more impressive." Goldstone remembered:

> We got through the hearings, and had all the arguments summarized. And I went over to get Lee Rankin's advice. He would spend hours with me, and he would work out alternative scenarios; if you do this, then Penn Central will do that, and so on. And I said, "What shall I do?" And [Rankin] said, "That is up to you. I am your lawyer, and I'm giving you my best advice on the risks you're running, and the procedures, and the options, but the decision is yours." And it was a very lonely position, but he was absolutely right; he said, "I'm not going to tell you what to do." But Rankin also said, "Whatever you decide, I will back you and defend you with everything I've got; I mean, you know I'm behind you whatever you decide." He quite rightly wouldn't help make decisions.

Goldstone told the next chapter of the story in his contribution to the New York Preservation Archive:

> So then we went back into Executive Session, with the full Commission; everybody was there. And we just went around the table, clockwise. I said, "I want you all to just speak your piece." Goldstone was glad that "They weren't interrupted, and everybody just said what they thought. It turned out that they unanimously wanted to turn down the application: they all had personal slants, and different reasons for doing so. I was the last one. I hadn't wanted to influence them. And so when they said, "Well, what do you think?" I said I had already drafted an opinion, and if they had all agreed the other way, it would have been a minority opinion of one! Up to that point, I don't think any of them knew how I had made up my mind. When he told F. Lee Rankin, the city's counsel, this, he said, "That is marvelous; you've really got an independent, unanimous opinion. Nobody was railroaded if that comes out in the appeal, as it will, that's really wonderful. That's wonderful!"

In 1969 the Penn Central Railroad persuaded the city to approve broadened enabling legislation. The railroad desired to transfer at least 50 percent of its unutilized development (that is, air) rights above Grand

Central Terminal to the then unprofitable Biltmore Hotel site—one of many properties owned by the railroad in the vicinity of the terminal. The city amended its initial air rights legislation to make possible a greater radius of transferability and to remove, within the Manhattan central business district, the 20 percent FAR (floor area ratio) coverage ceiling on an individual receiving lot. This would permit the railroad to carry out its massive Biltmore redevelopment scheme, for which its architect, again Marcel Breuer, developed drawings of equal detail to those worked up for proposals on the terminal site. After the legislation was adopted, however, the heretofore booming market for office space in midtown Manhattan produced a glut of unrentable floor space, and the railroad ceased work on the Biltmore project. It thereafter placed reliance on lawyers rather than architects and decided to pursue its interest exclusively in the courts. Goldstone completed his tenure with the Landmarks Preservation Commission in 1974, leaving the position with a status of heightened authority and influence.

Gilbert was unamused by the railroad's new plan: "This new impossibility has been designed by the distinguished Marcel Breuer, who understands the principle of the cantilever and the abhorrence of real-estate men for any midtown vacuum." Breuer was portrayed on the front page of *The New York Times* pointing contentedly toward a drawing of "his immense slab which looks like an elongated meat cleaver descending upon a prune soufflé. The accompanying story seems to make it clear that neither zoning regulations, nor the City Planning Commission, nor the Landmarks Preservation Commission, or any uprising of the maddened standees on the 5:07 to Larchmont had the power or energy to put a stop to the project. The thing is to be done, and the only wonder is our own lack of wonderment." So said Gilbert.

The fight for preservation seemed to have no end, not as long as the LPC lacked any compulsory mechanisms. The Municipal Art Society took on the issue and formed various committees to explore the idea of expanding the Landmarks Preservation Commission's powers. Goldstone recognized the need for added protection and supported the idea of amending the law, but faced with the realities of the LPC's limited staff and financial resources, he was reluctant to add too many new responsibilities to the LPC's purview. In 1973 the law was amended, giving the LPC the power to designate and protect interior landmarks (the old law only concerned external features) and scenic landmarks. The amendments also reinstated continuous designation determinations, ending the moratorium that restricted designations to a six-month period every three years. Could the terminal be safe at last?

CHAPTER SIX

Penn Central Strikes Back

The combat over the landmark status of Grand Central Terminal did not end in 1969—it merely shifted venues. For just as the Landmarks Preservation Commission sought regulatory powers, on October 7, 1969, Penn Central filed a lawsuit against the City of New York in the Supreme Court of New York State. Despite its name, the Supreme Court of New York was actually a New York trial court. Secretary of the Landmarks Commission Frank Gilbert received the lawsuit papers and later recalled "the young law student who brought the papers in from the law firm Dewey, Ballantine.... I think they were asking for $8 million a year in damages." The award the railroad sought was either too low—surely the replacement of the terminal with an office building was worth a lot more to the Penn Central—or too high, as interfering with plans for an office building did not cost the railroad that much. The suit thus seemed to be a version of a strike suit, meant to deter the city from proceeding with the landmark designation.

In its filing, Penn Central alleged that the LPC's refusal to approve any of the railroad's plans was so financially burdensome that it amounted to an unconstitutional "taking" of property without just compensation. This would have violated the Fifth and Fourteenth Amendments of the US Constitution, which protected citizens from having their private property taken for public use without just compensation and ensured that no person can be deprived of property without due process of law. The railroad valued this taking as $8 million in lost earnings for every year the Breuer project was delayed.

A second constitutional argument offered by Penn Central's legal team was that the effect of the landmark ordinance unconstitutionally discriminated against Penn Central by designating the terminal a landmark when the City of New York did not require other nearby landowners to bear the same financial burden. In other words, Penn Central claimed that the absence of hardship on other nearby property owners singled Penn Central out for unfair treatment.

The suit also challenged the landmark character of the terminal as "highly debatable and at best doubtful." This was a collateral attack on the statute itself, an alternative to pleading that the loss of revenue made the landmarking of the terminal under the statute impermissible. Pleading in the alternative, that is, pleading two incompatible grounds, is permissible under modern procedural rules. The firm of attorneys representing Penn Central/Union General Properties—Dewey, Ballantine, Bushby, Palmer & Wood—continued that "the esthetic quality of the south facade is obscured by its engulfment among narrow streets and high-rise buildings. It is hardly seen at all except for a short distance to the south of Park Avenue."

Furthermore, the railroad's law firm argued, in what amounted to an indictment of Penn Central's own earlier air rights venture, "The terminal is set against the backdrop and contrasting lines of the Pan Am Building, which appears to hang over the terminal and to dwarf it." Thus the construction of the Pan Am Building itself became a justification for demolishing the terminal rather than a compromise meant to save the terminal. "This argument was a little like the defendant accused of parricide begging for mercy because he is an orphan," John Belle, the head of the team that restored Grand Central Terminal, later wrote. These arguments, if taken at face value, questioned any individual landmarks law based on aesthetic values.

In Irving Saypol's Court

The City of New York, of course, denied each of the relevant allegations, and the matter eventually went to trial before Judge Irving Howard Saypol, a trial term judge in the New York court sitting in Manhattan. Judge Saypol had risen from unprepossessing circumstances to a place on the bench. He did not come from a wealthy or high-status family. He was as New York-born and -bred as the terminal itself, earning his law degree at Brooklyn Law School and practicing in his own firm until 1945, when he entered government service. There, he started his career as a federal prosecutor, and in 1949 he became US Attorney for the

Southern District of New York. There was, arguably, no more prominent district in the federal judicial system—the Southern District handling a wide variety of commercial, financial, and criminal cases. In his short tenure, Saypol was involved in several high-profile anti-Communist prosecutions, including the Alger Hiss, William Remington, Abraham Brothman, and controversial Julius and Ethel Rosenberg cases. As a state judge, Saypol presided over some of the most dramatic cases brought in Manhattan. Judge Saypol was perfectly content in the public spotlight.

His *New York Times* obituary described Saypol as "a stern and imposing figure with a hard, square jaw, bushy eyebrows and steady blue eyes that peered out from behind rimless spectacles.... His manner on the bench was customarily crisp and, to make his courtroom points, he could mix street talk with Latin." According to the obituary, in 1964 Judge Saypol fined a lawyer for contempt because she wore a brown suede hat in court. Calling her hat a "grotesque" and "flamboyant turban," he admonished that "bizarre hats" were "something no self-respecting judge can tolerate." In August 1966 Saypol held then congressman Adam Clayton Powell in criminal contempt of court, calling him "a mischievous delinquent." One could guess from Saypol's track record that both parties in *Penn Central v. New York* would have to toe the mark, indeed that the city might have an uphill battle convincing the judge of the merits and legality of individual structure landmarking.

Penn Central's team of lawyers thought that the case was straightforward. Grand Central Terminal's revenues were below its expenditures, and the historical preservation law (the Bard Act) guaranteed the regulated property owners a reasonable return on their property, which the law defined as the excess of revenues over expenditures. Accordingly, the company introduced evidence to show that it had been operating Grand Central Terminal at a loss of nearly $2 million a year for years, and that as things stood, it could not earn a reasonable return on its property. This was well below the 6 percent net annual return on assessed valuation the law defined as "reasonable." (Evidence submitted by the city merely reduced the terminal's annual deficit for 1971 from more than $1.9 to approximately $1.1 million.)

Penn Central also alleged that denial of the certificate to construct the Breuer Plan precluded it from millions in rent per year from UGP during construction and $3 million a year for fifty years thereafter.

Because Penn Central received no net revenue from the terminal and was compelled by the landmark regulation to operate and maintain it at a deficit, the railroad thought it had an open-and-shut legal case. Another high-rise on a different location would not be of the same value as the Grand Central parcel, the development partnership claimed after an investigation of potential alternatives. On top of this, Penn Central added to the bill that the rejection of the Breuer Plan cost it millions from rent that could go to support the terminal. It stopped short of adding the money it had advanced to Breuer for his work to the losses it faced under the landmark designation.

Penn Central's lawyers could also have argued, but didn't, that the terminal was the third station on the site and that each of the previous stations had been demolished due to changing ridership patterns and railway needs. If historical significance was the grounds for the landmark designation, historical context surely showed that each iteration of the station was a product of ridership and revenue, not aesthetics. Also, the railroad made no mention of the fact that the Landmarks Preservation Commission might have approved a plan that was more Beaux-Arts inspired, like the twenty-story building scheme proposed by the railroad sixty years earlier.

For its defense, the Landmarks Commission relied on the city's law department. It assigned three lawyers to work on the case: James Nespole, Victor Muskin, and Yvette Harmon. Nespole was the lead attorney. A New Yorker, educated at City College and Columbia Law School, he joined the bar in 1958. Muskin, an NYU Law School–trained counsel, was named an assistant corporate counsel for the city in 1969, after he had returned from service in the Peace Corps. Harmon had attended Cornell Law School and joined the city's law department in 1969. All three were relatively junior in experience to their Penn Central opponents. The city's lawyers would get daily transcripts of what was said in court, and Nespole led in questioning the precise wording of the record. Still, the city's case rested on expert testimony. Vincent Scully, the distinguished Yale professor of architecture, traveled from Hartford, Connecticut, to testify about the importance of Grand Central Terminal. Frank Gilbert recalled: "We brought in, and our attorneys brought in, a Yale historian, an architect, an old historian, and he testified." Leonard Koerner, another of the city's corporate counsel, recalled: "We all met with Vincent Scully the night before his testimony. Other witnesses included the head of the planning commission, Jack Robertson, architects, and real estate people coming in as to the potential for the site." Scully "said that when he comes into the train in Grand Central his heart palpitates from excitement." Saypol was not impressed. According to Gilbert, the judge jibed, "I guess you saw the homeless outside the bathroom." Koerner was watching the trial, and admitted, "So we had a pretty good idea things weren't going to go too well."

The city contested the argument that the landmark designation was an unconstitutional taking and presented an expert witness to testify that the proposed skyscraper could be built at a lower cost at the site of the Biltmore Hotel rather than the terminal. Frank Gilbert stated that "the friend of the court briefs, amicus briefs, began coming later. At the trial level, as the case was heard before Judge Saypol, there weren't any amicus briefs at that point. That type of brief belongs on the appellate level."

Murray Drabkin, a distinguished bankruptcy lawyer, professor of law, and bankruptcy law reformer, had been hired by the developers to guide the scheme through the regulatory process. He testified in court about the proceedings before the Landmarks Preservation Commission and found no fault in the way the it had handled the application. But that did not help the city (although a finding that the city or the LPC had acted wrongly would have doomed its case).

In the meantime, everyone on the city's legal team was beginning to sense how Saypol would decide the case. Gilbert acknowledged, "It was a difficult month for us, and that Judge Saypol, I think it's safe to say, was no fan of New York City government." During the trial, Penn Central's attorneys objected to Nespole's questioning, objections that Saypol upheld, with the result that Nespole continually had to rephrase questions. In a last effort to save the case, the city put into the record a letter dealing with $11 million worth of tax exemption that had been given to the railroad. While it proved that city officials were very interested in the help given to the railroad, it was irrelevant to the takings question.

Friends of the LPC tried to intervene on its behalf. The Municipal Art Society made a motion to participate in the role of friend of the court and produced a brief by a distinguished group of lawyers and former judges including former mayor Robert F. Wagner; Bernard Botein, former presiding justice of the Appellate Division, State Supreme

Court; Whitney North Seymour Sr., former head of the American Bar Association; Francis T. P. Plimpton, former diplomat and former president of the Association of the Bar of the City of New York; Samuel I. Rosenman, former State Supreme Court justice and counsel to Presidents Franklin D. Roosevelt and Harry S. Truman; Bethuel M. Webster, long active in city judiciary councils; and other prominent New Yorkers. It was a list of heavyweights. "This is not a proposal to replace the terminal with a new facility vital to the handling of plaintiff's business or even to building a facility in addition to the terminal essential to railroad purposes. Rather it is a plan to build an office building to produce revenue." The amicus brief further argued that the plaintiff railroad received a tax exemption for the railroad portion of the terminal and that if it was in the business of owning office buildings it would need to explain how it was still entitled to a tax exemption. In effect, the brief argued that the tax relief was a set-off to the lost revenue. Again, however, it was not relevant to the takings question, as it could not guarantee fifty years of further tax relief.

The court case dragged on for years, primarily because in June 1970, prior to the trial court's decision, Penn Central declared bankruptcy. Over the course of the next two years the trustees appointed to oversee the consolidation and repayment of the railroad's debts entered a series of contracts with the State of New York to ensure vital commuter operations in Penn Station and Grand Central Terminal. The Metropolitan Transportation Authority of New York (the MTA) and the Connecticut Transportation Authority (the CTA) assumed ownership and operation of these commuter services and employed Penn Central to operate them on their respective behalf. The MTA also entered into a sixty-year lease with Penn Central for the use of Grand Central Terminal. The authority agreed to pay a maximum annual rent of $454,415, and Penn Central would give a credit toward MTA expenses of running the terminal of at least $2 million annually for sixty years. The changed circumstances were undoubtably the main reason Judge Saypol took so long to publish his decision. Harmon Goldstone opined, "Judge Saypol wouldn't render a decision for almost a year.... I think he just hoped it would all go away by itself."

In the meantime, under the lease the MTA became Penn Central's tenant and was alone entitled to the rents and other economic benefits of the terminal. However, the air rights above the terminal were specifically excluded from the coverage of this lease. The cumulative effect of these necessary legal agreements was to "leave Penn Central with no possible source of return from the Terminal save [air] development rights." Everyone involved clearly was panicking over the city's financial crisis, no entity more than the MTA.

The impact of the lease on the terminal's survival was uncertain. Roberta B. Gratz wrote in a *New Yorker* article on November 8, 1974, that the city was contemplating withdrawing Grand Central's landmark designation in fear of losing the legal battle and paying Penn Central/UGP damages upward of $60 million. Though Judge Saypol had not yet ruled on the matter before him, it was rumored that he was leaning toward the plaintiffs. "This was when Grand Central was really almost lost," recounted Gratz. "Kent Barwick [the executive director of the Municipal Art Society] alerted me. I wrote this story to bring to the public's attention what was going on behind the scenes. The rest is history." The public did have reason to worry. "We were in no hurry for him to decide the case because we were pretty certain as to what his opinion would be. It would be against the city," Frank Gilbert reflected.

In the meantime, critics of the terminal's landmark status scorned those who would arrest needed development for the sake of preserving "useless remnants" of the past. They agreed with the owner of the fifty-year-old American Radiator Building, at 40 West Fortieth Street, also being considered for landmark designation. Commercial buildings were "not built for the ages but to last a commercial length of time," said a spokesman for American Standard, the building's owner, which was fighting designation.

The bad news kept on coming for the city and its Landmarks Preservation Commission when the Court of Appeals, the highest court in the state, vacated the landmark designation of the Morgan House. In brief, the Lutheran Church of America had bought the former J. P. Morgan Jr. mansion located in midtown Manhattan. The church wanted to erect an office building on the site of the hundred-year-old mansion and opposed the mansion's landmark designation. It had tried to get the zoning changed to permit a high-rise building there, but to no avail. The church was told to wait until its plans had favorable zoning. The Lutheran Church went ahead with its lawsuit anyhow. In the course of his testimony, Richard

Bernstein, who was then head of the City Planning Commission, admitted that denying the zoning request was "a polite way of saying no" to the church. The case went to the Court of Appeals, which found that the designation was an impermissible burden on the Lutheran Church and its use of the property. The city lost the case, but the building was not demolished and is now the centerpiece of the J. P. Morgan Library.

Still, the Landmarks Commission was demoralized by the court's decision. Gilbert: "Up until the Grand Central decision, which is 1978, you wondered.... When you listen to, in New York City, in my case, nine years of some people saying that you're not legal, all your work may be lost or wasted. You don't believe them. You believe in what you're doing; you're optimistic, but it has an effect on you." There was no jury to persuade, one way or another, only the judge, as the case was an equitable one—petitioners sought an injunction against the city. And Saypol was not particularly impressed by the city's array of experts.

For most of the public, the delay between the trial and Judge Saypol's opinion put the issue of Grand Central on the back burner, although the Landmarks Commission tried to keep it in public view. In a 1974 *New York Times* interview, Goldstone touted the "intangible returns that landmarks can bring—the sense of history preserved, the living evidence of a more gracious past, the pride of a city with roots"—and also "the very real economic benefits that accrue when a landmark or historic district is protected by official designation." An October 22, 1974, *Times* article noted that "others hold that the preservation law is "clearly confiscatory" if an owner is forced to retain a building, or to keep it in its existing form, if "there is no economic use for it," as D. Kenneth Patton, president of the Real Estate Board of New York, put it. While not considering himself an opponent of preservation—"I've always favored the principle of selective preservation," he said—"Mr. Patton contended that the Landmarks Commission had not developed enough of a systematic approach to granting relief to owners of property financially hurt by a landmarks designation." He suggested some form of public subsidy, tax abatement, or transfer of development rights to other properties. In reply, commission officials said that while they "have no power to make direct grants" to owners of landmark properties, they have helped certain owners to get needed relief through tax breaks and the transfer of development rights.

Events outside the courtroom were influencing Saypol, although he did not say as much. In 1975, when Saypol issued his decision, New York City was again teetering on the brink of municipal bankruptcy. Public works projects were halted midway, leaving the steel skeletons of new schools to rust. Another landmark—the elegant but disintegrating Tweed Courthouse behind City Hall, which was to be razed and replaced with a parking lot—was spared only because the city could no longer afford to tear it down. Private developers also packed away blueprints and placed planned construction on hold.

Judge Saypol Rules

Saypol's decision in the Grand Central case did not arrive until 1975. It was a long time between the case being heard, in 1972, and 1975. He waited a record length of time before he handed down his decision. "The station is probably in no immediate danger," *The New Yorker* noted imperturbably, but Frank Gilbert knew the lawsuit was not going the city's way:

> Judge Saypol called the lawyers in for week-long proceedings in front of him.... The lawyer for the railroad, John Wood, who's one of the named partners in Dewey, Ballantine, Bushby, Palmer, and Wood, and Judge Saypol were on the same wavelength, and they spent the week discussing more than 100 findings of fact. The railroad's findings of fact were all adopted by Judge Saypol, and the city was sitting there and basically listening.... I say, John Wood and Judge Saypol had a great week together."

Gilbert continued his recollection:

> Near the end of this, we were coming out of the courtroom one afternoon, and I turned to Mr. Wood and said, you know we've done you a big favor. We kept your client from building a building that would be vacant now because there's not a big demand. We'd appreciate very much a letter from your client thanking us for the help we've given him, and John Wood started to answer, he said you don't really think that, and at that point he realized I was pulling his leg

{ *Chapter Six* }

and didn't expect a letter from his client, but I think that was the best moment of the week.

Saypol ruled in Penn Central's favor, at least in part on the theory that landmark preservation is not within the state's police power. The judge wrote his short opinion and filed it on January 21, 1975. He stated, "Aesthetics is not for decisions here" and that Grand Central Terminal was "surrounded . . . by the heavily travelled roadway around its perimeter on three sides, it leaves no reaction here other than that of long neglected faded beauty." Clearly he was no fan of the terminal or its groundbreaking design features. The point he noted was that "the authorities empowered to make the designation may do so but only at the expense of those who will ultimately have to bear the cost, the taxpayers."

Judge Saypol also found the city's air rights compensation package to be too small to make up for the loss of development rights at the terminal because the Landmarks Preservation Commission did not prohibit a similarly large structure nearby. The ground rent required of UGP by Penn Central for a lease of the Biltmore Hotel site was $2 million more than the terminal lease, and rents would be lower than at the "superior location." Saypol's opinion also agreed with Penn Central that the cost of operating the terminal exceeded its revenues from tenants and concessionaires without considering other factors. These were the findings of fact that Wood had persuaded Saypol to accept.

Fred Prapert of the Municipal Art Society, who became interested in preservation in his own Midtown neighborhood at this time, later remembered that Saypol and Penn Central (the latter surely ironically) did not include the importance of a rail terminal to the city's population. With this in mind, Prapert thought, Penn Central was getting a fair return. (In a larger sense, mass transportation of all kinds always runs at a loss in pure dollars and cents. The value to the passengers, and thus to the city, is far greater than the dollar amount the carrier loses. That is why cities give tax breaks and other incentives to rails, buses, and other metropolitan carriers.) Saypol's ruling that there was an unconstitutional taking of private property for public use without just compensation to the plaintiffs gave Penn Central the right to build either of Breuer schemes or to demolish the terminal in its entirety. The question of damages was severed, pending the appeal. It was a crushing loss to the terminal's defenders and to preservation itself—if it stood.

Leonard Koerner recognized the broad damage the constitutional portion of the Saypol decision posed. "I know this is a takings conference, but our whole argument was that there was no taking. Instead what we were saying was a taking would only occur if the appellant satisfied its burden of showing that it could not earn a reasonable rate of return and what we essentially said was given an opportunity in the court they did not do that." The argument actually had two stages, as he recognized. First, was the landmark designation of the terminal actually a taking of Penn Central's property rights? In other words, was the city, through the LPC's power, and the state, through the Landmarks Law, allowed to take property from a private owner on the basis of historic or aesthetic value? Second, was the compensation adequate and appropriate? The trial judge stated that "any regulation of private property to protect landmark values constitutes a compensable taking," noting that such a rule would "eviscerate" the legislature's scheme, but that was simply inevitable. There was no middle ground.

Gilbert was philosophical about the decision. He felt that Judge Saypol's ruling was "just the way he saw the case. I don't think there was favoritism involved. Dealing with the case, he saw the case one way. He liked what the developers and the railroad were saying, and he didn't like what the city was saying. He was the commander, the ruler of the court room, and we were there paying attention to him." It seemed to Saypol, Gilbert supposed, that in view of these circumstances and in the view of the absence of a reasonable return on the property, the burden of maintaining the property as a landmark fell solely upon the landowner. Saypol found that the cost of operating the terminal exceeded its revenues from tenants and concessionaires and did not regard the transferable development rights either as providing compensation to the railroad or as minimizing the harm suffered as a result of the landmark designation.

A City on the Brink

In April 1975 the city had run out of money for the first time due a confluence of factors related to union contracts, Medicaid reimbursements, and fifteen years of questionable bookkeeping. Governor Hugh Carey was willing to advance state funds to allow the city to pay its bills under the condition that the city turn over its financial management to the state. This led to the creation of the Municipal Assistance Corporation (MAC), which was authorized to sell bonds to meet the city's borrowing needs. Its opponents, in the press, referred to it as "Big MAC," because of its authority to overrule city spending decisions. MAC, which was chaired by the financier Felix Rohatyn, insisted on significant reforms, including a wage freeze, a subway fare hike, the closing of several public hospitals, charging tuition at the previously free City University, and tens of thousands of layoffs. These spending cuts were intended to reassure banks and bond holders of the city's debt that they would be repaid.

In addition, in an effort to bring some order to the budgeting and management of New York City, the state created the Emergency Financial Control Board (EFCB) in September 1975 during a special legislative session. The creation of the EFCB was comparable to putting the city into receivership. The EFCB had authority over the finances of the city—it could control the city's bank accounts, issue orders to city officials, remove them from office, and press charges against city officials. In practice the EFCB was more hands off, and the mere threat of removing people kept the city in line. The governor made the majority of appointments to the board. The state law creating the EFCB required the city to balance its budget within three years, change its accounting practices, and submit a three-year financial plan. The board had the power to review and reject the city's financial plan, operating and capital budgets, contracts negotiated with the public employees unions, and all municipal borrowing.

Many prominent preservation advocates worried that the city would not appeal the Penn Central decision due to its dire financial straits. "We think the public has a right to protect the great buildings of the past and we mean to fight for that right. It is a soft-headed fallacy to believe that our cities exist to perpetuate a civilization," wrote Peter Blake in *New York Magazine*, "or to permit us to communicate so as to create a wiser democracy. They really exist for the sole purpose of making money." Kent Barwick, executive director of the Municipal Art Society, said that the decision was "a tragic blow to the government's efforts to make New York a livable city," and that "we think the public has a basic right to protect the great buildings of the past and we mean to fight for that right."

A *New York Times* letter to the editor argued that "everything from New York's celebrated skyline to its smallest historic survival is vulnerable. The problem is not alleviated by lethargy and conspicuous disinterest at City Hall. What is being sacrificed to political pragmatism and investment opportunism is the city in the only terms that history recognizes. It is an unconscionable giveaway, by men and minds that will never make history at all." "The implications of Penn Central for advocacy are so great," architecture critic Paul Spencer Byard wrote, "that the public perception will shift from seeing preservation as a matter of pleasure to seeing it as a public necessity." Other critics included Brendan Gill, who was succeeded as architecture critic at *The New Yorker* by Paul Goldberger, who later wrote that "while Gill alone did not save Grand Central Terminal, he did as much as anyone to establish the climate that made that possible, through his writing and his civic activism." At Gill's memorial service in 1998, George Plimpton eulogized: "The only things Brendan hadn't been able to save in his lifetime were the Polo Grounds, Ebbets Field, the Maisonette, Alger Hiss, the Reichstag, the Edsel, and the passenger pigeon."

Many supporters of preservation worried that Judge Saypol's opinion would have far-reaching consequences beyond New York. Ada Louise Huxtable thought it was a "disturbing case in many of its particulars. Not least is the gravity of its effect on the city's heritage," and that "there is much for the lawyers to consider on appeal." In another editorial she wrote for *The New York Times* she urged, "The appeal on the adverse decision on Grand Central Terminal is crucial to the city and the nation. New York is in the difficult position now of testing preservation legislation, much as zoning law was tested in the 1920's," and that "to deal with metropolitan form and function is not to chase the lost dream of the City Beautiful. It is to shape the tough and inescapable realities that control New York's efficiency, livability, well-being and style." Later that year, when the Landmarks Preservation Commission put together an exhibit on Grand Central Terminal, Huxtable wrote in *The New York Times* that the proposed Breuer tower "is like a slap in the eye ... [and] (along with the Pan Am Building) would squeeze the old building in a brutally arrogant embrace. The grand civic gesture has been replaced by the grim economic gesture."

As the issues extended beyond the city limits, so criticism of the decision went beyond the local papers. For example, *The Christian Science Monitor* reported that it was "really heinous," and the "facts are that Penn Central is in no shape to build a 59-story office building and the New York office market needs another tower like a hole in the ground." The newspaper also quoted future mayor Ed Koch that "Congress can be justifiably concerned that while Penn Central continues to receive millions in federal funds, it does not consent to construction plans that are contrary to the public's wishes." In short the paper cleverly pointed out that "Penn Central has little room to demand that it be compensated for what has been called a 'confiscatory' landmarks designation. Having used up so much public funding, the least the railroad can do is to compensate the American public by maintaining the integrity of this columned, people-churning hall."

The day following Judge Saypol's 1975 decision, *The New York Times* ran a front-page story in which the Municipal Art Society named Kent Barwick executive director. The story continued, "It was learned last night that the Municipal Art Society would announce within the next week the formation of a citywide committee to work for the preservation of the terminal and to support the city in its expected appeal." Beverly Moss Spatt, chair of the Landmarks Preservation Commission, was quoted: "Grand Central as it stands today is its own best defense, a landmark to the entire world. We cannot in good conscience encourage the compromise or destruction of a building that is so important."

The next day, the city's decision was announced: it was "99 per cent sure" it would appeal, according to deputy mayor Stanley M. Friedman, who spoke on behalf of the city. "I think we have to appeal—this decision goes to the heart of the landmarks law," Friedman said. "Grand Central is one of the greatest buildings in America." But that 1 percent haunted preservationists, and for good reason. The cautionary note was not lost on the city's lawyers. With Penn Central claiming that landmarking the terminal had cost it $60 million so far, W. Bernard Richland, a member of the city's corporate counsel, was worried that the city, already verging on a fiscal crisis of catastrophic proportions, would be liable for damages to Penn Central. Richland recommended to mayor Abraham D. Beame that the city not appeal Saypol's decision. "Bernie wanted us not to appeal," John Zuccotti, the former chairman of the City Planning Commission, remembered. "He had some thought that we were exposed. He was very concerned. I remember the Penn Central people coming to see us and they urged us not to appeal, too. We debated the issue in front of Abe and he said appeal."

Jacqueline Kennedy Onassis Intervenes

Also in *The New York Times* piece appeared a report that the Municipal Art Society would announce within the next week the formation of a citywide committee to work for the preservation of the terminal and to support the city in its expected appeal. "There we were," said one staffer who had joined the Municipal Art Society staff two years earlier, "just the two of us in this small office answering the phones when a soft spoken voice at the other end of the line said she'd like to speak with Kent Barwick." She said she had read the article in the *Times* and wanted to get involved. "I asked her for her name and she replied, 'Jacqueline Kennedy Onassis.'"

Jacqueline Kennedy Onassis was the former First Lady of the United States. She was famous for her beauty, taste, and fashion and as well as her love of history and architecture. Over the past decade and a half, she had become a genuine and effective advocate for preservation and aesthetics. When John F. Kennedy was elected thirty-fifth president of the United States in 1960, he brought his historically minded, Sorbonne-trained wife with him. Her most famous effort to showcase the history of Washington, DC, was over the White House itself. Remembering a childhood visit to the White House, Mrs. Kennedy told *Life* magazine, "From the outside I remember the feeling of the place. But inside, all I remember is shuffling through. There wasn't even a booklet you could buy. Mount Vernon and the National Gallery and the FBI made a far greater impression."

Soon after her husband's inauguration, Mrs. Kennedy enlisted the famed decorator Mrs. Henry Parish II to help with the restoration of the White House as well as making it a home for her and her young family. Within two weeks, the $50,000 budget had been spent on refurbishing the private living quarters. Still, Mrs. Kennedy planned more. After she looked into borrowing some antiques from the Winterthur Mansion in Delaware, its director Charles Montgomery put forward the idea of a committee of people whose goal would be to acquire antique furnishings for the White House. The Fine Arts Committee was born, and Henry du Pont was made its chairman. "He was widely considered to be the greatest collector of Americana and the most qualified authority on the subject of American historical decoration at the time," the JFK Library later noted.

Mrs. Kennedy convinced *Life* magazine to prepare a fully illustrated article outlining her plans, which ran in the September 1961 issue accompanied by an interview with Hugh Sidey, in which she stated, "Everything in the White House must have a reason for being there. It would be sacrilege merely to redecorate it—a word I hate. It must be restored, and that has nothing to do with decoration. That is a question of scholarship." The article garnered high readership and pushed Congress into action on the White House with Public Law 87–286, which officially declared the White House a museum. This act allowed the Fine Arts Committee and the curator's office to assure potential donors that their gifts would not be auctioned off or kept in the private collection of any president. It further protected the rooms of the White House from being radically altered in the future and clearly defined the project as historic preservation, rather than mere redecoration.

At this same time the federal government was growing larger while past efforts to house the government workers were halted for various reasons. During the Dwight D. Eisenhower administration, these plans were renewed, and a proposal for monumental, strikingly modern office buildings flanking Lafayette Square received funding from Congress. Early in February 1962, Mrs. Kennedy relayed to David Finley, then chairman of both the National Trust for Historic Preservation and the Commission of Fine Arts, that both she and the president were concerned about the proposed designs, worrying that they would be incongruous with other buildings on the square. In France, where she had studied, there was a law that provided that certain buildings of historical or architectural importance could not be destroyed. It would be nice, she ventured to Finley, for Congress to have such a law. As historian Arthur Schlesinger Jr. recalls her telling her husband, "The wreckers haven't started yet, and until they do, it can be saved." She then wrote to Bernard Boutin, head of the General Services Administration (GSA), to whom Finley had introduced her. "All architects are innovators, and would rather do something totally new than in the spirit of old buildings.... I think they are totally wrong in this case, as the important thing is to preserve the 19th-century feeling of Lafayette Square." She asked Boutin "to write to the architects and tell them to submit a design which is more in keeping with the 19th-century bank on the corner. It should be the same color, same size, etc." On April 18, 1962, Mrs. Kennedy wrote to Finley that the GSA agreed with her and adopted her positions.

Ralph Walker, a Fine Arts Commission member who was a former president of the American Institute of Architects, loudly took the opposing view. "To keep on using bad architecture and trying to preserve it [when] there is practically nothing that is worth preserving—the rest is junk, architecturally—it is junk.... I hope Jacqueline wakes up to the fact that she lives in the twentieth century." Dorn McGrath, George Washington University's prominent professor of urban planning, later quoted in the *Washington Post*, disagreed. Mrs. Kennedy's Lafayette Square "began the process of making a creative use of space in critical Washington locations, increasing the density in parts while maintaining the historical context. Her basic ideas, implemented by architects, demonstrated that one need not throw away 19th- and 18th-century architecture in order to live in the 20th century." The GSA would later publicize the lobbying effort on its website as "a watershed event for the historic preservation movement."

Lafayette Square was not the First Lady's only imprint on Washington, DC, during her brief tenure. She pushed for renovation of older buildings for theater and arts uses along and near Pennsylvania Avenue. William Walton, who as later chairman of the Fine Arts Commission was the authority over the "design and aesthetics" of all construction within the District of Columbia, was quoted in *The New York Times* that Mrs. Kennedy wanted to use one Pennsylvania Avenue building as "an opera house like she had seen in a trip to Panama City." Her drive made certain that theater and arts uses were a part of the first plans for Pennsylvania Avenue—plans that were later realized with the restoration of the National Theater and the Warner, and the use of the historic bottom two floors with new construction to create the Lansburgh Apartments.

John Carl Warnecke, the architect who helped Kennedy on the Lafayette Square plans, noted that "her focus was preserving the character that revealed the history of our country. She had the gut instincts to know what to approve and what not to." Members of Congress, in urging the passage of the National Historic Preservation Act in 1966, called Mrs. Kennedy's preservation efforts a model, "not only for preservation in this city, but for large and small communities throughout America." Wrote Roberta Brandes Gratz, an architectural historian, "Jackie, the great arbiter of good taste in fashion, food and architecture, raised the consciousness of the nation to the importance of historic preservation."

After her husband's assassination, Mrs. Kennedy disappeared from public life but found controversy in 1968 with her marriage to her longtime friend Greek shipping magnate Aristotle Onassis. "America has lost its saint," mourned one newspaper, as later recalled in *Town & Country Magazine*. "Cardinal Richard Cushing of Boston, a mentor to Jackie, felt it necessary to go public, saying that those who wrote him pleading with him to stop the wedding from taking place were misguided." Onassis died in March 1975 in Paris of respiratory failure while Jackie was in New York creating more rumors. In September of that year she started to work at Viking Press after its president, Tommy Guinzburg, suggested that she become a consulting editor. Still, the most important thing she did that year was to pick up the telephone to call the Municipal Art Society, offering to help in the fight to save Grand Central Terminal.

A press conference was announced soon after her call to promote the formation of the Committee to Save Grand Central and Kennedy Onassis's involvement in it. "Jackie Onassis will save us," architect Philip Johnson proclaimed to *The New York Times*. "Europe has its cathedrals and we have Grand Central Station (*sic*)," said Johnson, vice chairman of the committee. "Europe wouldn't put a tower on a cathedral." The committee also announced a national branch chaired by National Trust president James Biddle and American Institute of Architects president William Marshall Jr. Architect Hugh Hardy said, "We intend to demonstrate that Grand Central can again function as the symbol, marketplace, and economic engine with which a preeminently important part of midtown Manhattan can be rejuvenated." The *Times* noted that Mrs. Onassis, who "rarely lends her presence and name to a public cause," created great excitement in the crowd. "'I think this is so terribly important,' Mrs.

Onassis said in her quiet voice. We've all heard that it's too late." The public, she said, has been told "that it has to happen, but we know that it's not so," a reference to her work in Washington, DC. "Even in the 11th hour, it's not too late," said the former First Lady, who explained that she chose to help save the terminal because "old buildings are important" and "if we don't care about our past, we cannot hope for our future."

Fred Papert remembered, "There is not the slightest doubt, and I think I know it as well as anybody, it would not have been saved without her. The city would not even have appealed the bad lower-court ruling. Anyhow, she had that irresistible quality, and won them all over. When the Municipal Art Society, after she died, gave a dinner at Grand Central, Caroline [Kennedy, Jackie's daughter] made a speech and said that her letters that her mother wrote on behalf of these causes sometimes embarrassed her brother John and her, "because when you read one of those letters—nobody could say no to one of those letters, whatever the subject was. In any event, she saved us from Flynn-Walsh as I remember, and undoubtedly her presence—not as a celebrity, because in the case of Grand Central she was really the brains of that whole operation."

Joel Harnett, chairman of the City Club of New York and cochairman of the new committee, explained that there are "acres of space in this area not being utilized. If a new building is placed on top of the terminal," Harnett said, "it would be a prescription for civic insanity." Also included in the new committee was a who's who of New York City, including author Louis Auchincloss, president of the Museum of the City of New York; Thomas P. F. Hoving, director of the Metropolitan Museum of Art; US House Representative Ed Koch; David Malamud of the American Institute of Planners; T. Merrill Prentice Jr., president of the Municipal Art Society; architect Paul Rudolph; and Percy E. Sutton, Manhattan Borough president.

The chairman of the new group, former mayor Robert Wagner, sent a message to the media that the eighty-eight-member committee has a "distinguished group of private attorneys standing ready to support the city's case with an amicus curiae [friend of the court] brief." He did not identify the lawyers. He also said that he had told Mayor Beame that the committee intended to draw public attention to the plight of the terminal and to "sound an alarm in New York and across the country that the battle against the thoughtless waste of our manmade environment is farther from being won than many of us had thought." "What is at issue here," Wagner continued, "is the very concept of landmark preservation." This was a not so subtle threat to Mayor Beame to go ahead with the defense of Grand Central and appeal Judge Saypol's ruling, because it was now disclosed that the railroad's lawyers had offered a deal to Beame and the City of New York. If the city didn't appeal, Penn Central would not sue for damages. If it did appeal, the railroad would demand $60 million.

Even with Wagner as chairman there was little doubt who the real star was. Committee member Lorna Nowvé remembered, "We had all sorts of speeches. And there were hordes of people. Of course everybody came to see Jacqueline Onassis. I mean, let's not fool ourselves, but they realized that this was a challenge to a landmarks law that nobody really quite understood." Fred Papert later said that Jackie Onassis "became, really, the managing partner, the general of it all, without even the slightest doubt. There wasn't a move that we would make that we didn't talk to her—quite brilliant, in fact." "Not only did she join the committee but she called and wrote Mayor Beame to convince him to file the city's appeal. She went to the press conferences, breakfasts, whatever the event, she was there, and when she spoke it made a difference," John Belle later noted.

Though Mrs. Onassis's involvement was a net positive for the movement, it had its shortcomings, according to Gregory Gilmartin. In his book about the Municipal Art Society, *Shaping the City*, Gilmartin explains, "Some used Mrs. Onassis' involvement to paint preservation as the hobby of people who never rode the subways. But these were far outweighed by the advantages. Jacqueline Onassis brought to the Municipal Art Society a visceral belief in preservation.... She attracted news cameras as a flame draws moths. People hesitated to rebuff her. They took her phone calls." Perhaps, as future chair of the commission Laurie Beckelman suggested, it was Jackie's letter and phone calls to the mayor that finally convinced him to file the city's appeal.

The City Appeals

The Committee to Save Grand Central's plan was simple. It wanted to raise public awareness to get people to start thinking about what would be lost if the Grand Central Terminal court case failed. It was the time of the bicentennial of the Declaration of Independence, and Grand Central Terminal was becoming a popular symbol. The committee set up a storefront office in the Biltmore Hotel at Forty-Third and Vanderbilt across the street from the terminal. Lenora Nowvé remembered, "It was incredible to see just handing out fliers—and nobody wants to pick up fliers in New York City. It's the last thing you want to do. But say, 'Save Grand Central,' people would actually stop and they'd take the flier. They'd come to our little, little nook, which was also a little bookstore." New Yorkers were implored to either join the committee, volunteer their time, send money, or start petition drives. "Only a strong public protest can keep Grand Central from going under," one of the pamphlets read. "This case is a test of our civic pride—our sense of history and our appreciation of the amenities we have in the present. Little by little, many of our finest landmarks are becoming endangered species. New York has much to be proud of and Grand Central Station is one of its proudest monuments. Let's save it."

Some newspaper editorials were less enthusiastic. They accused members of the Municipal Art Society and the Committee to Save Grand Central of trying to save a spirit that was long gone, now merely a fantasy of their own creation. One such editorial stated "that saving Grand Central was as absurd and impossible as having a Walden Pond in New York." Doris Freedman, an important board member of the Municipal Art Society, led the counterattack against this negative publicity by contacting Congressman Koch for support on the federal level. Freedman was one of Koch's earliest supporters in his mayoral campaign and prodded him to work behind the scenes rallying support from the Metropolitan Transportation Authority lease on Grand Central Terminal.

On February 14, 1975, supporters of Grand Central Terminal got a boost from the federal government. William J. Murtagh, the keeper of the National Historic Register within the Interior Department, said that he had accepted the terminal for listing on the basis of an application by the New York State Office of Parks and Recreation. Though the designation did not come with any formal protection, it did signal that the federal government supported the cause. The committee kept historic preservation in the headlines by sponsoring rallies at Grand Central with cultural celebrities including Dick Cavett, who was master of ceremonies; Benny Goodman, Henny Youngman, Tony Randall, Robert Klein, Mary Travers, and Virginia Capers. Former mayor Wagner and Bess Meyerson, the former Consumer Affairs Commissioner, were also present. They also heard Manhattan Borough President Sutton call on the public for support to save "this giant among landmark structures" from falling "prey to the wrecking ball," *The New York Times* reported.

Papert later summed it up nicely by proclaiming, "Those are the kinds of fights you want. You want fights where there's a really good, non-participatory democracy; non-NIMBY [not in my back yard] argument for doing it. Because if we don't largely limit ourselves, our energies, to those fights, then we're not going to have any ammunition left when the serious ones come up." Nowvé highlighted the importance of the appeal: "I think that politicians in other cities were waiting to see what was going to happen, because they didn't have such instruments in place. And I think perhaps before they were going to write or were going to explore preservation policy locally, they were going to wait to see what was going to happen with this."

The campaign had convinced Mayor Beame to have the city file an appeal to Judge Saypol's ruling. He chose Nina Gershon Goldstein to write the appeal. Goldstein was a lawyer in the Appeals Division who had been a staff attorney of the Appellate Division of the Supreme Court of the State of New York, Mental Health Information Service, from 1966 to 1968. A professor of law and political science at the University of California, San Diego from 1969 to 1970, she cared deeply about environmental concerns. She came up with the argument, "in calculating the economics of the station—what the expenses were, what the income was, and why it didn't work—they [Penn Central] did not take into account the value of that station to somebody running the railroad." In other words, "You have to have a station for the railroad to come in, so you have to assign some value to that, and when that value was added, it turned out that Penn Central was making a fair return. And on that argument hinged the reversal of a lower-court decision." Papert later related that Goldstein "came up with a series of arguments that disputed Saypol's findings that there wasn't a reasonable return." Wrote Belle later, "This was truly one of the great cases of the city's law department." He recalled, "The really important thing was Nina's attitude. She felt the city should and could win and brought incredible determination, energy, and strength to the case."

Dorothy Miner joined in the appeal preparation representing the Landmarks Preservation Commission. She had earned her law degree from Columbia Law School in 1961 and a degree in urban planning from Columbia University in 1972. In 1973 she became counsel for the LPC. One of the main issues Miner impressed upon her colleagues was the need to look at landmarking not as something selectively focused on a single property but as another form of land-use regulation. Like building, zoning, and health codes, landmarking should be addressed as a code that was part of the city's overall land-use policy. Belle recalled Miner saying, "I'm not trying to take away from [anyone else's credit]... but the main work and briefs were done by the city's law department."

Another notable contributor was Beverly Moss Spatt, the chair of the Landmarks Preservation Commission at the time of the appeal. In addition there were lawyers who wrote the amicus briefs supporting the landmarks law. Ralph Menapace, general counsel for the Municipal Art Society, assembled a legal team consisting of, among others, Jack Kerr, Paul Byard, and Peter Sloan to write the society's and the American Institute of Architects' amicus brief in the appeals process. There were also briefs filed by the New York State attorney general and the Citizens Housing and Planning Council of New York.

The stage was set for the second act of the legal drama.

Cornelius Vanderbilt, 1850 Matthew Brady daguerreotype. (Library of Congress)

Grand Central Depot, ca. 1861–1880, exterior view. Photographed by C. K. Bill. (New York Public Library)

Grand Central Station, 1902, designed by railroad architect Gilbert Bradford. (Library of Congress)

This unusual photograph of the interior of the old Grand Central Station, replaced in 1913 by the present Terminal, in New York City was "discovered" recently by D. Koller, Photographer, in the files of the Engineering Department. Taken in 1902 and showing the first bulletin board, left, of the 20th Century Limited, it is the only picture known to be in existence showing the old train gates and approach to the trains at the platforms. Old memories will be awakened in many people by this photograph and some may even recall the polished cuspidor shown sitting in solitary grandeur between the gates.

Grand Central Station train shed, 1902. From *Central Headlight* 6, no. 10 (October 1945): 4. The caption reads: "This unusual photograph of the interior of the old Grand Central Station, replaced in 1913 by the present Terminal, in New York City was 'discovered' recently by D. Koller, Photographer, in the files of the Engineering Department. Taken in 1902 and showing the first bulletin board, left, of the 20th Century Limited, it is the only picture known to be in existence showing the old train gates and approach to the trains at the platforms. Old memories will be awakened in many people by this photograph and some may even recall the polished cuspidor shown sitting in solitary grandeur between the gates."

Grand Central Station waiting room, 1904. Detroit Publishing Company photograph collection. (Library of Congress)

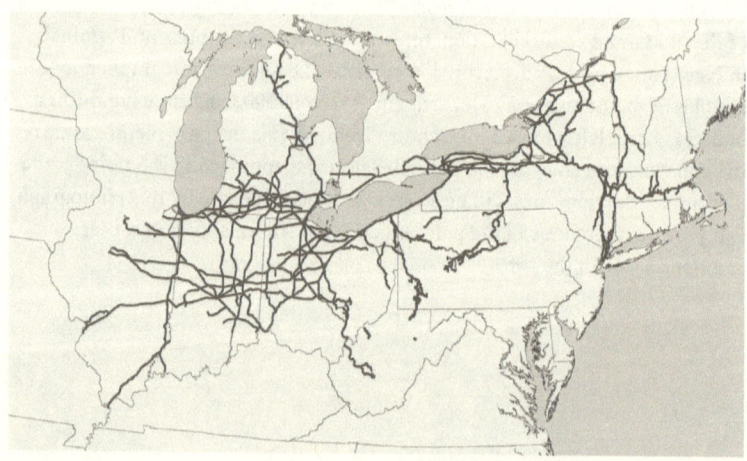

Map of New York Central Railroads, 1918. (James R. Irwin)

Pennsylvania Railroad Station, New York City, Seventh Avenue and Thirty-Second Street, looking toward Long Island. Painting by Hughson Hawley and the Pennsylvania Railroad Company, 1910. (Library of Congress)

Grand Central Terminal as viewed from Forty-Second Street, ca. 1910. (Library of Congress)

Incline from subway to suburban concourse, Grand Central Terminal, ca. 1915. (Library of Congress)

→

Proposal for a "Grand Central Air Rights Building" at 175 Park Avenue by Marcel Breuer and Herbert Beckhard, 1969, above Grand Central Terminal. (Marcel Breuer and Herbert Beckhard, Architects)

Jacqueline Kennedy Onassis on the Landmark Express, April 1978. Photograph by Helen Hayes for Amtrak.

US Supreme Court justices: William J. Brennan Jr., Byron R. White, Harry A. Blackmun, William H. Rehnquist, Potter Stewart, Thurgood Marshall, Lewis F. Powell Jr., John Paul Stevens III, and Chief Justice Warren E. Burger., 1976. (Library of Congress)

Grand Central Terminal, 1985. (Metropolitan Transit Authority)

Ceremony at Grand Central Terminal to dedicate a foyer in honor of Jacqueline Kennedy Onassis. Photograph by Fred Papert, 2014. (MTA)

CHAPTER SEVEN

Appeals in the New York State Courts

Nineteen seventy-five was arguably the worst year for New York City. The city was in a severe recession, with high unemployment and a lot of empty office space. Suburban communities were luring corporations, industry, and residents from the city. The financial problems the city experienced that spring and summer were growing worse. Congressman Ed Koch remembered hearing testimony before Congress about the city's fiscal situation and thinking that "it was like somebody escaping from the Warsaw ghetto and saying they're killing people there. Nobody believed it." New York State had effectively taken over the city's budget and was cutting services, firing city employees, and freezing wages. A sanitation worker strike left garbage everywhere, but worse was yet to come. October 1975 turned out to be the foulest month of the year in more ways than one.

Bankruptcy Averted

New York City was indeed deep in crisis. Four hundred and fifty-three million dollars of the City's short-term debts would shortly come due, but only $34 million was on hand. If New York could not pay its debts, the city would officially be bankrupt. Federal help was repeatedly refused by President Gerald Ford and his advisers. The only hope left was pension funds, and the Teacher's Retirement System pulled out of negotiations the night before the payment was due. Mayor Beame told a crowded benefit dinner the previous evening, "The problems were simpler and less complex in [Al] Smith's day, and there even seemed to be a greater sense of responsibility on Washington's part." On the morning of October 17, New Yorkers woke to a series of grim headlines "Balk by UFT [United Federation of Teachers] pushing city to default," in the

Staten Island Advance, and "Teachers Reject 150-Million Loan City Needs Today," in *The New York Times.*

The financial crisis was not just a New York City crisis, for New York's debt was held by banks throughout the United States and around the world. "By some estimates, New York's default would bring down at least a hundred banks, and expose others to liability for selling suspect or fraudulent products," *The New Yorker* would later write. Some economists even warned that New York's default would harm the US government with a falling dollar. The Dow Jones Industrial stock market index dropped ten points at the opening bell (a lot at the time), the price of gold began to rise, and, as reported by the United Press International wire service, "trading of bonds of other cities and states slowed to a near standstill, and even the prices of most credit-worthy bonds fell." One newspaper in North Carolina ran a cartoon of a bum lying on trash, under the Brooklyn Bridge, with the caption, "We're going down, America, and we're taking you with us."

President Ford ignored pleas from around the world, including the prime minister of Germany and the president of France, about the dangers of a New York default. His press secretary, Ron Nessen, said that Ford would continue to monitor the situation throughout the day but wouldn't change his mind about granting assistance to the city (a situation eerily similar to the Lehman Brothers bankruptcy crisis in 2008). In Nessen's words, "This is not a natural disaster or an act of God. It is a self-inflicted act by the people who have been running New York City." The teachers' union was in a bad spot. The head of the union, Albert Shanker, later called it blackmail. If the city went bankrupt, a judge could order thousands of teacher dismissals, undo the raises the teachers had recently negotiated, and override any pension laws, stripping retirees of their pension checks. A little after two in the afternoon the teachers' union announced that it had changed its position and now would invest its pension funds to deal with the $150 million shortfall. "No one else was coming forward to save the city," Shanker said.

The crisis of the day was averted, but twelve days later President Ford created another one by delivering a screed about New York City at the National Press Club. "What I cannot understand—and what nobody should condone—is the blatant attempt in some quarters to frighten the American people and their representatives in Congress into panicky support of patently bad policy. The people of this country will not be stampeded; they will not panic when a few desperate New York City officials and bankers try to scare New York's mortgage payments out of them." Then, he added against the advice of his staff, "I can tell you, and tell you now, that I am prepared to veto any bill that has as its purpose a federal bailout of New York City to prevent a default." (Perhaps one should add that New York City residents had long paid more in federal taxes than they received in federal benefits and payouts.) The next day, the *New York Daily News* ran the now famous headline "Ford to City: Drop Dead." The headline scared New Yorkers into cutting deals that were painful but necessary. Although Ford would later approve federal support for New York, New Yorkers remembered the headline. The following year, Jimmy Carter received the third-highest vote share a Democratic presidential candidate ever received in New York City, and narrowly won New York State, which gave him enough electoral votes to give him the presidency, revealing the impact of one speech.

The Appeal Begins

That October saw the start of the appeals process for the Grand Central Terminal case. The city was joined in its appeal by New York State and twelve leading architectural and civic organizations. Ralph Menapace, Whitney Seymour, and their teams met often with the amicus groups and the city's Law Department to strategize and frame the legal arguments.

This pool of talented lawyers with different legal specialties lent their experience and skills to aid the city with research and ideas. Menapace, whose corporate legal experience differed from the regulatory law practiced by most of the counsel in the Law Department, had the personality and the ability to bring a new perspective to the effort. Seymour at that time was one of the great lions of the bar and the former head of the American Bar Association. He lent his prestigious name and his experience with the courts to the Grand Central case just as it moved into the crucial appellate stage. The two men were very different: Seymour was a great public speaker, and Menapace was the modest but effective strategist behind the scenes. The supporting army of young lawyers and protégés who sat at the feet of these two masters would later continue the preservation battle beyond Grand Central—including Jack Kerr, who, after working with Menapace and then Seymour, joined the New York Landmarks Conservancy Board and carried the tradition to subsequent preservation cases such as the fight over St. Bartholomew's Church.

Oral argument took place on October 21, 1975, in the State Appellate Court for the First Department. The state's intermediate appellate court comprised of five judges, with only a majority needed to decide an appeal. *The New York Times* predicted that "further appeal, regardless of the outcome, will almost certainly be made to the Court of Appeals, the state's highest court." Two dozen Grand Central supporters, organized by the Municipal Art Society, attended the appeal hearing to support the appellants (the city).

The court's bench included Francis T. Murphy, who wrote the opinion in the case. A graduate of Fordham University and New York Law School, Murphy had been a member of the New York judiciary for forty years. He served fifteen years as a trial judge and twenty-five years as a justice of the Appellate Division's First Department, and after the Grand Central case, he served twenty years as the court's presiding justice. In addition to hearing some 63,000 appeals during his tenure as presiding justice, Murphy wrote widely on issues embracing legal and social reform. In an article announcing his retirement, *The New York Times* said of him, a "protégé of a once-prominent Bronx Irish Democrat machine, the wily, powerful judge is an unreconstructed liberal on criminal justice questions. He has often been the lone, dissenting voice in support of defendants' rights, and a caustic critic of prosecutors and the police."

Judge Theodore R. Kupferman was known as the Great Dissenter of the Appellate Division's First Department, "famous for his one-page dissents, usually written with a punchline," according to the *New York Law Journal*. In one case he wrote, "It does not take Gertrude Stein to know that a contract is a contract is a contract." His dissents outnumbered his majority opinions, 625 to 165. He served on the City Council from 1962 to 1966, when he was elected to Congress to represent the Upper East Side of Manhattan, filling a vacancy left when John V. Lindsay became mayor of New York City, and remained in Congress until 1969, when he became a trial court judge. In 1971 he was appointed by the governor to the Appellate Division, where he specialized in commercial cases.

Judge Harold Arnoldus Stevens was the first Black justice to serve on the New York Court of Appeals, the state's highest court. While attending Benedict College in South Carolina, Stevens was shocked by the lynching of a Black woman and her two brothers accused of murdering a sheriff. The event "cemented" his determination to become a lawyer. "There was no voice of protest raised," he said. "I was inspired to study law because it was our best bet to eliminate things like this." In 1936 Stevens became the first African American and the first non-Catholic to graduate from Boston College Law School. He later converted to Catholicism. Though originally from South Carolina, he had to attend law school in the North because of segregation. After marrying his childhood sweetheart, the couple moved to Manhattan, "for he had fallen in love with the city." In a *New York Times* interview, Judge Stevens recalled "a long, hectic trip South ... to deal with the problems of Negro sleeping car porters, and the relief and joy he felt when, returning at night across the Jersey meadows, he saw the twinkling panorama of city lights. 'I can't imagine living anywhere else,'" he said.

Stevens was elected to the New York Assembly from the 113th District and then to the Court of General Sessions in 1950. He loved the law and said, "There is poetry and drama in law.... It never grows stale. Every case is a human story. A tragedy for some, a triumph for others ... a system of continual growth and progression." In 1958 he was named associate justice of the Appellate Division of the New York Supreme Court. "As a realist ... I'm aware this appointment is breaking new ground. I recognize the fact, and I'm grateful to have the opportunity. But color doesn't restrict or inhibit the performance of my legal duties," he said in a 1968 interview. Stevens was named to the highest court, the State Court of Appeals, in 1974, as an interim appointment and lost the election to permanently fill the post. The next year he was reappointed presiding justice of the Appellate Division of the Supreme Court. He retired in 1977.

Judge Arthur Markewich was elected to the State Supreme Court in 1954, served a fourteen-year term, was reelected, and was elevated to the Appellate Division by Governor Nelson A. Rockefeller in 1968. Born and raised on the Upper West Side, he earned a bachelor's degree from Cornell University in 1926 and a law degree from Columbia in 1929. Markewich is most famous for being the justice who presided on the panel of Appellate Division that in 1976 disbarred Richard M. Nixon in New York State.

Judge Vincent A. Lupiano, a member of the Supreme Court since 1954, had served in the Appellate Division's First Department, embracing Manhattan and the Bronx, since 1974 and wrote the dissent in the Grand Central case. There was no animosity between the judges over the case, however, and presiding Justice Murphy later said, "Justice Lupiano was a man of great wit and learning, a dear friend and colleague whose presence will be greatly missed" at the time of his passing.

The case seemed to present simple questions: Was landmarking Grand Central Terminal a taking under the Fifth and Fourteenth Amendments (the latter applying the Fifth Amendment to the states through the doctrine of "incorporation")? Did Penn Central lose its property rights by some arbitrary and capricious action by the city that affected its property rights and not others? The reasons for the litigation had not changed. Penn Central was arguing in the newspapers before the appeal at the time "that the development rights over the terminal are its only source of potential revenue since it entered an agreement with the Metropolitan Transportation Authority in 1972 in which the M.T.A. took over the operation of the terminal." The city disputed this claim, arguing that "under this absurd theory, the owner of a landmark which is capable of yielding him a reasonable economic return would be entitled to destroy it if he assigns the income stream to another party."

In its formal answer to the city's appeal, the railroad said it had been "assiduous" in trying to improve its revenues from the terminal when it proposed that an underground mall be created and when it sought to convert the terminal's waiting room into a bowling alley. It said that the mall was not feasible, however, until passenger traffic decreased further and that the bowling alley was not permitted by the Public Service Commission. Furthermore, it said, the "commercialization" of the terminal had progressed so far that might be desirable to eliminate "some of the concessions which have disfigured the building."

The Municipal Art Society, the National Trust for Historic Preservation, the Citizens Union of the City of New York, and the City Club of New York all filed briefs supporting the city's landmarking of Grand Central, stating, "The hub and focus of the system that supports mid-Manhattan—the single most important contributor to New York's economic base—is Grand Central Terminal." The amicus briefs continued that the filers all "consider the unaltered continuance of the Terminal to be a matter of national significance and view any decision to invalidate its landmark status to be considerable threat to efforts throughout the country to protect and preserve the man-made environment."

The New York State attorney general's office had joined the city's corporate counsel to declare that the developers were "striking a blow at the city's landmarks law and the state's basic police power as it applies to zoning and the use of land." Police power is a doctrine that asserted the state could regulate businesses for the health and welfare of the citizens of the state. Here, the landmark law was considered a legitimate exercise of the state's police power. After all, the landmark law was a creation of the state.

The brief for the state continued that if Penn Central's definition of a "taking" was upheld, land-use restrictions of all kinds were in jeopardy wherever they resulted in a "mere diminution of value of the property regulated." Like the members of the Landmarks Preservation Commission and the city's counsel, the state attorney general was aware of the potential reach of an unfavorable ruling on the appeal. All zoning might be at risk. The attorney general argued that zoning ordinances have only been declared "confiscatory" where owners have demonstrated that their property has been rendered "unfit, at present, for any conforming use." Justice Saypol's ruling, it worried, "would paralyze landmarks preservation everywhere and would sanction violence to the fabric of the city."

In reply, the railroad asserted that the Grand Central case rested on facts "specifically and peculiarly relating to the terminal." Penn Central was not striking at landmarking of districts for historical or aesthetic value. Instead, it insisted that individual landmark parcels do not enjoy the "mutuality of benefit and burden" of landmark districts. "In the case of an individual parcel singled out from its neighbors," the railroad maintained, "the burden is placed on one person while the benefits are general to the community."

This time around, the city was ready for the financial question. Nina Goldstein of New York City's corporate counsel's office had mastered the financials. She argued in court that "the rental potential must include the value of owner-occupied space," and contended that in financial statements, the railroad had shown a loss on the terminal by including expenses generated by the trains without any offsetting income. LPC secretary commissioner Frank Gilbert agreed with Goldstein's approach. The Appellate Divisional Court "was a very crucial stage in the case" in reference "to the financial report that was submitted by the railroad." Goldstein suggested that only one-third of the space in the terminal was producing income—a total of $4.5 million in the previous year—while all expenses were being charged against that income.

For the railroad, John Wood retorted that even the city's expert had agreed that the deficit was at least $1.1 million and that expenses relating to railroad operations had not been included. To support the claim that it was actually sustaining a loss from terminal operations, Penn Central submitted a "Statement of Revenues and Costs" for the years 1969 and 1971. Wood was not done. He explained that under the agreement with the Metropolitan Transportation Authority the company made a flat commitment of $2 million toward the expenses with the agreement that it would retain development rights above it. Thus, Wood argued, the railroad was receiving no return at all. Under this lease the MTA became Penn Central's tenant and was alone entitled to the rents and other economic benefits of the terminal. However, the air rights above the terminal were specifically excluded from the coverage of this lease. The cumulative effect of these necessary legal agreements was to "leave Penn Central with no possible source of return from the Terminal save [air] development rights." Wood said the site had less desirable proportions and that building over the railroad tracks would be excessively costly.

In her rebuttal, Goldstein contended that 56 percent of the space in recently constructed Midtown office buildings was still vacant and that the $9.50 per square foot rental calculated by the builder to break even—which she argued was a low estimate—was above the $7.50 then charged by the neighboring Pan Am Building. Wood rejoined that Grand Central was different. "It's a splendid location . . . probably the best in New York City."

The Appellate Court agreed with the city and the Landmarks Preservation Commission and reversed Judge Saypol's ruling. In its 3–2 ruling, Judges Murphy, Kupferman, and Stevens found "that Grand Central Terminal has a special character, special historical and aesthetic interest and value as part of the development, heritage and cultural characteristics of New York City." And that "Grand Central Terminal is a magnificent example of French Beaux Arts architecture; that it is one of the great buildings of America, that it represents a creative engineering solution of a very difficult problem, combined with artistic splendor; that as an American Railroad Station it is unique in quality, distinction and character; and that this building plays a significant role in the life and development of New York City." In effect, it was not so much the financial or even the constitutional questions that particularly moved the majority, as the aesthetic and cultural value of the terminal to the people. This was a very New York City decision.

Still, the majority opinion gave space to both sides of the question. "On the record before us," Judge Murphy wrote,

> Plaintiffs [actually, the appellees, as the order of the parties had changed when Penn Central won in the lower court, and the city appealed] have failed satisfactorily to show: (a) an inability to increase the terminal's commercial income by transforming vacant or underutilized space to revenue-producing use; or (b) that unused development rights over the terminal could not have been profitably transferred to one or more nearby sites (see New York City Zoning Resolution, § 74–79 et seq.); or (c) that Penn Central's agreements with the Metropolitan Transportation Authority and the Connecticut Transportation Authority provide a basis for invalidating the terminal's landmark designation.

Unlike Judge Saypol, Murphy did not accept the railroad's findings of fact. "For example, the expense items included "Station Master and Staff," "Information Clerks," and "Gate Usher." Such large cost items (for 1971) as "maintenance, repairs and service plant operation" ($1,141,679), "cleaning" ($632,753), "policing" ($438,566), "materials and supplies" ($69,692), and "utilities" ($660,710) were related to the entire terminal operation and not segregated as between the railroad and real estate portions thereof.

Judge Murphy went on to state that the compounding financial error gave no value to the retail operations in the huge area used for railroad operations. All but one of the judges agreed with the city's stance that because Penn Central needed a railroad station for its main business of transportation it must have tracks, platforms, concourses, waiting rooms, ramps, ticket windows, and other such public amenities in order for it to conduct operations. The "reasonable" rental value of such spaces cannot be left out of an examination of the whole property to give a "reasonable" return. "Obviously, if the entire expense of operating a railroad terminal is offset only by nonrailroad rents generated by the commercial and concession use thereof, even the most profitable terminal will show a 'deficit.'" Frank Gilbert recognized that "the Appellate Division made new findings of fact which included the fact that the railroad had failed to show that it was incapable of obtaining a reasonable return from the Terminal."

The Appellate Division opinion continued, "To support the claim that it is actually sustaining a loss from Terminal operations, Penn Central submitted a 'Statement of Revenue and Costs' for the years 1969 and 1971. These statements, which were prepared for the instant litigation, improperly attribute a considerable amount of railroad's operating expenses (and some taxes) to their real estate operations." Instead, these figures were properly "related to the entire terminal operation and not segregated as between the railroad and the real estate portions thereof. Moreover, and to compound the error, no rental value whatsoever was imputed to the vast space in the Terminal devoted to railroad purposes. This was their own figures, and this was essential, vital to the Appellate Division in reversing the Trial Court's opinion."

Judge Murphy also broadened the finding to the entire project of landmark designation. He observed,

> Changing attitudes now acknowledge that [urban] landmarks merit recognition as an imperiled species alongside the ocelot and the snow leopard. Over fifty per cent of the 12,000 buildings listed in the Historic American Buildings Survey, commenced by the federal government in 1933, have been razed. The threat to the remainder continues undiminished as the recent loss of Chicago's Old Stock Exchange and the precarious status of New York's Grand Central Terminal attest. If this trend is not reversed the nation at its bicentennial in 1976 will mourn the loss of an essential part of its architectural and cultural heritage rather than celebrate the visible evidence of its past.

The decision also made noted that the "Amtrak Improvement Act of 1974 (88 U.S. Stat 1526) in accordance with the congressional declaration that it is national policy to preserve historic sites, seeks to encourage the preservation of passenger railroad terminals of special significance and architectural quality, such as Grand Central Terminal, by authorizing the Secretary of Transportation to provide them with financial and other assistance."

Context helped the appellant's cause. New York City's rich history was reflective of the great deal of time, money, and talent invested in building its own architectural heritage. Structures such as the Brooklyn Bridge, the Metropolitan Museum of Art, the New York Public Library, and Grand Central Terminal are important and irreplaceable components of the special uniqueness of New York City. The city's people had already witnessed the demise of the old Metropolitan Opera House and the original Pennsylvania Station. Stripped of its remaining historically unique structures, New York City would be indistinguishable from any other large metropolis.

After recognizing the importance of Grand Central Terminal as an endangered historic and significant structure, the court covered other issues. It looked at other case law to inform their decision. The judges looked back at the trial court ruling that "the authorities empowered to make the designation may do so but only at the expense of those who will ultimately have to bear the cost, the taxpayers" and offered that while the difference between a taking and a regulation "is sometimes difficult to discern, it nevertheless exists." Though "fraught with trouble" *Lutheran Church in Amer. v. City of New York* (1974) and *Matter of Trustees of Sailors' Snug Harbor v. Platt* (1968) were two of those cases. The majority said the Landmarks Preservation Law asserted "the right, within proper limitations, of the State to place restrictions on the use to be made by an owner of his own property for the cultural and aesthetic benefit of the community" and the Court of Appeals in the *Lutheran* case was "correct in refusing to declare the entire law unconstitutional on its face" despite the economic impact of the law on the particular parcel.

In *Lutheran Church in Amer. v City of New York*, the New York Court of Appeals dealt with a landmark devoted to a charitable use and ruled in favor of the church charity. The courts further adopted a concept first enunciated in the appellate court in *Matter of Trustees of Sailors' Snug Harbor v. Platt*. The court applied, as the standard: does the designation "prevent or seriously interfere with the carrying out of the charitable purpose"? But in the Penn Central case, the landmark parcel was not devoted to a charitable purpose, and no claim was made that it could not be used for its prime function—as a railroad terminal. Thus the test to be applied was the same as in zoning cases: have the plaintiffs demonstrated that the regulation at issue deprives them of all reasonable beneficial use of their property?

Murphy's opinion explained that in reaching its decision for an appropriate taking of private for-profit property, a three-pronged test was necessary. First, the regulation must be good for the public. Second, the law should be a reasonable way of achieving the stated public good. Finally, consideration should be given to the effect of the economic viability of the parcel involved. The New York Appellate Court cited, as the relevant case, the US Supreme Court case *Goldblatt v. Hempstead* (1962). In that case Herbert W. Goldblatt filed a complaint against the town of Hempstead, New York, claiming that a town ordinance regulating dredging and pit excavating on his property prevented him from continuing his business and therefore took his property without due process of law in violation of the Fifth and Fourteenth Amendments. The Supreme Court conceded that the law in fact did prohibit a prior use by Goldblatt, who had operated a gravel pit for thirty years. But the Court held that depriving the property of its most profitable use did not make the law unconstitutional. In Penn Central, the New York Appellate Court believed the first two requirements were met by the clearly stated purpose of the Landmarks Preservation Law and the unavailability of any reasonable alternative (short of condemnation) for the preservation of a landmark.

The final consideration in the majority opinion was that Penn Central's Grand Central Terminal had a reasonable financial return, even if the railroad was not receiving it. The opinion cited *Salamar Bldrs. Corp. v. Tuttle*, (1971), a zoning case where a New York Court of Appeals decision held the de facto ban on a housing development due to statutory lot size minimums to be a valid exercise of the police power. In that decision, the court held that "restrictions upon the unencumbered use of property, quite apart from its professed purposes, will have an adverse effect upon its market value. That hardship is inevitably the product of police regulation and the pecuniary rights ... of common weal ... and in our view, such burden has not been met."

Penn Central had argued that the Landmarks Preservation Law unconstitutionally discriminated against the company because it already received partial tax exemption as a railroad, and that despite the statutory hardship relief, it was left with no monetary compensation for the denial of its skyscraper scheme. The majority of judges found no basis for this and "has already been disposed of by us." While Penn Central might have shown that the landmark law diminished Grand Central's most profitable asset, that was not the constitutional test. "The validity of the Landmarks Preservation Law, as applied to Grand Central Terminal, does not depend on a showing that the landmark parcel will be undiminished in any degree by the regulation's restrictions; only that it will not "deprive the individual property owner of 'all beneficial use of his property.'" In fine, Murphy concluded, Penn Central had "shown hardship but not confiscation."

Judge Lupiano dissented. He remarked that no one could dispute the "historical, aesthetic and cultural significance of Grand Central Terminal" and "the contribution of the terminal to the uniqueness of New York City," disagreeing at least here with the trial court assertion that the terminal was "tired and faded." His dissenting opinion focused on what Judge Murphy phrased as "whether plaintiffs have satisfactorily established that the law, as applied to them in this case, imposes such a burden as to constitute a compensable taking." Even though aesthetics was not really the question, Lupiano was impressed that the Penn Central development scheme was designed by "renowned firm of Marcel Breuer" with a "high-quality building." That was not a finding of fact, of course, as only the design, not its execution, was available for viewing.

Even though Judge Lupiano disagreed with Judge Saypol on the beauty of Grand Central Terminal, Lupiano did agree with the lower court's ruling. In this, he relied heavily on the opinion of Associate Judge John Van Voorhis, serving as special master in the reorganization proceedings involving the New York, New Haven, and Hartford Railroad Company in the US District Court for the District of Connecticut. Lupiano reused Judge Van Voorhis's finding to conclude,

> It is doubtful that the City could insist upon its [Grand Central Terminal] being maintained at Penn Central's expense as a memorial to the golden age of railroading. The building, as it is, is expensive to maintain, and even under the broad scope of the police power in modern times it is doubtful that it can be so constricted without there

being a taking without payment of just compensation as required by the state and federal constitutions. This is particularly true in view of the similarity and close proximity to the Pan-Am Building which, it might be argued, could constitute discrimination denying the equal protection of the law.

Lupiano continued that the Landmarks Preservation Commission, by forcing Penn Central to maintain the exterior of Grand Central "in good repair," impinged on the railroad's property rights. "Maintenance is a prerogative of management. To transform that prerogative into a duty is to clearly lessen Penn Central's estate."

The dissent then stated that Penn Central had the right within zoning conventions to develop Grand Central to its most "profitable ways." The Landmarks Law forced Penn Central to "pay substantial rentals for a lease of the terminal," which Penn Central made with the Metropolitan Transit Authority, "when told that the only use to which he can put it is an unprofitable railroading use." Judge Lupiano also took umbrage at the idea that Penn Central was not making the most of the terminal for revenue. "Penn Central has been assiduous in attempting to increase its terminal income. Indeed, the commercialization of the terminal had reached such a point that one of the things discussed in the proceedings before the Landmarks Commission was the desirability of eliminating some of the concessions which have disfigured the building." And that "the simple assertion that there is room for development of additional office space, stores or recreational facilities is highly speculative."

Lupiano's minority opinion noted that the contract Penn Central entered into with the MTA for commuter rail service went directly to operating that service and not to Penn Central's general revenue. "The $2.5 million credit was the price it paid for withdrawal from commuter service. Viewed in this context, the credit is chargeable not to the operation of the terminal, but to the Penn Central itself. However, this does not alter the fact that the several agreements leave Penn Central with no possible source of return from the terminal, save development rights." The Landmarks Preservation Commission recognized that the development air rights that the zoning amended in 1969 covered more potential transfer sites "fraught with obstacles." The City Planning Commission and the Board of Estimate must approve. There was also the potential for neighbors to protest the transfer to other buildings for violating existing zoning. The fallout from transferring the air rights was impossible to predict. "For these and numerous other reasons it is difficult to assign a monetary value to the transfer rights." In other words, since a value could not be assigned, it might just be worthless.

The New York Times reported that the decision brought "unrestrained joy" to the city, architects, and historic preservationists. "It's the best Christmas present the city could ask for," said Beverly Moss Spatt, chair of the Landmarks Preservation Commission. "It shows that someone cares about architecture besides just the architects," said Philip Johnson, who had been one of the earliest critics of Penn Central's building plans. The terminal, however, was now operated not by Penn Central but by the Metropolitan Transportation Authority, which leased it from Penn Central. The MTA had recently embarked on a restoration program for the building, which included the first cleaning of the interior stonework and ceiling frescoes since the station was completed in 1913.

The December ruling, touted as a Christmas present to the City of New York, was barely unwrapped when the railroad decided to appeal this reversal to the state's highest court, the New York Court of Appeals in Albany. When the New York Court of Appeals case was being prepared, Goldstein no longer worked in the appeals division of the city's Law Department. Leonard Koerner took over and argued the case, working closely with Dorothy Miner, who had been hired by the city to become the LPC's full-time counsel. Mayor Abraham Beame and Jacqueline Kennedy Onassis with the Committee to Save Grand Central Station, alongside performers Jerry Ohrbach, Tammy Grimes, Kay Medford, and Bobby Short, rallied in front of the statue of Commodore Vanderbilt (on the south side of the terminal) on April 21, 1977, one week before the New York Court of Appeals heard oral arguments, to give the lawyers moral support. On April 27 the New York Court of Appeals began hearing Penn Central's request to have Grand Central Terminal's landmark status voided.

With bankruptcy still looming, the expense of defending yet another appeal was a problem for the city. W. Bernard Richland headed the city's Law Department at the time. He later wrote that his office was "decimated" and "on the brink of disaster" during the crisis. But under his guidance, the office nevertheless defended the Landmarks Law and the landmarking designation of the terminal. The railroad, itself in dire financial straits, hoped for a knockout blow, the two parties staggering like boxers in the last stages of a twelve-round bout.

In the Court of Appeals

Presiding over the Court of Appeals was Charles D. Breitel, a longtime Republican. During his tenure, from 1973 to 1978, New York State's highest court grew in prestige. The chief justice, Sol Wachtler, said at Breitel's passing in 1990 that Judge Breitel "was a brilliant jurist who will be remembered for his remarkable contributions to the jurisprudence of this state." Tom Goldstein, then the legal correspondent for *The New York Times*, wrote late in 1978 that with the lineup of judges having been the same for four years, the court had "recaptured its place among the top rank of state courts." A particularly noteworthy opinion was one Breitel wrote in 1972 upholding the state's liberalized abortion law of 1970. Judge Breitel also wrote an opinion in 1976 that invalidated a moratorium on $1 billion in New York City's short-term notes. In that opinion he wrote that although the city was in "dire straits," its financial woes were not in the same league as, for instance, "nuclear decimation." The decision set off a renewed and panicky scramble in New York City to hold off its numerous creditors.

James W. B. Benkard, a prominent New York corporate lawyer who was honored for his extensive pro bono work, said that Judge Breitel "was a brilliant, complex, energetic, and quietly ambitious man whose modesty and rigorous standards never allowed him to quite appreciate what a remarkable life he led." Breitel really did "love the law"; indeed, he once wrote that he "love[d] the court system," not a commonly expressed view. He cared deeply for the Court of Appeals, which he unabashedly described as the "greatest Court in the nation . . . surpass[ing] the Supreme Court by far." *Fordham Law Review* stated at his retirement in 1978 that "the New York Court of Appeals will lose one of the ablest leaders and foremost jurists in its proud history."

On June 25, 1977, the Court of Appeals' seven judges unanimously upheld the Appellate Division decision in *Penn Central*, and concluded that the landmark restrictions were permissible. City planner Norman

Marcus recalled that the Court of Appeals affirmed on all the grounds given by the Appellate Division, but viewed the "reasonable beneficial use–reasonable return on the property" question in a new light. The reasonable return to which plaintiffs were entitled in the Court of Appeal's "neo-Henry Georgian [single tax] perspective" could only come on the "privately created and privately managed ingredient" of the terminal's value. The terminal was exempt from real estate taxes, and there was no way of measuring a "reasonable return" or of using real estate tax abatement as a means of creating one.

Judge Breitel found that the Penn Central case was not a zoning case. Even though it was similar because the restrictions imposed on the use of the property are comparable to zoning restrictions, the "purposes are different, and in determining whether regulation is reasonable, the purposes behind the regulation assume considerable significance." He said that zoning regulates construction of new buildings. Individual landmarks are not the same as historic district regulation because all owners in the district benefit from a "general community plan." The case was also different from an eminent domain case where there is a clear taking and compensation must be paid. Landmark law is a "limitation on exploitation" of the highest potential on the land, something shared with zoning and historic district regulation, but it still is different because the law is shouldered by one owner. "Discriminatory zoning is condemned because there is no acceptable reason for singling out one particular parcel for different and less favorable treatment" except when the reason is a "cultural, architectural, historical, or social significance attached to the affected parcel." Nevertheless, the regulation required a "reasonable return or equivalent private use of his property," in response to which Breitel distinguished it from *French Investing Co. v. City of New York* (1977). Once again distinguishing *French* from *Penn Central* (as had Murphy), Breitel found that the regulations in the former case deprived the original site of any possibility of producing a reasonable return, since only park uses were permitted on the land. The transferable development rights were left in legal limbo, not readily attachable to any other property, due to a lack of common ownership of the rights and a suitable site for using them. Hence, the plaintiff was deprived of property without due process of the law. The regulation of Grand Central Terminal, by contrast, permitted productive use of the terminal site as it had been used for more than half a century, as a railroad terminal. In addition, the development rights were made transferable to numerous sites in the vicinity of the terminal, several owned by Penn Central, and at least one or two suitable for construction of office buildings.

Overall, it was the uniqueness of the terminal that seemed to entrance the Court of Appeals. It declared that "Grand Central Terminal is no ordinary landmark." It is not an ordinary piece of land or property. It is a railroad terminal, "set amid a metropolitan population, and entirely dependent on a heavy traffic of travelers to make it an economically feasible operation. Without people Grand Central would never have been a successful railroad terminal, and without the terminal, a major transportation center, the proposed building site would be much less desirable for an office building."

Penn Central's submissions were flawed, the court explained, because they did not include an imputed rental value for the terminal's facilitation of railroad activities. "Since Penn Central is in the passenger railroad business it, of necessity, must have a terminal.... The reasonable rental value of such [terminal] space cannot properly be omitted from any meaningful analysis of the property's capacity to yield a reasonable return." Because Penn Central had not demonstrated that the terminal would be unprofitable even with the rental income imputed for purpose, the court held that it had not carried its burden of demonstrating a taking.

The court offered a functionalist rationale as well for its finding. This was not exactly what anyone had argued, but it was highly relevant. The terminal's function, history, and setting were created by "society as an organized entity, especially through its government, rather than as a mere conglomerate of individuals" and "has created much of the value of the terminal property." This was a new and important concept created by the Court of Appeals. The judges stated that "railroads have always been a franchised and regulated public utility, favored monopolies at public expense, subsidy, and with limited powers of eminent domain, without which their existence and character would not have been possible." Historically, railroads relied on government for their rights of way, and land, grade, and crossing eliminations. "Penn Central and its predecessors have benefited mightily from this assistance." Importing historical benefits to the rail company as though they were present benefits was not an unprecedented step, however, as landmark law itself always looked to the past.

Judge Breitel's opinion also made the point that even though the terminal might not be making money, it contributed to the other properties Penn Central owned. The court used the example of a flagship department store at a regional shopping mall. "The flagship store may not produce enough income to justify its construction or maintenance, but it may draw enough customers into the other, smaller stores." Those "smaller stores" included the Biltmore, Commodore, Barclay, and Roosevelt Hotels, to which Penn Central could transfer the air rights. Even though the court said there are "many defects in New York City's program for development rights transfers," that in itself did not make the development rights worthless. Penn Central failed to "demonstrate affirmatively that the regulation eliminates all reasonable return.... When a less expensive alternative is available, especially when a city is in financial distress, it should not be forced to choose between witnessing the demolition of its glorious past and mortgaging its hopes for the future. The landmark preservation provisions of the Administrative Code represent an effort to take a middle way."

Ironically, Breitel's opinion for the court faced some criticism from the people who were trying to save Grand Central. Frank Gilbert of the Landmarks Preservation Commission thought it was too radical: "We did not think that this opinion by Judge Breitel and the Court of Appeals would hold up.... This was a very interesting and very progressive opinion. It left an awful lot of things up in the air." He also later called it "too revolutionary" and "hard to apply." The city's defense team wrote a brief objecting to the position. Koerner, who would later argue the case in front of the US Supreme Court, worried how Judge Breitel would take any criticism of the opinion; "he was so powerful in New York, and since as an institutional litigator we would do 30 cases or more a year in the state court of appeals at that time, I had to write him a letter and I explained that while we loved what he did we really couldn't urge it on the Supreme Court." Allan Nevins noted too that "no other court has ever used such a test which, if one considers it, is practically impossible to administer: How, for example, would one value Grand Central Terminal if it were in Des Moines instead of on Park Avenue? Moreover, that test was not obviously consistent with the legal doctrines previously discussed which had emerged to date from the U.S. Supreme Court."

Penn Central was likely to appeal to the US Supreme Court. Grounds for the appeal were the Fifth and Fourteenth Amendments. Koerner thought that Breitel's opinion had both gone too far on the zoning question and not gone far enough on the claim that the designation was singling out one building from a neighborhood. To him it was troubling that it was not a zoning case,

> "that we had singled out Penn Central's property, Grand Central terminal. That is precisely the opposite approach of what we wanted. We wanted to say we weren't singling out anybody, that the benefits and the burdens were being shared equally throughout the entire city, that everybody including the owners of Grand Central were benefitting by having all these landmarks, and to single out someone we said would be wrong and that is not what we are doing. . . . The other point Breitel emphasized was that he said the city at this period was in fiscal distress, which was true. He seemed to indicate that because of the fiscal stress we would be able to use a regulatory power, that is the police power, rather than the condemnation power. Obviously that's not a principle that can work. Either you can regulate or you can't regulate; it cannot depend on the finances of the city. That was a problem.

Still, many landmarks supporters were thrilled with the decision. "It is the most important decision that the preservation movement has ever had," said Beverly Moss Spatt, who added that it was "the high point" for the Landmarks Preservation Commission. L. Kevin Sheridan, chief of the appeals division of the corporate counsel's office, said: "I think we have pulled New York City landmarks out of the water—if this had gone the other way, landmarks would have been over in New York City." Sheridan, whose appeals division argued the case on behalf of the Landmarks Preservation Commission, called the decision "very strong, very far-reaching," and said that the court's argument that Grand Central Terminal's value comes in part from public contributions "goes even beyond what we urged." Said Margot Wellington, executive director of the Municipal Art Society, which had spearheaded the public battle on behalf of the terminal, "We were fortunate that in the years of fighting this case we had a building as symbolic to the whole nation as Grand Central is." She continued, "This was a case not about one landmark but about all landmarks."

Public support was divided along the lines that Koerner had predicted. *The New York Times* opinion piece that came out four days after the decision stated, "It is encouraging to see cities protecting their heritage and quality, and it is even more encouraging to see the process turned into a law that is sensitive to both individual rights and social needs. If we shape our buildings and our buildings shape us, as Churchill said, the law shapes both. The Grand Central decision carries that process farther with fairness and vision." Critics worried that the decision rested too firmly on the city's condition and the terminal's unique landmark status. The *New York Law Journal* had a piece in September attesting that "the Grand Central case is sui generis: the opinion [is] tailored to the Grand Central context." It was exactly the type of argument the city did not want to engage.

Richard Wolloch, the author of that law journal essay, worried that the sentimental value attributed to the terminal by the populace, the easements for the railroad right of way, the tax advantages, and the mass transit connections all had a tangible value that, in turn, gave value to the terminal structure. "Although the quantification of the value that these items bestow upon the Terminal was difficult to measure, the New York Court of Appeals insisted that the task could and should be performed." This new formulation for the valuation of a reasonable return stated that the assessed value of landmark property (for the purpose of tabulating a reasonable return) equals the commonly assessed value of the landmark realty less the value of the landmark that is attributable to social investment. The new formula Breitel supposedly applied depressed the private property assessment value of the landmark so that the 6 percent return yielded a lesser dollar amount based on a lower realty value. Wolloch saw the Penn Central case as a situation in which there was no reasonable return at all. The Penn Central Transportation Company claimed that, as to the terminal, it was consistently in debt; nevertheless, the New York Court of Appeals said that the terminal could take a loss and at the same time appreciate the value of adjacent Penn Central properties such as Park Avenue and several adjacent hotels so that it might realize an overall reasonable return. The attribution of value to adjacent properties by the terminal stems from the convenience of travel to and the centrality of the terminal that benefits these properties. "The aggregation of these appreciated properties adjacent to the landmark is an ancillary feature of the new method of landmark realty valuation which rarely benefits anyone but the large urban realtors because few people are able to amass several buildings in such an expensive commercial district."

Wolloch surveyed the entire landscape of regulatory takings. Thus far, land use regulation challenges had followed one of a series of overlapping tests in analyzing the reasonableness of restrictions on the property owner. The reasonable return test guaranteed a reasonable return on the realty investment of the private property owner whose property is restricted by a land use regulation. Under this formula, governmental regulation that deprives the property owner of a reasonable return amounts to an unconstitutional restriction on the owner's beneficial use. The beneficial use test forbids intrusive governmental regulation if it deprives the private property owner of a substantial portion of the beneficial use of his realty. The public interest test allowed governmental regulation of land use even to the point of denying all beneficial use if the regulation promotes a clear and necessary public interest. The nonprofit test was a variation of the beneficial use test: regulation of not-for-profit institutions was unreasonable if it deprived the owner of a substantial portion of the structure's charitable use. The social investment test held that only the value of the realty that is the product of the property owner's efforts should be guaranteed a reasonable return. The Court of Appeals in *Penn Central* stated that "a property owner is not absolutely entitled to receive a return on so much of the property's value as was created by social investment." Wolloch read the court as saying that the sentimental value attributed to the terminal by the populace, the easements for the railroad right of way, the tax advantages, and the mass transit connections all had a tangible value that, in turn, gave value to the terminal structure. Finally, the *Penn Central* Court of Appeals test was an extension of the social investment test where there was no reasonable return at all.

Koerner rationalized the innovative decision somewhat differently from Wolloch: "Judge [Charles D.] Breitel is the presiding judge. Now you have to understand he's a very strong presiding judge. He rules the court with an iron hand. He's very smart. Now he has a number of grounds for his opinion but this is the one that no one argued. The one ground is the air rights have value." But Breitel looked at a bigger piece of the social and economic reality than the findings of fact presented to the court.

> Penn Central as a railroad had a monopoly power. They got the right of eminent domain, they got the right to settle in the middle of the city in the most expensive area of the city, they had the right to have direct access to the subways and the trains, they had the right to have grants of property, they had the right to develop the property around Grand Central Terminal for their own benefit. They had all these rights, and they had all these benefits, and now it's time to give back.

How central was it to the Court of Appeals decision? In other words, was it an obiter dictum? Unnecessary to find for the city? The answer lay in the marble palace in which sat the justices of the US Supreme Court.

CHAPTER EIGHT

Briefs and Oral Argument in the US Supreme Court

Penn Central v. New York City at the appellate level in the state courts presented both easy to understand urban space issues and complex legal concepts. What was a reasonable return, and what was best use of private property? How did individual rights and public interest intersect—or were they opposites? There was a lot of case law on takings, both physical and regulatory, by the time Penn Central appealed its case to the US Supreme Court. Case law had determined that the government could take, but on what basis and with what return or cost depended on the details of the taking. Was it a zoning case? A regulatory takings case? An example of eminent domain or the police power of the state?

The one difference between the state courts of appeal and the US Supreme Court, a difference that gave hope to the railroad appellant and concern to the preservationists, was that the Supreme Court was not comprised of New Yorkers with a sentimental attachment to the terminal and to the greatness of the city itself. Those attachments had shown through all of the state court opinions, even those of Saypol and Lupiano that had favored Penn Central. How would the tug of memory and the elevating power of aesthetics play in the High Court?

The Landmarks Preservation Commission and the city had three lines of argument for the Supreme Court hearing. First, they could posit that landmarks were simply another type of land-use tool, like zoning, and that all zoning required was a reasonable return on the property. Second, they could maintain that the value of the terminal lay not only in the actual revenue, but in the convenience for those who were using the mass transit facility. These were hidden revenues of great benefit to the public as a whole and to the city in particular. Finally, they could offer the value of the terminal as a landmark monument, a unique and valuable public space. What they did not want to rely on was the more amorphous social value of the terminal and the evil monopolistic character of the railroad in Breitel's obiter dictum.

Leonard Koerner led the city's legal team writing the brief for the Supreme Court. The team included Dorothy Miner; Allen G. Schwartz, from the city's corporate counsel's office; and L. Kevin Sheridan, his colleague. Sheridan was (in)famous for the paperwork that covered every surface in his office and forced visitors to stand (according to recollections preserved at the New York Preservation Archives Project). The city's team also included Ralph Menapace, who had argued the case in the New York courts, Paul Byard, and Jack Kerr. Byard was an architect and a lawyer who was already involved in the renovation of historic city buildings. Kerr was an expert in landmarks conservancy, with a background in archeology. He was one of the counsel who lost the *Lutheran Church* case, and he was determined, he later recalled, not to lose this one.

They divided the brief writing tasks among themselves. Kerr worried that individual landmarks had not been established as one of the permissible uses of police power under the Constitution, unlike historic districts. The latter included large geographic areas of many connected properties and affected everyone equally, very much like zoning. By contrast, individual landmarks seemed like spot zoning, where a municipality signals out one property owner for special reasons. Spot zoning may be legal, if the owner convinces local government that the proposed use of the land or the structures requires an exception to the surrounding zoning. For example, a small plot of land allowing a corner store would be fine but a carve-out for a noxious use like a bar or slaughterhouse would not be. In the first case, the differing land uses are mutually compatible and supportive. In the latter case, the residential nature of the area would be harmed by a conflicting land use. Some courts, however, reject spot zoning proposals when they harm local communities. Menapace spent a lot of time with economists trying to figure a way to argue that having to maintain Grand Central as a railroad station was not a hardship to Penn Central. Miner focused on Fifth Amendment takings law.

The city's lawyers tried to align the precedents to support their case. Precedent is a vital source of law in the American system, alongside codes, the text of the Constitution, statutes, and treaties. Precedent from New York (the state is the sovereign; New York City municipal rulings did not have the force of precedent) was best. Case law from other states, or from federal courts on allied subjects, might be persuasive but was not compelling. Thus, for the team, one important case was *Hadacheck v. Sebastian* (1915), an old case dealing with brick kilns in Los Angeles, but an important one because there the government essentially put the brick kiln industry out of business in Los Angeles. Better was *Queenside Hills Realty Co. v. Saxl* (1946), where a lodging house in New York City complained because it had to put in a sprinkler system, which would have decreased the value of the building by 30 percent. The Supreme Court decided that 30 percent was not enough to amount to a taking. And then in *Berman v. Parker*, a case familiar to everyone involved in *Penn Central* by this time, the Court said to the department store owner, "This is a law designed to make Washington more beautiful. It's an aesthetic law." The Court concluded it was a proper exercise of the police power, and that aesthetics can be subsumed under the police power. Berman did receive some compensation, but he lost the store. Justice William O. Douglas wrote, "In the present case, the Congress and its authorized agencies have made determinations that take into account a wide variety of values. It is not for us to reappraise them."

Koerner thought that the city could still rely on *Goldblatt v. Hempstead*. He recalled the case well: "This was a gravel and mining and sand excavation program in Hempstead, which is a part of Long Island. The town felt that this business was incompatible with what they're trying be, really a suburb. They essentially put him out of business and said, 'You have the land, you have to bring it up the water table and use it for something else.' It essentially took away most of their value. They went up to the Supreme Court, and the Supreme Court cited that *Hadacheck* case, the one involving the brick kilns, and said, 'Look, we said you can be reduced in value, you can still earn a reasonable rate of return, go away.'"

Koerner found one more precedent in the city's favor: *Maher v. City of New Orleans* (1975). The case was a challenge to the designation of the French Quarter in New Orleans as a historic district that went all the way up to the state supreme court. The owner had a single-family residence, and he wanted to build a multiple residence, and said, "You can't tell me what to do." The court said, "Yes, we can." It noted , "You had put your relative in that residence. You weren't even getting a fair rent. You can divide up the residence but you can't change it." Koerner recalled that "the important thing about that case is that cert [certiorari, the writ by which the Court asked for the papers from the lower courts and heard a case on appeal] was denied by the US Supreme Court. It recognized at least the principles of landmark designation, and okay for a district. But now Grand Central took it to the next step for individual districts."

Watching from the sidelines, Frank Gilbert was still worried. After all, Penn Central had won the first round. "Although the appellants suggest in their reply brief that the factual conclusions of the New York court cannot be sustained unless we accept the rationale of the New York Court of Appeals . . . it is apparent that the findings concerning Penn Central's ability to profit from the Terminal depend in no way on the Court of Appeals' rationale." The railroad and its lawyers were very conscious that they were in a box because of the finding about reasonable return. The "appellants' position appears to be that the only means of ensuring that selected owners are not singled out to endure financial hardship for no reason is to hold that any restriction imposed on individual landmarks pursuant to the New York scheme is a 'taking' requiring payment of 'just compensation.' Agreement with this argument would of course invalidate not just New York City's law, but all comparable landmark legislation in the nation. We find no merit in it."

Friends of the Court

Friend of the court briefs were arriving. Most important perhaps was the brief of the federal government, crafted in the solicitor general's office. The premises of the brief were straightforward: in order to promote the general welfare, federal, state, and local governments may regulate the use of private property. The scope of legislative discretion in this area is broad, and economic regulations enjoy a presumption of constitutionality. Furthermore, historic preservation is a valid objective of government regulation.

The brief continued that New York City's law and federal statute established that some properties, wherever located, deserve special treatment in order to preserve and improve the quality of life in the city as a whole. This effect on the quality of life may be present whether a number of such buildings are located together in a single historic district or are dispersed throughout a city, state, or nation. Penn Central did not challenge the designation of Grand Central Terminal as a landmark, and so it was in no position to argue that it was injured by arbitrary or unprincipled action. The decision that the terminal is a landmark would be unassailable in any event. Tracking the New York Court of Appeals opinion, the federal government's brief said that the terminal was "no ordinary landmark."

The federal government brief then came to the financial return question. "Once it has been established that a regulation serves a substantial public purpose, the only open question is whether the regulation obliterates any beneficial use of the property. Appellants do not raise the beneficial use of the property. Appellants do not raise the beneficial use question here and could not reasonably do so. The landmark designation does not affect the use Grand Central Terminal has had since its inception. It was, and will continue to be, a railroad terminal containing office space and concessions."

The amicus brief for the United States continued that the attention to the uses of the entire bundle of rights was consistent with the decisions in regulated industry cases that the regulated entity need not be allowed to earn a reasonable return on every component of investment. "It is enough if the entity receives a reasonable return on every component of investment or it is enough if the entity receives a reasonable return on the investment taken as a whole." The brief cited *Atlantic Coast Line R.R. Co. v. North Carolina Corporation Commission* (1907), in which "the Court upheld against the constitutional challenge to an order to the railroad to run an additional train at a loss, concluding that calculation of gain and loss, and of reasonable return, must be made with respect to 'the nature and productiveness of the corporate business as a whole.'" The fact that the case came from a time, 1907, when rails ruled the nation's economy, did not matter. It was the holding that mattered as precedent.

The result was the same when a utility sought to abandon an unprofitable service. The Court had held in *Puget Sound Traction, Light & Power Co. v. Reynolds* (1917) that abandonment need not be permitted as long as the company was earning an adequate return on its total investments. Again, it did not matter that the petitioner was a utilities company rather than a railroad; the doctrine was the same. These cases indicated that investments and property rights cannot easily be carved up for "takings" purposes, and they reinforce the submission that as long as the terminal still earned a reasonable return when put to its intended use, the argument that some discrete part of the original bundle of rights has been made worthless is immaterial.

Other supporting briefs for the city added arguments that were closer to Breitel's opinion. The Pacific Legal Foundation brief submitted that it was a well-established principle in both federal and state courts that the costs of a public good should be distributed to those who will benefit. The State of California brief concluded that the only difference between *Penn Central* and *Maher* is that the landmark buildings in New Orleans designated for preservation are apparently located in one area, whereas in New York historical buildings are apparently spread throughout the city. This distinction is without a difference since in both instances significant buildings are regulated in a similar manner. In *Maher* the issue was resolved by analyzing whether the regulatory action denying construction was valid. This case should be judged in the same manner.

The California brief also addressed a case that seemed to be on point in favor of Penn Central, but was in the amicus' opinion not so. In *Benenson v. United States* (1977), the Court found that the sum total of government action aimed at preventing demolition of the Willard Hotel in Washington, DC, so as to facilitate acquisition, constituted a taking. There were numerous attempts to negotiate acquisition of the property. On two occasions legislation was enacted that affected the owners' use of the property. Also, during this time the government's purpose changed from demolishing the hotel to preserving it! Finally, attempts to seek approval for new uses were frustrated because of the government's desire to acquire the property. The court concluded from all these governmental acts that a taking had occurred. In addition to the factual differences, in *Benenson* the Court concluded that the owners could make no economic use of the property as a result of the governmental actions.

The State of New York had supported the city throughout the litigation and submitted its own amicus brief for the attention of the High Court. Unlike the inverse condemnation cases relied on by Penn Central, the state argued that the railroad retained full and unhampered use of its present property. As the state appellate courts had found, the railroad earned a reasonable return, if not a profit. Under the doctrine of police power no more is required. For example, in *New Orleans v. Dukes* (1976), New Orleans had enacted an ordinance "'to preserve the appearance and custom valued by the [French] Quarter's residents and attractive to tourists.'" The Court concluded that the legitimacy of the use of the police power for such an objective was "obvious."

A brief from the National Trust for Historic Preservation (NTHP) expanded on the state police power doctrine. The primary responsibility for determining which measures will promote the public welfare lies with the state, and substantial deference must be paid to the state's judgment. "The settled rule of this court is that it will not substitute its judgment for that of the legislative body charged with the primary duty and responsibility of determining the question." The NTHP brief did not stop there. "Legislatures may implement their program step by step... in such economic areas, adopting regulations that only partially ameliorate a perceived evil and deferring complete elimination of the evil to future regulations."

Daniel M. Gribbon represented Penn Central. Gribbon was a legend in the District of Columbia bar, a senior member of the Covington and Burling firm there. He earned his law degree at Harvard Law School and clerked for Judge Learned Hand on the Second Circuit before his service in the US Navy during World War II. In the years between the war and his appearance in *Penn Central*, he chaired committees of the American Bar Association and the DC professional responsibility board. He was a veteran of the Supreme Court bar and had argued many cases to a successful conclusion. In a 1998 interview Gribbon recalled the Penn Central case, but it was not one he thought most important in his career. "Another case of significance, and this one I lost, was *Penn Central Transportation Company v. New York City*, which shed a new light on the principle of 'takings.'" Ruefully, he added, "All that I was able to salvage was a dissent of three justices: Chief Justice Berger and Justices Stevens and Rehnquist. It may be wishful thinking on my part, but it seems the law on takings in the intervening years has moved closer to their view. That's what you tend to say when you lose a case."

Preparation for Oral Argument

Koerner recalled the preparation of the case at great length in the New York Preservation archives:

> Well, I'll give you some of the history. When I took over the case after the Court of Appeals, I had the case in the Court of Appeals, a new mayor came in, and that was Edward Koch, who you may have heard about. He brought in a new Corporation Counsel. So the Corporation Counsel came in January, and we were getting ready to file a brief in the Supreme Court, and it was January '78, in response to the brief of the petition[ers, i.e., Penn Central].

The new corporate counsel was Allen Schwartz. Schwartz had worked for the city in prior years but came out of private practice to lead the Law Department. He would later sit on the district court bench for the Southern District of New York.

Schwartz sat down with Koerner, "interviewed me, discussed the case" and decided not to change horses in midstream. This in the face of petitions from a number of leading New York firms that wanted in on the action, now that the city had won in the state courts. Koerner thought, "That took a lot of guts, because I worked on that case with one other person, Dorothy Miner, and Kevin Sheridan supervised us. We didn't have the staff a big firm would have, and [Schwartz] had faith in our ability to do the work." Koerner was delighted with the amicus briefs. "We won on numbers in terms of amicus briefs." Equally important, the amicus writers had developed elements in the Breitel opinion.

Penn Central had implied throughout the litigation that it had been unfairly singled out. Koerner's chronology refuted that implication. "The nub of the case," stated Koerner,

> was that Grand Central has not been singled out. There was a landmark law in place before the announcement that Penn Central was going to build on top of Grand Central.... This case must therefore be judged on the basis that Grand Central is indeed profitable in its present use as a railroad for passenger service and that part of the issue regarding air rights was whether the $3.8 million return on the Biltmore site was so unfair as to emasculate the land use regulation, not whether Penn Central was entitled to the highest and best use.

Dorothy Miner, part of the oral argument team for the city before the US Supreme Court, praised how Koerner's oral argument captured the borderline justices:

During Lenny Koerner's oral argument [the justices] had a great number of questions. What he's good at is answering the question while bringing them back to what he wanted to argue as he moved it forward. That's a very adept lawyer and one of the most important characteristics of appearing before the Supreme Court. It's one of the times when oral arguments really mattered. His answers, not the whistle stop train, made the decision what it was. He showed the justices that if the railroad ever closed down and stopped using the Terminal, we would have another set of facts and they would be entitled to come back and present them. And that was the most critical thing of all in terms of proving fairness.

The oral argument for the city was concluded by assistant attorney general Patricia M. Wald, speaking on behalf of the United States as amicus curiae. The administration of President Jimmy Carter had expressed its commitment to historic preservation as a national policy. The Supreme Court customarily allots time for the representative of the federal government when the federal government has submitted an amicus brief. Wald declared that historical and cultural foundations of the nation should be preserved as a living part of our community life and development in order to give our people a sense of their history.

Wald recalled she "always . . . played a very anomalous role in this whole litigation. It was not a litigating division and although I had had some litigating experience, a fair amount before I took that job, I certainly didn't have any in the job. I had no relationship with the lands and natural resources division except in terms of their legislative priorities." Wald was familiar with the case of course, in a general way. "One day Wade McCree who was the Solicitor General at the time came to see me. And he said you know there is a tradition in this department that all heads, all assistant attorneys general, this is 1978, get to argue one case in the Supreme Court. And I said at the time I was busy, I think I was trying to get FISA passed which was the foreign intelligence act, and an omnibus judgeship bill to get President Carter 150 new judges, etc." McCree was insistent. "He said we think we have a good one for you to argue." Wald recalled her response. "It was a little bit like a barrister [the English attorney who argued cases before the crown courts] being called in and the brief is already written and indeed the brief already had been written by the lands and natural resources division."

Wald did not protest,

> so they gave me the brief and in retrospect I was certainly a bit of a dummy, I think, in terms of the merits of the case. They gave me a brief and I read it and read the cases, etc. And then [future federal court of appeals judge] Frank Easterbrook, who was then the Deputy Solicitor General, came to see me for 15 minutes. I think he had somebody with him but I don't remember who it was, from lands and natural resources. I don't even remember what they talked about, but it wasn't anything very much pointed in terms of what I would say at the oral argument or what points I would raise.

Wald recalled that "Easterbrook had been down to see me as the deputy solicitor, and there is a big footnote in the U.S. brief from [Richard] Posner. Posner and Easterbrook later became of course the economics and law types, but the U.S. was citing, thinking it was in its favor obviously, a Posner analysis which they said showed that basically what had happened here was like a non-monetary landmark tax on it, etc. So that's basically it." Both Easterbrook and Posner would go from the University of Chicago faculty to seats on the Court of Appeals for the Seventh Circuit, and there they would offer the law and economic jurisprudence for which they are now famous.

The issue for Wald and for the United States was whether the federal government had a legitimate interest in the litigation. "Subsequently, I talked with Lois Schiffer, a good friend of mine, who in the Clinton administration became the head of the lands and natural resources division and was at this time the head of the general litigation part of the division. She said, 'my god, they didn't even moot court you.'" [That is, they did not practice a question-and-answer session with Wald.] She had never argued in the Supreme Court before, either. "I was a little bit of babe in the woods. So I asked her, seeing as how I was not present at the creation of the brief or any of the strategy that went into it, I asked her subsequently when this panel came up, if she could go back in her memory and remember some of the background."

Schiffer was not offish, but she was not particularly helpful, either. Wald recalled:

{ *Chapter Eight* }

She said that they had gotten a letter from the National Trust asking them wouldn't they like to come in and do it, and she said "you know in general they decided that they would but she referred to it as a quote ho hum case." I said, well, was there any dispute about... what attitude you would take, what points you would make, and she said she didn't remember much about the brief at all. She was the head of the litigation section, but she couldn't remember whether or not she had even reviewed it. But she said one question was, did the U.S. actually have any relevant interest in this seeing as how these are primarily state and locally administered programs. And so there was a little question about whether the U.S. really did have a pertinent interest. They decided that it had, but there was no significant dispute inside the department about what attitude they would take or anything else. And so that's how it came to be. Well I'll let it stay there.

The Justices

When the time came for oral argument, sitting in the curved array of raised seats at the front of the Supreme Court courtroom were the nine members of the Court. Republican Presidents Richard Nixon and Gerald Ford, and then Governor Ronald Reagan all criticized the rulings of Chief Justice Earl Warren's Court as too lenient on criminals and too activist, and all three presidents sought to appoint conservative justices. Nevertheless, the legacy of the Warren Court remained strong throughout Warren Burger's tenure as chief justice. That is to say, albeit with some qualifications, the Burger Court upheld many of the precedents of the Warren Court, even in regard to due process and criminal law. How the justices would view landmark law was uncertain, however.

Justices William Brennan and Thurgood Marshall generally took liberal stances, while John Paul Stevens, Potter Stewart, and Byron White often took centrist positions. William Rehnquist, Chief Justice Burger, and (to a lesser extent) Lewis Powell made up the conservative bloc of the court. During his time on the court, Harry Blackmun shifted from the right toward the center, allowing liberals to claim more victories as the 1970s continued.

Burger was serving on the federal appeals court bench when President

Nixon appointed him to the center seat. Burger was known as tough on criminal matters, something that Nixon had promised voters he would be in his 1968 campaign. Burger took a great deal of interest in his role as head of the federal judiciary, pressing for reforms in both administration and law. His goal was greater efficiency, and part of this was closer administrative relations with state courts and with Congress. Although he was not regarded as an innovative judge, he brought a gravitas to the Court that, in previous years, had come under fire for its liberality and activism.

President Nixon's second appointee, after two failed candidacies, was Harry Blackmun. Blackmun, from Minnesota and a close friend of Burger's, was supposed to be just as conservative, but proved over time to belong to the liberal wing of the Court. Most closely associated with his opinion for the Court in *Roe v. Wade* (1973), Blackmun would become a predictably strong supporter of women's rights and affirmative action.

William Rehnquist joined the Court in 1972 as an associate justice. In 1986 he would become its chief. He was raised in Wisconsin but made Arizona his home. He served Republican administrations in the Department of Justice and was elevated to the High Court without serving in any of the lower federal or state courts. Capable of warm personal relations with his fellow justices and judicial clerks, his strongly held views made him a controversial figure. He was a conservative in religious matters, defended school prayer, favored a very narrow view of the Fourteenth Amendment, and stoutly opposed affirmative action and expansive views of civil rights.

Nixon's fourth appointee was John Paul Stevens. Again, expected to join the conservative bloc, Stevens proved a true maverick. His opinions spanned both wings of the court and were deeply learned and heavily annotated, and in time he became one of the most respected jurists of his day.

Already on the Court was William Brennan, a Democrat in New Jersey politics, and an ally of Chief Justice Warren when Brennan joined the High Court bench in 1956. His support for liberal causes was predictable and well known. Brennan also had a reputation as a court politician, working hard to bring together majorities for the judgments he favored. This sometimes meant changing portions of his draft opinions to accommodate other justices' views to bring them on board. He would be known as the liberal lion of the court. Brennan may have had a special affection for the terminal, growing up across the Hudson River from it. Was such an attachment an impermissible bias, or was it a deeper appreciation that someone lacking his experience might not share?

Appointed by President Lyndon Johnson, Thurgood Marshall had risen from near poverty to become the foremost litigator for the Legal Defense Fund of the National Association for the Advancement of Colored People, and then solicitor general of the United States, a Court of Appeals judge, and finally took a place on the High Court. Marshall was the strongest voice for civil rights on the Court and an ally of Brennan in almost all things.

Potter Stewart, appointed by President Dwight Eisenhower, was a moderate, supportive of civil rights, but not of civil liberties. His position on pornography became, unfortunately, too well known, as he was quoted as saying that he could not define it, but he knew it when he saw it. A Midwesterner, his social views were conservative, and he dissented in the cases on birth control and religion in the schools.

President John F. Kennedy's nominee, Byron White, was the second longest serving member of the Court at the time of *Penn Central*, and was, like Stewart, a pragmatic jurisprudent. He looked closely at fact situations rather than sweeping doctrines. He had starred at school as an athlete, and in government service, and was a steadying influence on the Warren Court. He was a reliable vote for civil rights, and the rights of prisoners. He was not, however, a great friend to reproductive rights.

Conferences and Drafts

After oral argument, the justices conference on the case. Speaking in order of seniority, the chief going first, they indicate how they will vote and why. Then they return to their chambers and draft, or comment on others' draft, opinions. Their clerks, former outstanding law school students, help to craft the opinions to varying degrees. David Carpenter, Brennan's clerk in the 1977–1978 term, knew that Brennan's views would be the key to the city's success. "And he [Brennan] did mention this case to us at the jurisdictional stage. He said that sooner or later we're going to have to take one of these landmark zoning cases, and he read to us from the jurisdictional statement during one of our daily meetings. But that's really all I remember at this stage."

Brennan would need all of his skill to form a majority for the city. The justices kept notes during the oral argument, and then during the judicial conference that followed, once the case had been submitted. Justice Blackmun's notes suggest that he did not believe a benefit was conferred, along with the burden, to a private landmark owner. He noted that the lack of benefit was "enough to push [him] over," presumably to rule against the city and the Landmarks Preservation Law.

A law review article by Harvard Law School professor Frank Michelman had made its way into the chambers. Michelman's specialty was property law, and his 1967 economic analysis of takings law apparently was required reading for the clerks. He offered judges a three-part test to determine whether the Fifth Amendment had been violated, but also whether the takings could be justified by balancing the loss to the owner with the social value to the community. First, weigh the "net efficiency gains secured by the government action in question" versus the losses to the owner, the "settlement costs" in monetary compensation, then the "demoralization costs" incurred by not indemnifying them at all. The last calculation included a variety of factors, including noneconomic ones like fears of other owners whose property might be taken at a later time. Like so many law review pieces, much of it was speculative and overbroad, but the piece had received widespread attention.

Justice Rehnquist's clerk, Barton Carpenter, knew his justice was already working on his opinion. Carpenter shared his master's views. He thought that very few takings were justifiable. Still, this was an important case. Had Rehnquist the practiced political skills of a Brennan, his might have been the majority opinion, imperiling all landmark law. Carpenter recalled, "When I was a law student taking constitutional law with Henry Monaghan [at Columbia Law School] we spent a lot of time on the takings clause. I studied Michelman's article then. . . . I thought as a law student that Michelman . . . had made a serious attempt to make sense out of these decisions that were in quite a bit of disarray. I reread both articles when working on the opinion—and cited them both."

The two Carpenters revealed the ill-kept secret of the clerks at the High Court: the fact was that almost all of the justices asked their clerks not only for research aid, but also to write up opinions on portions of cases submitted to the Court (in addition to looking for other cases the justices wanted to hear in the thousands appealed to the Court every year). The two former clerks talked on the record at a Fordham Law School panel held years after the Penn Central case was decided. They were proud of their contribution to the two opinions. By this time, both of their justices had gone to their rewards, and here was the opportunity to tell the world what really happened. "The concept of "investment backed expectations" definitely came from Michelman's article, David Carpenter revealed. "But... I didn't call anyone at Harvard [Law School] to talk about it while I was working on the draft opinion. Nor did Justice Brennan. Michelman is a former clerk of Justice Brennan, though." In effect, the battle forming between Brennan and Rehnquist was something of a competition between the two Carpenters, and behind that, a debate over Michelman's contribution to the literature.

Another issue for counsel and clerks was the impact of Judge Breitel's earlier opinion. The Supreme Court did not have to take the opinion of the New York Court of Appeals into account at all. Breitel had broken new ground in it, but unlike some judges in the lower courts, he did not have a pipeline to any member of the High Court bench like Judge Learned Hand had to Justice Felix Frankfurter or Judge Henry Friendly had to Justice Brennan. Gribbon, who argued for Penn Central in both New York and the District of Columbia, did feel the Court adopted "one half of Breitel's opinion, that is, the notion that if we could make a reasonable earning on what was left that there had been no taking. Now that was novel as far as I was concerned." Lawyers watching the Court (court watching is a cottage industry) were also concerned about the impact of the Breitel opinion. As was noted previously, Frank Gilbert liked what Breitel had written, although he conceded that the chief judge's novel views might not have stood the test of time.

Oral Argument

On the morning of April 16, 1978, oral argument at the Supreme Court in Washington, DC, began. The Municipal Art Society board had mobilized over four hundred supporters of the city's case to travel to DC on what journalists called the "Landmark Express," showing public support for the terminal. It was appropriate that the Municipal Art Society members rode the New York–DC's Amtrak Metroliner, as it was originally a Penn Central train. The public effort to save Grand Central Terminal thus enlisted Grand Central's great rival, the Pennsy, in the cause of historic landmarks.

Koerner reported that "[oral argument] was more handled by Dorothy Miner, who was the counsel to Landmarks Preservation, and she was the one who rounded up the amicus briefs. The State of New York filed one, the Municipal Arts Society, the National Trust for Historic Preservation, all put in briefs in support." Koerner wryly added, "As Mr. Gribbon pointed out in oral argument, we won on numbers in terms of amicus briefs." Even in the cut and thrust of adversarial oral argument, the lawyers had their fun.

Koerner recalled the order of presentation and the preparation. Seating arrangements were visual statements of support for the lawyer facing the justices. "Everybody is sitting there. So there is Allen [Schwartz] and I and it's ten to ten and he asks, 'Where's your briefing notes?' And I wrote on a pad, 'Mr. Chief Justice and members of the court,' and he turned colors." Schwartz expected voluminous and detailed talking points. Koerner, who knew the case backwards and forwards by this time, was teasing his colleague. "That that is the way an attorney introduces himself or herself to the Supreme Court. As a law student, you learn that very famous introduction. In fact, lawyers in law school are actually taught not to use notes whenever possible." He didn't.

Gribbon did not share Koerner's picaresque sense of humor, but he was a worthy opponent for Koerner, Miner, and the other city lawyers. For the Historical Society of the District of Columbia Circuit he recalled the first time he was lead counsel before the court. "You have nine people before you, each with his or her own agenda, peppering you with questions. Most of the questions are directed not so much at the advocate arguing the case, but at one of the other justices. It is a little difficult to know how to handle that situation without alienating one or the other, or perhaps both, justices."

Gribbon opened. His approach and tone were careful, detailed, and unemotional. The issue was not about aesthetics, but property values. He conceded much of what the opposing counsel had argued. He told the Court, "Your Honor, the issue raised here is not, as some of the briefs seem to suggest, whether the City of New York may validly preclude Penn Central from constructing a building. Twenty-five years ago in *Berman and Parker*, this court, in unanimous opinion proclaimed for all that it is just as appropriate for government action to look to things that beautify and enhance the quality of life as it is to do away with things that are unsanitary." But "We are solely burdened and unbenefited, everybody else, not just the buildings, but the visitors, and the people who do it are the ones that get the whole benefit out of it."

Although he seemed to be swimming up water, he knew where he was going. "In most of the cases where there is a problem as to a taking, there has not been an exercise of eminent domain, it is government regulation which is operated in a way which may constitute a taking even though the exercise of eminent domain has not been tried." He did not classify the city's action as simply taking without adequate compensation. "It is claimed here that the *Goldblatt* decision of this Court establishes a different rule, a rule that says, you do not look in the case of regulation to what has been taken, you look rather to what is leftover." Fair enough. "Now that decision does contain some language with respect to the uses left to the property owner but I do not believe it establishes anything like proposition claimed here."

Again, Gribbon conceded what he had to concede. "Now far from saying, as it is urged here, that valid regulatory action cannot resolve in a compensable taking, the court, talking through Mr. Justice [Tom C.] Clark, acknowledged at the outset the basic principle on which we rest our case saying, 'Governmental action in the form of regulation can be so onerous as to constitute a taking which constitutionally requires compensation.'" Becoming bolder with each passing moment, Gribbon noted that the Supreme Court's rulings on takings were "confusing[,] an incompatible result of an explained and conclusionary terminology, circular reasoning, and empty rhetoric," but that he had no all-purpose tests to offer the Court in place of its own garbled precedents.

This was sure to arouse the ire of the justices. Gribbon recalled, "I was well into my argument when Justice [Thurgood] Marshall, who usually doesn't take much interest in matters of this kind, he was slumped back in his chair, he suddenly came forward [and] almost stood up and said: how did you get this property in the first place, did you steal it fair and square." Marshall did not pursue the matter, but it was pretty clear how he would vote when the time came. "Before I had recovered sufficiently to say anything, he had slumped back in his chair and never showed any interest in the argument thereafter."

Frank Gilbert was counting votes from the visitors' seats. "At that point we felt that Justice Thurgood Marshall was on our side." Later he spoke to the justice. "I said to Justice Marshall, I wonder if you remember, I've been quoting you as asking the lawyer for the railroad, 'How did you get the terminal in the first place? Did you steal it, fair and square?' And without hesitation, he said 'I'm still waiting for an answer' and that's a moment I treasure."

Gribbon was too experienced to be stunned for long. He returned to his argument. He was still reasoning from the contrapositive, that is, the negative reverse of his case:

> "I do put you, however that a review of the taking cases does disclose two guidelines that may usefully be applied here in determining whether the city's action constitutes a compensable taking. 1. When regulatory action is directed towards the elimination of offensive uses or condition, it has been held in many cases that the resulting loss to the property owner is non-compensable because it is one that he may be properly called upon to bear for the public good.

Grand Central had not engaged in offensive uses or creation of an offensive condition. "2. Such cases began as you all know with the elimination of common nuisances, and then went on to encompass other properties and uses which though not nuisances were offensive to the general tenor of the community such as breweries and billiard halls and livery stables." Well, no one in Grand Central had suggested putting a brewery, a billiard hall, or a stable in the terminal, although once upon a time, the cars were pulled by horses to eliminate a nuisance.

At last, Gribbon arrived at his destination, having taken a somewhat circuitous route. "Now the construction of a multi-story office building in Midtown, Manhattan, which Penn Central is prohibited from doing, is not only permitted by the zoning laws but it is actually encouraged as an efficient use of valuable land." Not only was the construction legal, it was a benefit to the general public. All Grand Central had to do was to "show any loss under the taking cases, whether it is an expectancy of profit here or whether it is a demolition, then it should be compensable."

His example was a familiar one. "When they take 3 acres out of 100 acres of land they do not look and say, "Well, you can do pretty well on the other 97 acres." They say, 'They have taken 3 acres and we will give you the value of it' and that I submit is precisely what we are faced with here."

Justice Blackmun wanted to know if the city had suggested some kind of compensation, or perhaps a smaller building over the terminal. Gribbon was now on surer ground. The question was a softball, and the counselor had a ready answer. "No, Your Honor. Nothing that small has been suggested simply because it would be an inefficient utilization of land. There are no other buildings really in that area that had been built in recent days that would build only that much floor space." One had to realize, he offered, that the real estate in the city was high-priced, and only a big building would repay the construction cost. The city did not care; "Nothing is going to satisfy because they want the air to roam freely over Grand Central Station. . . . Every indication that what is wanted is the preservation of Penn Central [*sic*—he meant Grand Central Terminal] in its pristine state." Finger pointing went both ways. Koerner had accused Penn Central of refusing to compromise. "They had no interest in that, because, in the end, the cost would have not made it worthwhile, because you would have to use the original limestone. There is no money in it. The money is in the height."

Gribbon's answer took him back in time. "Back in 1893, Mr. Justice [David J.] Brewer speaking for the Court said, 'The Fifth Amendment prevents the public from loading upon one individual more than his just share for the burdens of government.' Forty years later Mr. Justice Brandeis speaking for the Court, 'Particular individuals may not be singled out to bear the cost of advancing the public convenience.'" Read broadly, the Court had repeatedly invoked the Fifth Amendment to prevent tailored takings. "In 1960, the Court said the Fifth Amendment is designed to bar the government from forcing some people alone to bear public burdens which in all fairness and justice should be borne by the public as a whole." Gribbon was counting justices just as Koerner was. It was important to secure the vote of Justice Rehnquist. How better than to quote him. "Just a few years ago in a decision by Mr. Justice Rehnquist, I think the essence of these declarations was captured and the statement that the Fifth Amendment derives as much content from basic equitable principles of fairness as it does from technical concepts of Property Law." The city was simply being unfair to Penn Central.

In short, Gribbon did not want the Court to see the case as one about landmarks, that is, as a special category of property law, but simply as one more takings case. When the benefit was to the society as a whole, the burden should be borne by the society as a whole. How this would apply to the landmarking of a single building was unclear, but if the general argument was sound, then the particulars of the case did not matter. The unique character of the terminal was irrelevant, and he avoided any mention of it. "Significantly, neither the Court of Appeals nor the city and its supporting friends have anything to say about this fairness concept which has to be the lifeblood of the Fifth Amendment. Nothing they could say would alter the fact that full burden of the city's action in freezing the terminal falls exclusively on Penn Central."

Chief Justice Burger was thinking laterally about the issues of landmarking old church buildings, presumably when they had outlived their clerical usefulness. The case in point was *Lutheran Church*. "If the church which presumably has fee title to that property began negotiations for the sale of it to Hilton Hotel Corporation or someone to build a hotel there and some effort was made by the Congress to preserve it, would that be a taking in your view if they said, 'No, you cannot tear that down and build a Hilton Hotel. You cannot do anything with it. You have got to keep it the way it is.'" "They" in Rehnquist's scenario was the city. The chief justice was thinking in terms of zoning, although all parties and the Court of Appeals had denied that landmark designation was simply zoning. Gribbon explained, "That is the vice of this landmark law. It is not zoning, it does not purport to be zoning, it is on top of the zoning laws. There are vast pervasive zoning laws in the City of New York and this sits on top of them superimposed, and it permits highly-selective and particularized actions." Again, Gribbon wanted to avoid the landmark designation question. "The designation for example of the Public Library or of the Brooklyn Bridge or of the Statue of Liberty as historic landmarks does not mean anything." Or should not. "It is the unpredictable nature and the highly-selective nature of what not only has been done but indeed what the law contemplates."

Koerner's turn came next. The chief justice was still confused. "You do not contend this is a zoning case, do you?" he asked Koerner. "No,"

Koerner replied. "What we contend is this is another type of land use regulation with a very same test enunciated by this Court for all other land use cases for those applied here." Not zoning at all, for zoning is a different land-use tool. "What I am saying is that the entire community should pay the appellant if the restriction denies him the right to a reasonable rate of return. The problem here is that everybody is trying to analogize this case to zoning. But it is a different type of land use regulation. The promotion of which has the same effect on the community as the zoning, and that is to make the community more attractive." Only partially concealed in his response, though clear to everyone in the room, was the fact that *Penn Central v. New York City* was the first case where landmarked properties were not next to each other. Preceding cases had been about historic districts, where landmarked properties were next to each other.

It was not just another property use case, Koerner emphasized, bringing back the landmark issues that Gribbon had so earnestly avoided. Just as Gribbon wanted the Court to look away from the landmark designation, Koerner wanted to place it front and center. In the context of landmark law, Penn Central's terminal was not unjustly singled out, because the landmark had focused attention on many individual structures. "This is the nub of the case. The appellant has proceeded with the assumption that Grand Central Terminal has been singled out. That analysis might be correct if there had never been a Landmarks Preservation Law and in response to an announcement by Penn Central that they were going to build a building on top of Grand Central Terminal . . . the public reacted to it and passed a law that distinctively impacted on Penn Central." But the law was already in place. The landmark concept was not tied to Grand Central Terminal. It was a concept rooted in aesthetic values and urban life long before the railroad decided to turn the terminal into a high-rise. That law "sets out in advance the criteria for determining whether or not a building is architecturally or historically significant. The intention of the plan is to preserve all historical buildings, whether by accident they are a part of historic district or they are single and outside the district."

Judges reason by analogy. Justice Marshall wondered if the Landmarks Preservation Commission was "qualified to deal with due process?" like a court. Worried that the justice was edging toward the entire issue of administrative agency discretion, Koerner was quick to answer: "No." Marshall puckishly continued, "Aren't you giving it business?" Koerner explained, "What I am saying is that they have set up a procedure to determine which properties are historically significant." The commission's proceedings were open and based on set rules, but those rules were not the same as a court's. Well then, could it be likened to a zoning commission, Marshall ventured. Koerner replied, "It is like the Zoning Commission to the extent that its . . . " Marshall interjected, "But a minute ago, you said, 'Oh, no.'" Koerner, trying to be respectful, replied, "No, I was not able to finish." Marshall finished for him. "You were not going to get in the zoning business. I thought that is what you said." Koerner wanted to say what he wanted to say, and he would not be deterred. "No, what I said . . . " Marshall persisted, "But now you are going in zoning?" It is rare for someone to get the last word in one of these colloquies, but Koerner did. "No. What I am saying is that in both zoning and landmarks, you have expert commissions charged with the responsibility of developing a comprehensive land use scheme. The purpose of the scheme is to benefit the community."

Justice White had a question that did not involve zoning. "If the company at any time in the future, next year or the year after that, any time it can prove that the situation has changed and that the property is no longer economically viable, it will get relief." Koerner saw that Justice White was trying to be helpful. "That is precisely the answer. That is right." But Justice Rehnquist was not so well disposed to the city. "What again is the definition of being economically viable?" Koerner surmised that the oral argument had reached a critical point. "It was not required to be quantified in this case, but it has been traditionally meant that on his investment, he would be able to earn approximately 6%." Penn Central had insisted that the city's action meant the company would continue to lose money. Rehnquist supposed, "Like public utilities." Koerner agreed. "Correct!"

But Koerner suspected a trap. The trick to avoiding a trap is to know where it is set. "Well, then again, the answer to Your Honor's question is that in your application you are singling out that particular railroad and restricting its development of its property. The entire concept of this scheme is that we are not singling out Penn Central, we are treating it like every other landmark within the City of New York." Koerner thought that the trap was the singling out argument that Gribbon had made and Justice Rehnquist laid. The way out was to offer evidence that the terminal was not singled out, but was instead part of a much, much larger scheme of landmarks. "We have designated over 500 properties. Indeed, before a designation is completed, that designation has to be approved by the City Planning Commission which must determine whether it is consistent with the zoning plan and the master plan, and whether or not any urban renewal development might interfere."

Judge Breitel had made the air rights an important point in his decision. Perhaps Justice Rehnquist would use that, and the fact that no one on the city team was willing to defend Breitel's approach, to knock down the rest of the city's argument. Another way to avoid a trap is to spring it safely. "What we have left out and the appellant has not commented on [is] the air rights. We have never contended that the transferred development rights [TDRs] were equal in value to what the person lost, but that is not the test. The test is whether the transferred development rights constituted a valuable asset to the appellant." The city passed the test on TDRs imposed by the New York appeals courts.

Justice Stevens joined in the discussion. "Before you do that, let me just understand your theory. If there is no taking here, you do not even have to give them the TDR." Koerner: "That is correct." Justice Stevens: "Then why do we have to consider [them]?" Koerner responded, "Because the air rights are part of the comprehensive scheme in an attempt to at least recognize that we are going to try to do everything we can." Stevens persisted. Why were the air rights relevant? Koerner: "Because, Judge Breitel felt that the air rights . . . " Stevens: "Nobody is defending his rationale." Koerner was playing catch-up now, having made the mistake of bringing up air rights himself. He offered that air rights were important because they were part of the package of rights Grand Central defended. In the courts below, air rights were important. They were not important to Justice Stevens. Koerner must have regretted mentioning them at all. But he seriously thought that the discussion of air rights, and the part that air rights played in the high-rise real estate world of midtown New York City, had to be addressed. Stevens showed his cards at this point. "But your legal position is you do not have to be fair." The city was not going to get that justice's vote. Koerner somewhat defensively replied, "No, that is not our legal position."

Justice Stewart came to the city's rescue: "Your position is, as I understand is that there can be a taking sometimes under this contemplation." Koerner welcomed Stewart's support, and added, "There has not been [a taking] in this particular case and that the facts and circumstances of this particular case show there has not been." Instead, the city had not offered the company the "highest and best use" of the property rights above the terminal, those pesky air rights, but did not deny Penn Central a "reasonable return." With this, Koerner's time expired.

Next, Patricia Wald expanded on the amicus brief of the federal government. She had to show that the federal government had a legitimate interest in the outcome of the case. "Congress and the executive have declared in many statutes that it is a national policy, the historical and cultural foundations of the nation should be preserved as a living part of our community life and development in order to give our people a sense of orientation." She then proceeded, without interruption, to list the ways in which the "Federal Government is deeply involved in historical preservation." First, it preserved historic landmarks on federal land. Second, it employed eminent domain [confiscation with compensation] for other historic sites. Third, the national registry of historic sites having local, city, state and national significance had reached fifteen thousand buildings. Fourth, by statute it provided funds to states and cities to survey and "embark on preservation projects to preserve their treasures." Fifth, "all federal agencies pursuant to the 1966 Act and to an executive order, who license projects or spend money on projects in any state must take account of the need to preserve historic sites which are registered or which are eligible for registration." Finally, a series of federal laws, including the National Environmental Protection Act, required preservation impact statements when a building listed on the federal registry was endangered by a project.

Justice Stevens now asked the same question he had asked Koerner: "Is it fair to say that the federal policy has always been where there is a public benefit, the public shall pay?" Wald was ready and pulled no punches. "I believe that that is an overstatement for the following reasons. Naturally, the Federal Government has relied primarily upon state and local governments and their Police power and their particular historic preservation laws to bring about the preservation of buildings." What was more, the federal government had used its regulatory powers on land use for other purposes similar to preservation and did not in those cases compensate owners.

Chief Justice Burger had a concern about land that was part of the historic Bull Run battlefield. "The beneficial use that my farmer friend up at Manassas has in mind is to leave it to his children or to sell it as the case maybe. And he can get $1,500 an acre for it in some places now. Are you suggesting the United States government, or any government could take that property without paying him the going rate?" Wald offered a complex answer to the simplistic hypothetical. "I am not suggesting they could take it, Mr. Chief Justice, I am suggesting that a valid historical landmark statute could allow them to restrict its usage so that a particular historic framework or particular historic use would not be violated."

The chief justice seemed reassured, or perhaps he was not going to show that he could not understand her, but Justice Stevens understood all too well. "Mrs. Wald, just applying it to the historic landmark area, if the landmark designation causes the property owner to actually lose money on the property, then it's a taking. If it can still make a reasonable return, it is not a taking. Is that your test?" Wald could only reply, "[There is] No set of formula has a reasonable return or a beneficial use." Justice Stevens wanted a different answer. "You just say, just a marginal profit would not be enough. It has to be a reasonable return." Wald wanted to talk about uses, not compensation. "I would say a reasonable return is a beneficial use." Stevens pressed on. "In a reasonable return, how does one measure that if it is a lot less then it could be obtained by putting it to some other use? Is it still reasonable?" Wald stuck to her guns and returned to uses. "I believe so and I believe that is exactly what all of the cases have said, we do not take the test of the most profitable use."

Wald tried to clarify her answers, because answers to questions from the bench often had a staccato quality, an incompleteness. "I certainly believe that Constitution would require the owner, if he could not use it for a particular purpose to be able to go out and find the most profitable use consistent with the point of the regulation, namely the preservation of the landmark."

Chief Justice Burger reentered the conversation. "Do you mean you are going to make him do something with it?" Wald replied more broadly than she would have wished. "No, we are going to permit him to do something with it if he wants to." The chief responded, "What if he just wants to board it up?" Wald must have felt some frustration here. "If he wants to board it up and that does not, in some way infringe upon the historical preservation aspect of the property, then he could do that, it is the historical preservation; simply said, [to use another example] this is a beautiful church to look at from the outside and we do not care what happens, whether anybody goes in it or anything else. Then, he can just leave it stand there, if he wants to. On the other hand, [if] he wants to continue to run it as a church, then he could do that too."

There comes a point in oral argument when the Q and A have gone off the track. Wald and the chief justice had reached that point. Burger: "Who should pay the $10,000 a year insurance premiums on it and public liability in the meantime?" Wald: "Well, the church might be the wrong example, but in essence the owner continues with all of both the liabilities and the profits of ownership. But, any owner has certain options about how to use his property." Burger: "What profit have you got on a boarded-up building?" By now the example had taken the place of the issues. Wald: "If you boarded it up by your own choice then you . . . " Burger: "No, boarded it up because the government from your point of view would not let him sell it—would not let them sell it." Wald recalled later, "I just remember breathing a huge sigh of relief when my time was up."

Gribbon, who as the appellant had spoken first, had left himself some time for rebuttal after Koerner and Wald had finished. "I say the Court of Appeals finding to that effect is totally erroneous because it is based on this concept that we need only earn or return on the privately contributed ingredient. That destroys the entire finding." Justice White proposed, "Well, let us assume for the moment that we accept it. That it is economically viable, but nevertheless, it is perfectly obvious, you could make more if you build a big building on it." Gribbon replied, "I still say, even if you accept it, the decision is wrong and we are entitled to compensation. I do not think the fact that what we have left over is atonement for what has been taken from us."

Justice Rehnquist was persuaded by Gribbon's argument, but his questions were actually comments directed to other members of the Court. "In your brief at Page 17 you cite this Court's opinion in *Fuller* [U.S. v. Fuller (1973)], where you say that the government in a condemnation case can exclude from consideration of the jury the value that may be added by the fact that the government built a post office near the site 80 years ago. Is that substantial to your argument there?" Gribbon played along. "I think it is. I think that is a very important part of our argument. I think that this highest and best use is something that has to be looked at very carefully. . . . There was a loss to the property owner and he was compensated for it. Second, his entire property was not taken. He was compensated because he was no longer able to operate a chicken farm and it was clear that he could have operated a vegetable patch. The Court noted that, but, the compensation was because he was prevented from doing that." Gribbon summarized: "A statute such as this Landmarks Law creates unusual opportunities for arbitrary action." The danger in the passage of such a law is that "those who own property that is coveted for public use are rarely, if ever, going to be a majority at the post or in law-making bodies." The courts must protect the property owners against the wishes of the majority. Alexander Hamilton would have approved.

Sitting at the appellees table across the aisle from Gribbon, Koerner watched the bench. As he later recalled, he knew that Justices Rehnquist and Burger would not buy the city's case. "I wasn't sure about Stevens, but the other two were really, really unhappy. And I knew that Marshall and some of the others were—Brennan in particular—were supportive, but I really couldn't tell." After all, it was a case of first instance, and coming from New York City, a lot was at stake. It would be a landmark case in both senses of the term. He recalled with some amusement, "There were a lot of questions about a church. There is a church near the Supreme Court. They keep referring to some historic church. I know what they were talking about, but they kept saying, 'Would you let them go out of business? What would you do?'"

All analogies, parallels, irrelevancies, tests, measures, costs, questions, and answers were done. Chief Justice Burger announced that the case was submitted.

Waiting for the Court to Speak

Long after the case went to the Court, some of the participants left detailed accounts of their thinking about the events in Washington, DC, while waiting for the Court to announce its opinion. Koerner was openly grateful for the receptiveness of members of the Court. In questioning,

> Justice Brennan . . . was just applying the reasonable rate of return in saying that you have to look at everything. One thing that the opinion picked up, for which I give a lot of credit to the clerks in the Supreme Court, is the fact that Judge Breitel said to the owners of Grand Central terminal, I know I set forth this standard, if you think under this standard you can make a showing, go back to the Supreme Court and they will be obligated to review it. And Justice Brennan in his opinion specifically noted that, that if they could show that there was a hardship they could still go back there at any time. Now, I think that was helpful to us and they picked up on it.

Koerner regretted telling the court that it would be a different case and that a hardship might have been granted. "Obviously, in retrospect, I'm not sure that should have been the answer. . . . If the terminal could be used as a discotheque or a Union Station model, as you know where you have all those stores, maybe they can still earn a reasonable rate of return. So I might have just been too quick to close down the terminal."

Patricia Wald was equally candid. "But sure enough I thought it was interesting because one of the first questions I got in my brief period arguing as an amicus was exactly the one thing that I mentioned that the Justice Department worried a little bit about, what interest does the United States have in this case." The amicus brief from the solicitor general's office was not a key factor in the outcome, but "we had to answer of course that the United States had no program where they directly imposed these kinds of restrictions for landmark provisions. I went through the rigamarole about all of the national landmarks but they were grants and aids and tax credits." In oral argument, she had to deal with what could have been a very embarrassing question, whether the United States ever imposed directly restrictions like this for landmark purposes. "Of course I had to answer no. The rest of my argument it seemed to me was like the tail wagging the dog or the tail of the dog after Mr. Koerner's argument because they just kept going with the hypotheticals."

Justice Brennan's law clerk, David W. Carpenter, thought the case was well argued on both sides, which was not always true for that court term. He attended the oral argument, as most of the clerks routinely did. He thought that three things turned out to be significant to the opinion that occurred at the oral argument:

> First, very early in Mr. Gribbon's argument, Justice Stewart pressed him very hard on how this was any different than zoning. Justice Stewart said that height limitations are perfectly valid in the zoning context, and the effect on the property owner is the same whether the restriction results from zoning that applies to everyone or historic landmark law that applies just to you. He didn't see how it made any difference in terms of the Takings Clause that landmark zoning was involved and he thought the real problem, if any, was one of discrimination, almost equal protection. And there the obvious answer was to talk about the concept of average reciprocity of advantage, which Mr. Gribbon did, but Justice Stewart just wasn't buying it. He didn't view that concept as important to the law of takings. And that was one thing that turned out to be significant in the preparation of the opinion.

Carpenter continued,

> The second thing is that Justice Powell and I think Mr. Koerner was alluding to this, pressed very hard on what would happen if circumstances changed and it turned out that Penn Central was unable to use the terminal in the railroad business. He was very concerned whether Penn Central would have an opportunity to come in and get relief if circumstances changed, such that use of the terminal in its present form became uneconomic. That concern was subsequently reflected in the opinion, I think in a footnote.

Last but not least for Carpenter,

> There was a third thing that was significant which related to the way Penn Central had argued the case. It had presented a syllogism: air rights are property, this takes away air rights, therefore it's a taking. But the original plan for the terminal had included an office tower, not the 55 stories or whatever was proposed in the case, but I think 20 stories. A question was asked whether there was anything in what the Landmarks Commission had done that would indicate that they would have disapproved a lesser-sized structure more along the lines

of the original plan. And Mr. Gribbon was forced to acknowledge that there wasn't. And that was significant too because it meant that to a great extent the characterization of the law as having taken away all the air rights above the terminal really wasn't accurate and that too was reflected in the opinion.

David Carpenter admitted that he had more than a passing acquaintance with his justice's majority opinion. "Any Supreme Court opinion is a formidable thing to undertake, but this was certainly the hardest one that I worked on. In addition to studying the briefs and the record and reading all the Court's taking opinions, I read many law review articles about historic preservation; a lot of that was reflected in the first part of the opinion. And while I was working some on other opinions at the time, I spent probably two weeks trying to draft and redraft the opinion." Justice Brennan would then rework the draft.

> Justice Brennan had very much wanted to get the opinion to work on during Memorial Day. He was an early riser who took walks early each morning, and I delivered the draft to his house at 5:30 in the morning Memorial Day just as I think he was coming back from his walk. And then he worked on the opinion, worked his magic on it that day and gave his marked-up version of it back to me Tuesday. There were lots of footnotes to fill in and the like, which I did over the course of the next two days, and the Justice went over it again on Thursday and we circulated the draft opinion to the other Justices on Friday morning, June 2nd.

David Carpenter had been talking to his opposite number, Barton Carpenter, Rehnquist's clerk, while the two were working on drafts for their bosses. Rehnquist's clerk had a draft dissent ready "within an hour or two after the circulation of the draft majority opinion." Both men were exhausted, but David Carpenter was also apprehensive. "I told [Brennan] that Rehnquist had been lying in wait. Now, Justice Brennan was the nicest man I've ever known and very fatherly, grandfatherly. He put his arm around me and said don't worry it doesn't touch us, and he made me sit down and read the dissent—and he sat next to me while I read it." He was right, Carpenter thought.

Carpenter believed at the time the majority opinion may well have in fact persuaded Justice Stevens, but that "he may have wanted the case to come out 6–3 rather than 7–2 because he thought it was a tough issue for the reasons that Buzz [Barton Carpenter] has identified and thought it looked better coming out 6–3. In any case, he certainly followed *Penn Central* enthusiastically thereafter."

CHAPTER NINE

The High Court Decides

After oral argument, the justices retire to their chambers with their clerks. They restudy the briefs and their notes on the oral argument. They share their thoughts with one another and with their clerks. They meet once a week in a conference, during which, following seniority from the chief down to the most recently appointed member, they express their views. In the past these conferences could be rough-and-tumble events. Justice Felix Frankfurter, a former law professor, was notorious for lecturing his colleagues. Among them, William O. Douglas, also a former law professor, would simply leave "until Felix is done." Chief Justice Harlan Stone called these his "wild horses," and found it impossible to rein them in. Chief Justice Warren Burger allowed members of his Court to question and answer one another. By contrast, Chief Justice Rehnquist was very strict about time allotted to each justice.

The senior member of the majority side decides who among them will write the majority opinion. If a majority of the Court agrees to the logic of the opinion (its ratio decidendi) it becomes precedent. Sometimes the justices on the majority agree with the decision but not all parts of the majority opinion. Then the decision stands, but the argument of the majority opinion does not become precedent. Instead, one finds concurrences in part and dissents in part. Some members of the Court, notably Chief Justices John Marshall and Earl Warren, were renowned for their ability to achieve unanimity. Not so Chief Justice Burger.

The Majority Opinion

After the exchange of views at the judicial conference and the exchange of draft opinions subsequent to the oral arguments in *Penn Central v. New York City*, the Court produced a majority opinion and a dissent. In an opinion by Brennan, joined by Stewart, White, Marshall, Blackmun, and Powell, the Court held that application of the Landmarks Preservation Law preventing use of the air space above Grand Central Terminal did not effect a "taking" of private property by the government without just compensation in violation of the Fifth and Fourteenth Amendments.

Justice Brennan began his opinion, "Over the past 50 years, all 50 States and over 500 municipalities have enacted laws to encourage or require the preservation of buildings and areas with historic or aesthetic importance." The direction of city planning, the need to preserve something of the city's past for its future dwellers, the educational and emotional value of preservation—this is what the majority decision was about. Frank Gilbert tried to plumb Brennan's feelings, not just his rationale: "That's the direction he was heading in, and he goes into quite a discussion of details about the New York City law, and he formulates what historic preservation was all about. It wasn't about acquiring property by the municipalities."

The law, and under it the designation of the terminal as a landmark, did not interfere with the present uses of the building, but allowed the owner to continue using it as had been done in the past, permitting the owner to profit from the building and obtain a reasonable return on its investment. Nor did the law and the designation of Grand Central as a landmark necessarily prohibit occupancy of any of the air space above the landmark building, because under the procedures of the law, it was possible that some construction in the air space might be allowed, though it would be a small skyscraper. Finally, the law did not deny all use of the owner's preexisting air rights above the landmark building, since under a transferable development rights program, it was possible for the owner to transfer the development rights it was foreclosed from using as to Grand Central Terminal to other neighboring properties it owned.

The reasoning of the majority was clear. Appellants (Penn Central) could not establish a "taking" simply by showing that they had been denied the ability to exploit a property interest that they had believed was available for development. The Court noted that landmark laws were not like discriminatory or "reverse spot" zoning. The New York Landmarks Preservation Law did not interfere in any way with the terminal's present uses and plaintiffs' primary expectation concerning the use of the parcel. Borrowing from New York Court of Appeals Judge Breitel, Justice Brennan found that the restrictions imposed were substantially related to the promotion of the general welfare and not only permitted reasonable beneficial use of the landmark site, but also afforded plaintiffs opportunities further to enhance not only the terminal site but also other properties.

The majority opinion in *Penn Central v. New York City* established a three-part takings test. Where the government's action is not a taking, requiring just compensation depends, first, on the economic impact of the regulation on the owner; second, the extent to which the regulation has interfered with distinct investment-backed expectations—the sale value; and, finally, the character of the governmental action. Though not perfect, and constantly reinterpreted by the Supreme Court, the formula has thus far withstood the test of time. This is because, like other landmark law cases, the Court's decision embodies more than just a way to resolve a constitutional dispute. It represents a societal understanding of who we are, what we were, and who we wish to be.

There were the usual train of qualifications in the majority decision. It was true, as Penn Central's counsel emphasized, that both historic district legislation and zoning laws regulate all properties within given physical communities, whereas landmark laws apply only to selected parcels. But, contrary to appellants' suggestions, landmark laws are not like discriminatory, or "reverse spot," zoning: that is, a land-use decision that arbitrarily singles out a particular parcel for different, less favorable treatment than the neighboring ones. In contrast to discriminatory zoning, which is the antithesis of land-use control as part of some comprehensive plan, the New York City law embodied a comprehensive plan to preserve structures of historic or aesthetic interest wherever they might be found in the city, and as appellees noted, more than four hundred landmarks and thirty-one historic districts had been designated pursuant to this plan.

The Court majority found equally without merit the related argument that the decision to designate a structure as a landmark "is inevitably arbitrary or at least subjective, because it is basically a matter of taste," according to Penn Central's reply brief. The law had not singled out individual landowners for disparate and unfair treatment. This removed any suggestion of bias the state or the city might have had against

Penn Central, an imputation easily disproved by the tax and other benefits the railroad was afforded. The Court found that "the argument has a particularly hollow ring in this case. For appellants not only did not seek judicial review of either the designation or of the denials of the certificates of appropriateness and of no exterior effect, but do not even now suggest that the Commission's decisions concerning the Terminal were in any sense arbitrary or unprincipled." In other words, if the accusation of improper treatment of Penn Central were to be credited, the railroad would have to produce evidence of ill will by the state or the city. Of course, "a landmark owner has a right to judicial review of any Commission decision." But here the appellants did not identify "arbitrary or discriminatory action in the context of landmark regulation." In short, Penn Central could not have its cake (that it was singled out) and eat it (that there was no misconduct by the state or the city).

Penn Central had tried for a similar digestive feat in its next argument. "Appellants observe that New York City's law differs from zoning laws and historic-district ordinances in that the Landmarks Law does not impose identical or similar restrictions on all structures located in particular physical communities." Actually, the law did precisely that, although not every landmark stood where the terminal did in Midtown. From this fact, Penn Central had insisted "that New York City's law is inherently incapable of producing the fair and equitable distribution of benefits and burdens of governmental action which is characteristic of zoning laws and historic-district legislation and which they maintain is a constitutional requirement if 'just compensation' is not to be afforded."

In short, Penn Central pleaded that landmark designations had to be fair and equitable across the entire range of real estate—a palpable impossibility. The very nature of landmarking a single building was that the designation did not apply to the buildings around it. The Court saw the fallacy in the Penn Central argument. "It is, of course, true that the Landmarks Law has a more severe impact on some landowners than on others, but that in itself does not mean that the law effects a 'taking.' Legislation designed to promote the general welfare commonly burdens some more than others." Brennan had no trouble finding precedent for this in the brickyard in *Hadacheck* and the gravel and sand mine in *Goldblatt v. Hempstead*. Differential impact was similarly characteristic of zoning laws.

The Court was not a trial venue; it was concerned with law rather than fact, or rather, it accepted the facts as they were presented in the pleadings. But when a party could not or did not present any or sufficient factual evidence to support its legal arguments, the Court would take judicial notice. Here, "appellants' repeated suggestions that they are solely burdened and unbenefited is factually inaccurate. This contention overlooks the fact that the New York City law applies to vast numbers of structures in the city in addition to the Terminal—all the structures contained in the 31 historic districts and over 400 individual landmarks, many of which are close to the Terminal."

Social benefit and public interest were not usually part of property law, but Judge Breitel had added these elements to his decision, and they reappeared in the Supreme Court's majority opinion. "Unless we are to reject the judgment of the New York City Council that the preservation of landmarks benefits all New York citizens and all structures, both economically and by improving the quality of life in the city as a whole—which we are unwilling to do—we cannot conclude that the owners of the Terminal have in no sense been benefited by the Landmarks Law." A nice twist this was, suggesting that Penn Central lived in the city and benefited from the intangibles of a landmark terminal.

Often, the law reasons by analogy. After all, what is precedent but analogous prior cases? The Court did not regard landmark as zoning but did refer to the zoning analogy. "This is no more an appropriation of property by government for its own uses than is a zoning law prohibiting, for 'aesthetic' reasons, two or more adult theaters within a specified area ... or a safety regulation prohibiting excavations below a certain level." A broader analogy was to landmark law outside the state. It was moving ahead throughout the country. Whether that applied to the terminal was a matter one could argue, but the Court took notice of the times.

Having sustained the landmarks law in a general way, the majority had next to deal with the compensation issue. Penn Central claimed the city violated its own landmarks law by denying to the railroad compensation for lost revenue. The majority replied, "Rejection of appellants' broad arguments is not, however, the end of our inquiry, for all we thus far have established is that the New York City law is not rendered invalid by its failure to provide 'just compensation' whenever a landmark owner is restricted in the exploitation of property interests, such as air rights, to a greater extent than provided for under applicable zoning laws." The majority had to "consider whether the interference with appellants' property is of such a magnitude that "there must be an exercise of eminent domain and compensation to sustain [it]." What precisely was the impact of the law as applied to the terminal on Penn Central?

The Court concluded that, unlike government impositions in prior cases, the New York City law did not interfere in any way with the present uses of the terminal. "Its designation as a landmark not only permits but contemplates that appellants may continue to use the property precisely as it has been used for the past 65 years: as a railroad terminal containing office space and concessions. So the law does not interfere with what must be regarded as Penn Central's primary expectation concerning the use of the parcel." By this time Penn Central's primary interest, as the company defined it, was not mass transportation but real estate development. The Court, however, shifted the time frame of the Penn Central's aims from post–World War II to earlier in the century. In effect, the Court was adopting the city's view of Penn Central's purpose rather than Penn Central's view. By shifting the day-to-day burden of managing commuter traffic in and out of the terminal to the Metropolitan Transportation Authority, Penn Central was saying that it was no longer thinking like a railroad. The Court ignored this.

Actually, the majority was well aware that Penn Central did not regard rail service as its primary purpose. "On this record, we must regard the New York City law as permitting Penn Central not only to profit from the Terminal but also to obtain a 'reasonable return' on its investment." The Landmarks Preservation Commission's report emphasized that whether any construction would be allowed depended on whether the proposed addition "would harmonize in scale, material, and character with [the terminal]. Since appellants have not sought approval for the construction of a smaller structure, we do not know that appellants will be denied any use of any portion of the airspace above the Terminal."

In response to the appellants' argument that the development rights had been obliterated by the Landmarks Commission, the majority of justices concluded that the air rights "has not been abrogated" and that they were "transferable to at least eight parcels in the vicinity of the Terminal, one or two of which have been found suitable for the construction of new office buildings." Although Penn Central and its allies in the real estate business argued New York City's transferable development-rights program was inadequate, the New York courts had disagreed when they decided *Penn Central*. According to Justice Brennan's opinion, the lower courts found that, at least in the case of the terminal, "the rights afforded are valuable." Finally, "while these rights may well not have constituted 'just compensation' if a 'taking' had occurred, the rights nevertheless undoubtedly mitigate whatever financial burdens the law has imposed on appellants and, for that reason, are to be taken into account in considering the impact of regulation."

The majority opinion more or less ended where it began. "On this record, we conclude that the application of New York City's Landmarks Law has not effected a 'taking' of appellants' property. The restrictions imposed are substantially related to the promotion of the general welfare and not only permit reasonable beneficial use of the landmark site but also afford appellants opportunities further to enhance not only the Terminal site proper but also other properties."

The Dissent

Three justices dissented, joining in an opinion that Justice Rehnquist wrote. Justices Rehnquist, Stevens, and Burger thought that only zoning was an acceptable land-use government regulatory scheme and that only "in the most superficial sense of the word can this case be said to involve 'zoning.'" This was the backside of the zoning analogy. If landmarking was actually zoning, then it must follow the conventions of zoning law. "Typical zoning restrictions may, it is true, so limit the prospective uses of a piece of property as to diminish the value of that property in the abstract because it may not be used for the forbidden purposes. But any such abstract decrease in value will more than likely be at least partially offset by an increase in value which flows from similar restrictions as to use on neighboring properties." In zoning, all property owners in a designated area are placed under the same restrictions. The rationale for this is that no individual property owner is singled out, and no property owner is entirely deprived of the whole value of the parcel. Thus zoning is "not only for the benefit of the municipality as a whole but also for the common benefit of one another." The system is not a violation of the Constitution because it is reciprocal.

By contrast, "Where a relatively few individual buildings, all separated from one another, are singled out and treated differently from surrounding buildings, no such reciprocity exists." The dissent did not exactly define reciprocity, nor did it appear in the text of the Fifth Amendment, but it had some existence in precedent. A better description of the test the dissenters imposed was proportionality. "The cost to the property owner which results from the imposition of restrictions applicable only to his property and not that of his neighbors may be substantial—in this case, several million dollars—with no comparable reciprocal benefits. And the cost associated with landmark legislation is likely to be of a completely different order of magnitude than that which results from the imposition of normal zoning restrictions."

For the dissenters, the key issue was the financial one, dollars and cents, rather than any subjective assessment of nonfinancial value. "Unlike the regime affected by the latter, the landowner is not simply prohibited from using his property for certain purposes, while allowed to use it for all other purposes. Under the historic-landmark preservation scheme adopted by New York, the property owner is under an affirmative duty to preserve his property as a landmark at his own expense." Under this calculation, all landmark law relating to a single structure was questionable, unless the loss the owner suffered was minimal. "To suggest that because traditional zoning results in some limitation of use of the property zoned, the New York City landmark preservation scheme should likewise be upheld, represents the ultimate in treating as alike things which are different."

The dissent suggested that the majority had overextended the concept of zoning to the point where it actually undermined the Fifth Amendment. The majority had adopted the city's proposition that governments could force "some people alone to bear public burdens which, in all fairness and justice, should be borne by the public as a whole." The result was that the city had simply "destroyed—in a literal sense, 'taken'—substantial property rights of Penn Central." This was an impermissible deprivation of a constitutional right to property.

Of course, governments could and had taken property in other circumstances. But "Appellees [the city] are not prohibiting a nuisance." In public nuisance law, if a use of a property was dangerous or unhealthful to the public, a government could simply take or "condemn" the property without any compensation. This was not true of the terminal case. "The record is clear that the proposed addition to the Grand Central Terminal would be in full compliance with zoning, height limitations, and other health and safety requirements." The dissent found that the purpose was aesthetic. "Appellees are seeking to preserve what they believe to be an outstanding example of beaux arts architecture. Penn Central is prevented from further developing its property basically because too good a job was done in designing and building it. The City of New York, because of its unadorned admiration for the design, has decided that the owners of the building must preserve it unchanged for the benefit of sightseeing New Yorkers and tourists." The mass transit passengers' enjoyment of the building was not mentioned. It had no dollar value.

Justice Rehnquist's dissent disagreed with everything the majority opinion held. Rehnquist felt the monetary loss was "uniquely felt and is not offset by any benefits flowing from the preservation of some 400 other 'landmarks' in New York City." He found that the Landmarks Commission had imposed too much of a cost burden on less than one-tenth of one percent of the buildings in New York City for the general benefit of all the city. That was a wealth transfer not sanctioned by the Constitution. "The Fifth Amendment prevents the public from loading upon one individual more than his just share of the burdens of government, and says that when he surrenders to the public something more and different from that which is exacted from other members of the public, a full and just equivalent shall be returned to him."

Rehnquist offered a proportionality calculus to measure permissible taking. "The benefits that appellees believe will flow from preservation of the Grand Central Terminal will accrue to all the citizens of New York City. There is no reason to believe that appellants will enjoy a substantially greater share of these benefits." A fairer distribution of costs, or burden, was available. "If the cost of preserving Grand Central Terminal were spread evenly across the entire population of the city of New York, the burden per person would be in cents per year—a minor cost appellees would surely concede for the benefit accrued." The majority opinion would allow the city to "impose the entire cost of several million dollars per year on Penn Central. But it is precisely this sort of discrimination that the Fifth Amendment prohibits."

Rehnquist was not persuaded by Judge Breitel's or Justice Brennan's reasoning. He thought that they misunderstood the transfer rights question. The lower courts had opined that TDRs have an "uncertain and contingent market value" and do "not adequately preserve" the value lost when a building is declared to be a landmark. "Because the record on appeal is relatively slim, I would remand to the Court of Appeals for a determination of whether TDR's constitute a 'full and perfect equivalent for the property taken.'"

Instead, Rehnquist reached back to an earlier time of constitutional law and American history, when property rights seemed clearer, and cities were wiping away entire historical neighborhoods to give rights of way to railroads. "Over 50 years ago, Mr. Justice Holmes, speaking for the Court, warned that the courts were 'in danger of forgetting that a strong public desire to improve the public condition is not enough to warrant achieving the desire by a shorter cut than the constitutional way of paying for the change.'" Rehnquist was not unmindful of the realities of urban finances. He just did not weigh them on the same scales as the city itself:

> The city of New York is in a precarious financial state, and some may believe that the costs of landmark preservation will be more easily borne by corporations such as Penn Central than the overburdened individual taxpayers of New York. But these concerns do not allow us to ignore past precedents construing the Eminent Domain Clause to the end that the desire to improve the public condition is, indeed, achieved by a shorter cut than the constitutional way of paying for the change.

Initial Reactions to the Court's Decision

Leonard Koerner was nonplussed by the dissent:

> Truthfully, I didn't know what they were talking about. It all was very confusing, because the only way Landmarks can operate, as I made clear, is by restricting buildings. There is no other thing they can do; otherwise, it's not preserving landmarks. Second, if they can earn a

reasonable rate of return, what's left? I didn't understand what they were talking about. What is investment backed expectation? If you are designating a landmark you're going to undermine their investment. Of course, but that's true in zoning. What if [we] down zone the Upper East Side, which we did years ago. Everybody's investment expectations are going to go down. What's the purpose?

The Supreme Court decision was the final word for Penn Central. While Penn Central did seek a rehearing by the US Supreme Court, the Court denied the petition on October 2, 1978.

City planners like Jack Kerr were pleased that "the majority opinion noted that the law advanced a 'comprehensive plan' to preserve landmarks in the city." This analysis seems to draw an obvious line between spot zoning and regulations genuinely designed to serve a public purpose, such as the Landmarks Preservation Law. Kerr thought that "as a matter of common sense, it seems that it will be necessary for the government, from time to time, to pass a law that may affect relatively few properties." He understood that in the majority opinion's various asides and cautions, the Court may have been considering slippery slope concerns: that is, would the landmark law have no stopping point? The Court may have been attempting to prevent commissions and city preservationist groups from abusing the Takings Clause. While the potential loss to Penn Central definitely constituted a relevant, substantial sum, Penn Central had, thus far, failed to occupy the domain that the government took over. From a public policy perspective, it makes sense to prohibit a plaintiff from claiming Penn Central's part. Again, it would appear that the Court was looking less to a commonsense analysis of the effect and more to the nature of the intrusion and the public's perception of fair play. The Court's decision in Penn Central may have saved the terminal. Had the Court decided that a taking occurred, the City of New York would have had to acquire the terminal using the eminent domain provision of the Constitution.

Frank Gilbert had his own take. The variety of these impressions suggest that each of the players on the preservation side was touching a different part of the elephant, as in the old story:

> As you read the opinion by Justice Brennan, it's very interesting to see him using the description of Grand Central going back 10 years

to when the property was designated a historic landmark. He quotes the point in the commission's opinion: "Reduce the Landmark itself to the status of a curiosity." He's summarizing what the Landmarks Commission did, many years later, and it draws upon the Appellate Division's view about the failure "to impute any rental value to the vast space in the Terminal devoted to railroad purposes."

Gilbert saw how strongly the appellate opinions in New York influenced Brennan. What he did not note was that Brennan, from North Jersey, knew all about the Pennsy trains into the city. He had witnessed the demise of Penn Station and perhaps had an extrajudicial attachment to the one remaining great monument to the age of trains in the city.

Alexander Garvin, a city architect and planner, had his own version of the opinion's contribution. "Protecting the cultural patrimony is an important additional way of providing for the general welfare. As Justice Brennan explained in the Penn Central case: Structures with special historic, cultural or architectural significance enhance the quality of life for all." Garvin, naturally, was importing his own professional interest into the opinion. Not a lawyer but a working architect, he understood that "not only do these buildings and their workmanship represent the lessons of the past and embody precious features of our heritage[,] they serve as examples of quality for today . . . enhancing—or perhaps developing for the first time—the quality of life for the people." He also knew that when such examples of older architecture are gone, all that they represented goes with this. By contrast, "Protecting this scarce resource provides citizens with a profound connection to their culture and their history. This is the rationale for such disparate 'historic' districts as those of Williamsburg, Charleston, New Orleans, Santa Barbara, and Santa Fe."

Norman Marcus, writer of the "Transfer of Development Rights" section of the Zoning Code, recalled, "The decision was hailed as an example of 'maturity' on the part of a 'country that is finally recognizing its urban assets and the need to protect them for livable cities.'" He continued his high praise: "Two years too late for the Bicentennial, the Penn Central decision may well insure the quality of our Tricentennial." John D. Echeverria later wrote, "Historic landmark preservation represented a sound public policy and that this landmark in particular, which every Justice on the Court had undoubtedly visited, was worthy of protection."

Although defenders of the decision saw it as laying the groundwork for a realistic view of the takings doctrine, critics saw it as a "naked deprivation of property rights," and a subversion of the Fifth Amendment, in the words of law professor Steven J. Eagle. The ghost at the feast was compensation for lost value because of zoning. The syllogism went like this: if landmarking could deprive a legal owner of much of the value of his property and landmark law was akin to zoning law, then zoning could deprive an owner in similar fashion of property value. Some of the case law cited in favor of the city said exactly that. This worried the justices, in particular Potter Stewart, as it opened the door to judicial determinations on every zoning ordinance and variance. It was a nightmare scenario.

Justice Rehnquist's law clerk Barton Thompson, who served during the 1977–1978 term, recalled, "The only thing Penn Central had done was build a really great building that everyone liked." Those sorts of issues bothered the justices on one side. "But on the other side, they didn't want to do anything which could undermine the constitutionality of zoning. They didn't want to get into a situation where governments would have to compensate property owners in a normal zoning case, and the hypothetical that Justice Stewart asked at the very beginning of the oral argument really highlighted the potential dilemma." Thompson recalled that Stewart asked what would happen if there was a zoning regulation that had prevented Penn Central from building anything taller than Grand Central Terminal: "Would Penn Central be entitled to compensation in that particular setting? The justices were very concerned about the potential implications of ruling for Penn Central in a variety of other contexts. For that reason, the case could have gone either way."

Thompson reported that the justices who dissented worried about the underlying motives of the majority:

> So Stevens at this stage was, I think, very interested in questions of proportionality and justice and whether or not in this particular case there might have been other ways in which New York City could have made Penn Central whole. Looking at the oral argument of [subsequently appointed Judge] Wald, there was a series of questions

that Justice Stevens asked in which he was very interested in whether or not the federal government had ever engaged in historic preservation without providing compensation. And I believe he was absolutely convinced that there was a variety of cities and states around the nation that had found other approaches to historic preservation that wouldn't have forced this type of takings issue to come up before the courts.

Was the majority opinion an example of a liberal jurisprudence? Was the dissent a conservative reply? Court watchers are wont to divide the justices into liberal and conservative blocs. The members of the majority included both liberal and middle-of-the-road justices. More important for students of the Court, the decision was an activist one, for it advanced the law of property rather than constrained it. Most important, it was strongly deferential to the state and its agency, the city. Such deference was a mark of the later New Deal Court but was recalibrated when the Court had to deal with civil rights cases. In the 1980s, a conservative majority developed the jurisprudence referred to as "the new federalism," again deferring to the state when federal authorities challenged state law. One might thus see *Penn Central* as the first of the new federalism cases, although its author, Justice Brennan, was not an advocate of that jurisprudence. Instead, it was William Rehnquist, who became chief justice in 1986, who pressed for the new doctrine. Ironically, then, it was Justice Rehnquist who authored the dissent.

John Belle, in his history of the terminal, tried to find a way to bring the two opinions together, for as a city planner he knew that the landmark issue was only taking baby steps. "Associate Justice William H. Rehnquist wrote for the minority in dissent, If the cost of preserving Grand Central Terminal were spread evenly across [the] entire population of the City of New York, the burden per person would be in cents per year, a minor cost that the city would surely concede for the benefit accrued." For Rehnquist, the city was unfairly and illegally imposing the entire cost on Penn Central. But was it? Was the railroad as a railroad, a transportation company, so burdened, or was Penn Central's decision to reboot itself as a real estate development company the real cause of its problems?

It did not take long for conservative and libertarian scholars to provide their own analysis. At the time, they saw the majority deferring to New York City, the State of New York, and the federal government. Deference to the legislative or popularly elected branch has been a major trope of Supreme Court jurisprudence since the closing years of the New Deal. The majority had focused on the use question rather than the extent or face-value loss to the company. The Court assigned value to the preservation that was nonmonetary. In this sense, the Court had also relied on something like the "rational relation test." That test is ordinarily applied to Fourteenth Amendment due process review of state legislation. If the action is a legitimate subject for state regulation, and that regulation bears a rational relation to the subject, it passes muster. Was the landmark law rationally related to the legitimate public interest? This was the lowest level of constitutional measure of state action. (The highest is strict scrutiny, usually reserved for civil rights claims in which a state action must be a narrowly tailored response to a severe public problem.) The Court declined to give commensurate weight to the company's argument that it was singled out, that it had freedom to use its property in any way that did not constitute a nuisance, and that the company's loss of revenue was not nearly compensated by the taking.

In the law, the immediate impact of *Penn Central* was the elevation of the legal standing of preservation, but the longer-term impact was the test for regulations that deprived land owners of their profits. It was this that drew much scholarly attention to the case. When the dust had cleared and *Penn Central* was no longer up for grabs, commentators of all stripes moved from the case present tense to the case as precedent. Was *Penn Central* to become the lodestar of landmark law and landmark designations? Or would it be narrowed and picked apart as powerful economic interests and potent intellectual critics swarmed? In a common-law system like ours, majority opinions of the highest federal court become precedent for most subsequent cases bearing the same or substantially similar legal and factual patterns. Sometimes the High Court abandons part or all of a precedent, but *Penn Central* appeared to be safe, at least for the present. All cases of this moment overlap and implead multiple areas of law. *Penn Central*'s precedent reached out beyond landmarks to all manner of takings questions. No case in the common law system is the last word, however, and soon after the victory for the city and the

Landmarks Preservation Commission, critics in and outside of the court system were picking away at the majority decision.

The collateral impact on landmark advocacy was an important by-product of the decision. The Municipal Art Society, once a small but visible group, became a popular civic force with, like the city's own Law Department, a newfound respect. While this was an indirect result of the opinion in terms of the historical trajectory of preservation, it was a landmark of sorts in itself. It proved that a coalition of lawyers, city planners, architects, and preservationists could move mountains—the real estate establishment, the city, the State of New York, and the state and federal courts. Columbia University's Allen Nevins recognized the sea change. The business community now had a rival in policy and planning. He spoke in oracular tones: "In rejecting the Penn Central taking claim, the decision in *Penn Central Transportation Co. v. City of New York* makes it clear that historic preservation qualifies as just another form of land-use regulation as far as the law is concerned."

Among the men and women who argued the case or briefed it, opinions of its impact were mixed. Leonard Koerner worried whether *Penn Central* "helped us or hurt us? I think it helped us because it was so renowned. . . . Sometimes good facts help you. It was clear, some of the justices, even the ones who voted for us like Justice Powell, they had a lot of doubt. I wasn't sure how it was going to come out after the argument. . . . You put it all together, I don't think the preservationists understood how close it was." Dorothy Miner thought it was just part of the zoning plan looking at all the buildings, Koerner admitted, but he wasn't satisfied by her assessment. "She used to joke with me and say I'm not pro-preservationist, and I was just being realistic. It was a very difficult case." David Carpenter thought of the decision differently at the time. "At the time I thought Justice Brennan was making some modest efforts to bring a little content to an area of law that was, as Buzz [Barton Carpenter] said before, then quite formalist and in disarray." Penn Central's counsel Daniel Gribbon wondered how he could have argued the case differently. "I haven't for the life of me come up with any magic bullet that would have changed things. I don't think there was anything that I or anyone else for that matter could have said that would have persuaded Justices Brennan and Marshall."

Spokespersons for the real estate community were not pleased. They opined that the decision might be constitutional but didn't seem fair. *The Wall Street Journal* predicted that landmark designations would discourage the purchase of historical structures, and current owners would have strong incentives to demolish them before they were landmarked. Some law school professors agreed. Private property has and always will have a special place in the hearts of some legal academics. For example, legal scholar Thane Scott saw the case as the opening act of far-reaching "government involvement" in land use. In *Penn Central*, development and preservation met head on. While indirect effects, for example on environmentalism, might benefit, they might also be thwarted when local governments take private property for the public's benefit without compensation to the owner.

Law professors like Richard Epstein regard the case as a backward step. In *Takings*, his classic book-length essay on property, he offered that the majority's reasonable measure was actually no measure at all. The government had taken property without compensation, and calling anything else a reasonable return was simply ignoring the rule that taking must be fairly compensated. The law required that the taker must pay "fair market value." Sheldon Lobel believed, "One cannot envision a more favorable set of circumstances for a court to uphold a landmarks law. Everyone is familiar with the statement 'hard cases make bad law.' In *Penn Central* the more appropriate phrase would be 'easy cases make bad law.'"

While John Echeverria was triumphalist, the "Court's rejection of the company's 'takings' claim represents one the most famous government victories in the annals of land-use law. And the decision articulated several principles that have turned out to have enduring significance in regulatory takings doctrine." Both David Carpenter and Gribbon doubted the case would remain so important. Carpenter remembered, "One thing going in, I thought this was a reasonably important case but less important than a lot of the other cases that we had that term. I certainly never thought this was a case that we would be sitting around talking about 25 years later." Gribbon agreed. "I am surprised that the decision has taken on such importance. At the time it was important but I didn't think it was of the cosmic importance which it turned out to be." Wald, least prepared of all of the litigators, but perhaps the most important of them, added, "I certainly didn't recognize the significance, maybe because I wasn't a regular player in that field at the time.... So I think in retrospect it was a kind of braking case, I mean it put on the brakes, this is where we stop at least for the moment."

Penn Central's Long-Term Impact

Albert Belle's history of the terminal reports, "The ink was barely dry on the ruling when preservationists began making plans to use the Grand Central Terminal ruling by the nation's highest court to save other landmarks." Perhaps the preservationists were a little too optimistic? Lobel and others thought that was hasty:

> Real estate developers and land use attorneys should not take too seriously the claim that *Penn Central* is the *Euclid v. Ambler* of historic preservation. *Penn Central* was a close decision which upheld the landmarks law as applied to Grand Central Terminal. The change in the Supreme Court since 1978, Chief Justice Rehnquist's growing influence and the Court's recent land use decisions seem to indicate Penn Central was not the Euclid for landmarks but a sui generis situation.

While in landmark law the case was an instant icon, in the wider sphere of property law its impact was less straightforward. In his book *Preserving Grand Central*, Thomas Goodwin correctly judged that "the case did serve as precedent for many cases in the future, serving to establish a pro-government, progeny interpretation of the Fifth Amendments Takings Clause." Lawyer Leonard A. Zax, in his 1990 *LA Times* piece, agreed that Justice Brennan "also established a cornerstone of modern real estate law—that local governments must take account of private property rights and pay just compensation when regulations go too far and become a 'taking'—a legal term for the possession of property." And, "In a very real sense, we in the Washington area have Brennan to thank for the preservation of buildings like the Willard Hotel and the city's historic districts." A decade after the decision, all fifty states and more than five hundred municipalities had enacted laws to encourage or require the preservation of buildings and areas with historic or aesthetic importance.

City planner Norman Marcus stated that the timing of the ruling was crucial. "The Court's decision comes not only at a time of taxpayers' revolt but also at a time when recycled buildings have begun to rival new high rises in the conventional wisdom of the inner city marketplace. Its implication will not be lost on municipalities anxious to preserve their aesthetic, historic, and cultural past at minimal cost to the taxpayer"; also, "a comprehensive municipal program of landmarking will from now on be treated with all the judicial deference accorded classic zoning in the 50 year wake of *Euclid v. Ambler Realty Corp.*" Marcus went so far as to state that "the Penn Central decision has jostled this private market, thereby promoting building recycling, by removing any lingering expectation that the public purse stands ready to pay just compensation (top dollar) for preserving landmark structures already housing reasonable beneficial uses."

Gribbon had recognized this social component. "I think I let the argument become a question of whether the landmark program was socially desirable or not. Those demonstrators that were referred to, Jackie Kennedy Onassis and the vice president's wife, they didn't care who paid for this, all they wanted was to make sure that the landmark program continued." Gribbon did not lose the case, however. The notion that property rights were absolute lost. Would an absolutist Fifth Amendment stance not have sacrificed the rights of the many to enjoy the architecture of the terminal? Or was enjoyment not a constitutionally protected right?

Gribbon thought that the majority had put the compensation question off to the side from the start. "I think the basic argument, although it wasn't articulated, really came down to whether the Court was going to stand in the way of landmark designations rather than who should pay for it. On the matter of who should pay for it, the chairman of the Landmarks Commission said we have created a public park over Grand Central. And that's great but who is supposed to pay for it, Penn Central or the public?"

Nearly ten years later, the Court returned to the issue of takings for broad public purposes in *Keystone Bituminous Coal Association v. Debenedictis* (1987), finding that regional health and environment protection were grounds for taking, assuming that reasonable economic returns and investment possibilities are not entirely shunted aside. The balancing of interests had moved a little to the side of the owners, but the impact of *Penn Central* could still be felt. As time passed, along with the accumulation of precedent, the three-factor test would undergo, in the words of law professor Steven J. Eagle, a series of cycles (perhaps gyres would be a better physical metaphor) since *Keystone*. So the debate over use, regulation, competing interests, future investment, and past income will continue.

Who was right? The *Penn Central* majority employed a balancing test. Public interest weighed in the scales against the owner's property rights. Such tests are common in nuisance cases and not uncommon in other areas of law. In balancing tests, social and economic factors can have as much impact as pure legal doctrine. Penn Central's case was weakened by the massive infusion of public aid to the railroad in years past, but that factor would not be true in other landmark designations. In short, the leading authority on the subject concluded that the weighing of these factors in future cases had a "mystical" quality. But there is no question that *Penn Central* remains a landmark precedent in preservation law.

Perhaps the last word should belong to a historian in this history of the case. Allen Nevins, who as a historian teaching at Columbia University and living in the city was hardly an objective, outside observer of the litigation, thought that the opinion was a major victory for the future of Grand Central Terminal, and that it significantly promoted historic preservation everywhere. "The Court laid to rest the notion that aesthetic considerations alone are not a valid basis for the use of the government's police power." Nevins was a believer in positive government, a supporter of the New Deal and American involvement in World War II. He was also an advocate for cities. Hence, he agreed "that states and cities may enact land-use restrictions or controls to enhance the quality of life by preserving the character and desirable aesthetic features of a City."

CHAPTER TEN

The Terminal After *Penn Central*

Victory in the courts for preservation of Grand Central Terminal would have been incomplete without renovation of the terminal. The building in the 1970s was not a pleasant place. Austerity had begotten grime. The great windows were dirty, little light passing through them, as if the outside world did not want anyone to see what Penn Central's bankruptcy had wrought. *The New York Times* later recalled the terminal was "rendered largely pointless by the disappearance of long-distance trains—since commuters time their departures to the minute—the grand waiting room along 42nd Street became a more-or-less permanent shelter for hundreds of homeless people." To prevent the homeless from making a home in the terminal, the waiting room benches were removed, but the problem remained.

During the lawsuit, Penn Central had profitably sold off the Barclay, Biltmore, and Roosevelt Hotels. The railroad also dumped the adjacent Commodore Hotel in a complex deal involving tax breaks, leasebacks, and other investment arcana among the city, the state Urban Development Corporation, real estate mogul Donald Trump, and the Hyatt Hotel Corporation. In addition to restoring the hotel inside and out, the deal was intended to generate $2 million to clean Grand Central's exterior. "As an investment," Ada Louis Huxtable wrote presciently, "this could well be seed money for far greater returns in the start of a revitalized 42nd Street." But real estate deals, even those as touted as the hotel sales, did not change basic facts. "The truth is," the architecture critic Paul Goldberger wrote at the time, "the Grand Central neighborhood does not work as it is now—it is too dirty, too pressured, too troubled by a large homeless population and too lacking in amenity for everyone else." Still, the idea of preservation, he said approvingly, "is based on the idea that the terminal is not just a building, but the symbolic anchor of a neighborhood."

Would the *Penn Central* decision save the best social use of the terminal? Could the preservationists become renovators? John Belle said that the 1978 decision "set a standard that cities should protect their heritage. We as a city and a country were now being challenged to look at our built environment with fairness, vision, and integrity." But not at a single stroke. According to *The New York Times*, in 1980 the architects Gruzen & Partners studied the revival of the original 1910 tower design. They found many problems, including changed building codes, loss of corner space to the elevator cores, and the huge difficulties of delivering materials and planning construction. Historian Samuel Roberts reported that "early in 1982, offices and the stairway to the 43rd Street exit were closed because of leaks and cascading plaster, apparently caused by the gut renovation of the Biltmore Hotel across Vanderbilt Avenue. A month later, commuters dodged falling plaster and dripping water, which forced officials to close a waiting room and the terminal's sole locker room."

Still, help was on the way to the beleaguered terminal. In 1983 the Metro-North Railroad, a division of the Metropolitan Transportation Authority, officially took over the terminal and its operations from Conrail. Because Penn Central had been given the right to develop 1.8 million square feet of space by the 1978 Supreme Court decision, acquiring the terminal with these development rights still attached to it would make the acquisition costs unaffordable, so Metro-North leased the building. When Metro-North was created in 1983, among its first priorities were repair of the copper roof and the porous deck over Park Avenue. The result, however, was not quite what Metro-North expected. "By sealing the roof first and stopping the water from coming in," *The New York Times* reported in 1985, "in the past month, hundreds of homeless people have taken advantage of a Metro-North decision to open Grand Central Terminal all night and have been sheltering on cold nights in the terminal's waiting rooms, corridors and other marbled nooks and crannies."

The roof repair was just the first step. Skylights blacked out in World War II were replaced to allow more daylight to stream into the building. Brass fittings were polished. New doors were installed. Even the marble floors were cleaned every night. Ten elevators, some with bronze castings inside, were modernized. Metro-North also started looking to improve passenger flow to increase ridership by almost a million people a year.

Some critics (after all, it was New York City) were upset that the cleaning did not directly help the homeless. The *Times* reported in 1986, "Grand Central has become a home for thousands of homeless people. You have a huge social problem. They're choosing to ignore it and focus on the ceiling. Dare they afford to set up another Versailles?" Lee Stringer, the author of "Grand Central Winter: Stories from the Street," remembered "living in Grand Central, along with hundreds of other homeless New Yorkers. It has since struck me how perfectly right it was that a great public building should serve, above everything else, as a refuge." Unfortunately, Vanderbilt Avenue had become a haven for drug dealing, and surging crime seemed even more dangerous on dim and claustrophobic passageways and platforms. True, without the efforts of the MTA, Grand Central would clearly have been suffering far greater neglect and disrepair. Some maintenance projects were doomed, however. John Belle remembered, "Keeping the bathrooms clean and safe was growing impossible as more and more homeless New Yorkers used the space to bathe and launder their clothing. The railroad leased the restrooms to a private concession hoping they could do a better maintenance job."

Late in 1986 Metro-North began to think about removing the clutter of advertising in the main concourse. "There is a lot of pressure on the M.T.A. to rid Grand Central of all signs," the *Times* reported in 1986. "We would like to look at it in terms of overall view," said Marsilia Boyle, director of real estate for the Metropolitan Transportation Authority, which owned the terminal. "We've also been having discussions with the Municipal Art Society and other groups about how it fits into the neighborhood as a public place.... The arts groups were now demanding restoration, to keep it a more interesting place historically." The advertising revenue was not significant, and when the rental agreements expired the next year, plans to restore the ceiling to its former glory might end the gaudy and distracting displays. The giant Kodak sign, for example, would be replaced with a restaurant.

According to *The New York Times*, the odds were against Peter Stangl when MTA chairman Richard Ravitch appointed him to head Metro-North in 1981. The railroad was losing riders, only 81 percent of its trains were on time, and many of them were infamous for running their heaters in the summer and air conditioners in the winter. Ten years later, the

Times had changed its tune. "Metro-North was a real big mess, but Peter brought in new ideas and energy and made it a success story in New York and gave people in the mass-transit business around the country hope." The system, including Metro-North, the Long Island Rail Road, and the New York City Transit Authority, was working.

At the center of the project was the terminal. According to Samuel Roberts, by 1988 Stangl's goals included a full restoration of the terminal. Stangl outlined three goals: "First and foremost, we want Grand Central to be a terrific train station again. Secondly, it's important to restore the building's architectural integrity. And thirdly, we want to improve the way we use space for retail purposes." Stangl himself was a regular commuter on the line. Like the early leaders of the city's preservationist movement, he knew that political connections were vital to gain public support and funding for his plan. He told the *Times*, "You can debate about options. What you can't debate about is to make sure that the genius that went into this terminal is not wasted." The plan reported in 1988 suggests that some of the balconies overlooking the main concourse be set aside for "quality" restaurants, like those found in the Gare du Nord in Paris.

The MTA still had the problem of the homeless making the terminal their home. Homeless advocates were very worried and "would monitor the development plan very closely, with an eye toward making sure they would not sweep the homeless out," said Norman Siegel, executive director of New York Civil Liberties Union. "The homeless problem, to begin with, comes from gentrification and redevelopment, so we will make sure their rights are not violated." Under a recent court decision, Siegel said, homeless people could not be evicted from the terminal as long as they did not violate any criminal laws.

Then there was the giant Kodak sign, covering an entire wall. Frank Gilbert recalled, "The results are so impressive with a successful commercial area there, with the removal of the Kodak sign—that huge Kodak sign which was on one side of the Terminal." New York City critics being what they were, some argued that the Kodak sign itself had become a landmark, and should not be removed. "People even suggested it had acquired historic significance; it had been there so long." Others saw it as a welcoming beacon, albeit a kitschy one. Christopher Gray of the *Times* acknowledged that the sign, "which greeted millions of passengers with pastoral farm scenes and Alpine idylls, was, like the proposed skyscraper atop the terminal, simply in the wrong place at the wrong time." The financial hit was considerable—Kodak was paying a hefty $450,000 a year to promote itself—but Metro-North, signaling an enduring and—for a government agency—unusual commitment to enlightened self-interest, refused to grant a long-term lease. "I'll be sad to see that sign go because it's my scenery," said John McFadden, owner-manager of the terminal's cafe. "However, I guess all the restoration work in the terminal makes sense, just so long as a new generation of M.T.A. management doesn't decide to change it back to a more commercial look five years from now." Like other tenants, McFadden felt nervous about his future because the MTA had not revealed who would be invited to remain. "I'm hoping this cafe will exist as long as Grand Central continues to stand," he remarked, "but I have no idea what the M.T.A. is thinking."

The New York Times reported in 1989 that "Grand Central is a wonderful space, but it has some very real problems," quoting Bradley C. Mendelson, managing director of retail leasing for Edward S. Gordon Company, a Manhattan real estate concern. "At Grand Central, everyone is always late to the office or late to a train, which doesn't promote a mindset for shopping. And I don't think anybody believes the homeless problem will lend itself to a quick solution." The homeless too were not going away, not if their advocates had anything to say about it. "Even when restoration plans were announced advocates for the homeless attacked the plan, saying it would drive homeless people from one of the last remaining public areas in the city where they can seek shelter. On any given day, hundreds of homeless people loiter in the terminal, sleeping in the waiting room and begging for money and food," the *Times* reported in 1990.

Peter Smith, president of the Partnership for the Homeless, which operates the nation's largest private shelter network, said his organization was disappointed with the plan because "there was not even a hint that anything would be done to meet the needs of people." Smith said Metro-North had ignored his group's recommendation that a vacant map room on the lower level be a social-service center for the homeless. In the meantime, the nadir of the old terminal was not far away. In 1991 Amtrak switched the last long-distance and intercity trains to Penn Station. At 8:35 p.m. on April 6, the Rip Van Winkle lumbered off to Albany for the last time.

Restoration of the Terminal

A site so central to a metropolitan area as vital as New York City would not wither for long. A master plan for restoration, as opposed to the earlier piecemeal efforts of the MTA, was prepared by the architectural firm Beyer Blinder Belle, in association with Harry Weese & Associates and Seelye Stevenson Value & Knecht. The plan called for an intensified pace of restoration and several significant expansions. Originally the plan presumed that the great waiting room, then sheltering hundreds of homeless people, would become a retail center with a stage for theatrical and musical productions. Fast-food outlets, retail stores, and two movie theaters would go on the lower level. "Grand Central will be more than just a place to catch a train," Stangl predicted. "It will be a place to have a banquet or reception, to catch a movie, to go shopping or for dinner and to see local talent on stage. It will become a destination in its own right." Peter Malkin, chairman of the Grand Central Partnership, a coalition of neighboring property owners and businesses, was equally enthusiastic. "It's a terrific plan that complements the work we are doing to upgrade the area outside the terminal. . . . I especially like the idea of putting restaurants around the balconies, a step that will enhance the character and environment of the main terminal."

The new president of the Municipal Art Society, Kent Barwick, was in accord, but a little more wary of the commercialization the new plan entailed. "Our initial response is enthusiastic. It's the kind of planning that is called for on a very complex issue like Grand Central, where you need to strike a balance of restoration and commercialization." Early on, Metro-North officials said they believed that they could double retail revenue at the terminal to $14 million in five years and reach $20 million in ten years. To achieve that growth, the line planned to increase retail space in the terminal, to 150,000 square feet from the current 105,000. "We figured out a scheme that allowed us to buy a building losing a fortune," Susan E. Fine, director of real estate for the authority, remembered, and ultimately redeemed "the value of public entrepreneurship—taking risks beyond the MTA's core mission and trusting staff to get it done." But the cost, at inception some $425 million, was sobering. Cost-saving measures cut it down to $240 million, still a lot for the always cash-strapped MTA.

The architects retained the idea that the station was primarily a place of transition. Like Ellis Island, whose restoration in 1991 was also designed by Beyer Blinder Belle, Grand Central was one of the most thrilling symbols of the city's receptivity, its openness to people and to ideas. John Belle himself recalled, "When our firm was put in charge of this restoration we felt a guardianship and a personal responsibility for its rebirth. As the architect for the restoration, every detail became a personal obsession, the design of the new east staircase a personal crusade." Sadly, Belle, the lead architect on the project, did not live to see the return of intercity trains to Grand Central.

Once again Jacqueline Kennedy Onassis played a role. At Peter Stangl's and Kent Barwick's invitation, she came to hear the Beyer Blinder Belle team make a presentation of their plans. It was a memorable occasion. After a somewhat lengthy talk, the restoration architect thought that the former First Lady and Grand Central Terminal's champion had had her fill of the subject and was eager to leave. As she rose from her seat, he thought she was heading for the door. To his surprise she proceeded to engage him in an animated conversation about many of the derails of the plan. "This brief but intense conversation was an inspiration to the team that was drawn upon many times as future difficulties and frustrations sapped our spirits," Belle recalled. Once again, her presence and support made a difference.

A second highly visible sign of restoration came in 1990. The Kodak "Colorama" sign came down. Working mostly at night behind shielding drapes through the late winter and early spring of 1990, workers removed the Kodak images and screen piece by piece and cleaned the marble and limestone underneath. The morning it was finished and the protective curtain was taken down, the architects stood quietly watching the first commuters stream into the main concourse from the train platforms. As the sunshine burst through three windows that had not been seen since 1950, it was as if life were being breathed back into the building. Many commuters stopped in their tracks, speechless and amazed at the change that had so instantly brought back the majesty of the space.

The ceiling restoration project was next. The effect was electric. "It was almost comical," journalist Jack Taylor said. "People would bang into one another. When the first person stopped, the next person would bump in, and then they all started looking up at the ceiling." With the possible exception of Central Park's renovation, started in the 1980's under the direction of Elizabeth Barlow Rogers of the Central Park Conservancy, this may have been the greatest feat of historical preservation in the city's history.

By 1994 further restoration plans became much more concrete. Susan Fine said the new plan was "much less glitzy"—and therefore that much more feasible. "Once this work is done," she said, "the terminal will be in a good state of repair for the next generation." The MTA entered into an agreement with GCT Venture that same year that would form the basis for implementing the modified master plan: the Grand Central Terminal Revitalization Plan, the $200 million program completed in 1999. New escalators, redesigned ramps to the trains, and the return of the oyster bar all heralded the rebirth of the terminal. The cost? Well, in the end the MTA sold $84 million in bonds: $49 million for public improvements, and $35 million for retail-related work. It also used $109 million of its capital budget and received $4 million from the federal government, for a total of $187 million.

The renovation was a collaborative effort of architects, engineers, and the Municipal Art Society, but agreement was sometimes hard to secure. For example, the new eastern staircase, which threatened to diminish the room's amplitude, was an issue, but by increasing access to the concourse balconies, it added an observation deck that rendered the scene below an epic urban spectacle. America's foremost architect, Philip Johnson, a leader in the fight to preserve Grand Central in the 1970s, said, "It's a logical way to complete the Beaux-Arts approach to architecture, which was symmetry. And it brings back the balcony level into some sort of usefulness."

Ah—but the critics' carping was not silenced. There were some concerns that the balconies not become a private preserve of restaurant patrons. "You shouldn't have to book a table to get a view," Kent Barwick of the Municipal Art Society said. "There still ought to be a place—not to romance this too much—where a lonely sailor can go and look down." The reference to Leonard Bernstein's "On the Town," set in part in the terminal, was appropriate. Belle: "The loss of the matching staircase gave the Concourse a strangely unbalanced look, as if a limb had been amputated from an otherwise perfectly formed human body." John Beyer recalled later it "was exceedingly controversial, to the extent that there was a war between the New York City Landmarks Commission and the SHPO [State Historic Preservation Office] that had to be resolved in Washington by a special committee that heard similar controversies and made a judgment about what to do" with building the second staircase. Critics like Nicholai Ouroussoff complained about the new staircase even before final plans were announced. "Nor is the Grand Concourse itself sacred. A second grand stair—modeled after an early plan that was never realized—is being constructed along the east balcony that once belonged to Kodak.... The eye will no longer travel up to the spectacle of stone pillars above but will stop at the chewing faces of office workers and tourists. (One symbolic oddity: The east stair will be 3 1/2 feet higher than the west, visually distorting the main space.)"

Preservationists had to become pragmatists. It was simply not feasible, given the function of the terminal as a terminal, to cling to the belief that an artifact is best preserved in its original state. There were advances in structural design and materials, and there were new uses to consider. Belle wanted a more fruitful give-and-take in "the ongoing discussion between architect (instrument of change) and preservationist (all change is inferior to the original) [as] a far more equal debate. In the actual event "A screaming match [over the staircase] ensued that cleared the air and allowed work to continue." Everyone agreed that the architects should prepare drawings and models that reflected the original staircase design.

That resolution was easy compared to the battles over commercialization. Retail space in the terminal nearly doubled, to 170,000 square feet (almost four acres), from 105,000 square feet, only 75,000 square feet of which was occupied in recent years. Given tenant demand, the developers believed they could have leased 100,000 square feet more. "Those rents support the bonds which made possible the architectural restoration," said E. Virgil Conway, chairman of the authority. "But we did not let the commercial development intrude upon the beauty of the terminal." Not everyone agreed. Critics at *The New York Times* in 1995 worried about all the new retail: "One wonders why it is necessary to turn all the available space into sit-down and take-out food vendors. Perhaps a balance of restaurants, shops and waiting areas would be more desirable." Ouroussoff also worried that Grand Central would turn into other train stations where "the willingness to neglect the historical meaning of the terminal to lure middle-aged mall rats will alter the personality of the space forever. I preferred the company of the worn-down commuters, the loiterers, the needy and the homeless." Jennifer J. Raab, chair of the Landmarks Preservation Commission, said she was optimistic that a detailed master plan governing the aesthetics of storefronts would set clear standards. "We still have to be vigilant," she said, "but we've taken an important first step by being so careful."

The placement of the restaurants turned out to be crucial. Because they were located on the balcony spaces surrounding the main concourse, they allowed observation of activity below as well as offering opportunities for design innovation. Food stands would become part of a dining concourse, joined by stores in the old incoming train room, renamed Biltmore Hall (after one of the lesser Vanderbilts). Leases for these commercial venues were much desired, and soon new tenants were to fill the terminal; at least that was the plan. To no one's surprise, there were delays, unexpected costs, and shop owners who pulled out of deals. Critics at the *Times* wondered at the new offerings. "As Whitney Warren, one of Grand Central's original architects, put it in 1913, 'The up-to-date station resembles a bazaar.' Now Grand Central, looking as good as ever, is up-to-date once again."

When Grand Central Terminal was rededicated on October 1, 1998, it was not hard to understand why so many people had fought so hard to save the terminal. On that day, five thousand people filled the main concourse, which had been returned to its original grandeur. Many were thanked, and many remembered—among them Jacqueline Kennedy Onassis. In the meantime, Metro-North was expanding. Since 1985 Metro-North has increased the number of weekday trains from 471 to more than 600. In mid-2012, MTA chairman Joseph Lhota announced that the railroad would add 230 more trains, mostly in off-peak hours and on weekends, in what he described as the largest service expansion since Metro-North's inception. On-time performance has reached a record high (for 2011, 97.4 percent on the Hudson, 97.1 percent on the Harlem, and 93.7 percent on the New Haven for the morning rush; and 98.5 percent, 97.8 percent, and 95.1 percent, respectively, in the afternoon). So has annual passenger traffic. Since 1983, when Metro-North was created, ridership has doubled. It topped 82 million in 2011, when, for the first time, the number of Metro-North commuters surpassed their Long

Island Rail Road counterparts. It was fast becoming the largest passenger railroad in the country, and with an on-time record approaching 100 percent.

As Benjamin Baccash reported in his 2010 study of the Landmarks Preservation Commission's post-1978 efforts, the victory over Penn Central was "esteem building" for a regulatory agency hitherto regarded as "timid." Almost six hundred landmark designations followed, along with more than thirty historic districts and a dozen interiors. A full-time enforcement officer joined the commission, and it began to take the lead in designations, rather than simply responding to requests from other agencies and individuals.

Realtors protested and Mayor Edward Koch tried to mediate with another ad hoc committee, but the die was cast. The ad hoc Historic City Committee brought realtors, planners, architects, and preservation professions together to establish standards for inspection of buildings and districts, imposition of fines, and investigation of complaints. The city was now a full partner in the preservation project. This in turn meant that appointment as chair of the Landmarks Preservation Commission would be influenced by city politics. As the Koch administration gave way to that of Rudolph Giuliani, a new policy reemphasized the role of landlords. The uneasy balance between property interests and historic interests will always be part of preservation law.

In Europe, national preservation authorities have often played a decisive role in preserving the heritage of cities, but in the United States the power to implement urban architectural preservation has predominantly rested with local governance. Federal authority to protect historic properties does conserve important archaeological and natural sites like the Grand Canyon and the pre-Columbian Indian ruins of the Southwest, and monuments of great national significance such as the Statue of Liberty and Ellis Island in New York, but national laws can safeguard only an infinitesimal portion of the total heritage of the nation, with an especially limited effect on cities. In fact, fewer than 1 percent of New York's significant properties would be protected under federal mandate. Historic preservation remains the task of interested and influential local individuals and groups. *Penn Central v. New York City* did not change that.

But preservation does not mean that interiors will be neglected. In the new decade of the 2020s, the commuter traveler was the beneficiary of major improvements to Grand Central Terminal. The MTA and Metro-North at the terminal unveiled upgraded communications displays, as well as major safety improvements to stairways, escalators and elevators. Functionality went hand in hand with beautification, in the terminal's new entrance on Vanderbilt Avenue. Grand Central Terminal is alive and well.

Conclusion

There can be little doubt that *Penn Central v. New York City* is a landmark law case in all senses of the term. The history that has been shared in the preceding pages is a testament to that fact. It was truly a battle of titans, not only between the litigants, but for what was truly at stake in the case itself: the buildings that form the basis of a city, just as much as its people, art, music, businesses, and law. *Penn Central* was all of this and more.

Grand Central Terminal's fate was not the end of the landmark law story. Or at least, that is not what was important about the case. Landmark law brought together social, economic, and professional narratives that shaped, and would continue to shape, American property law and public policy. In the late twentieth and early twenty-first centuries America remains divided between those who would destroy the city in order to create and those who wish to preserve parts of the city in order to build a better future. *Penn Central v. New York City* was a partial victory for the preservationists in this contest, but it also cleared the ground for further confrontation.

In some sense, nineteenth-century New York City was built by Cornelius Vanderbilt and the New York Central Railroad. The company was wildly profitable, beating back competitors, creating great demand for economic development in midtown Manhattan, and in turn necessitating the need for bigger and better train stations. The Central's growth would lead to the construction of the most important privately owned public space in New York. Grand Central Terminal then fostered an entirely new kind of property district with its novel use of "air rights," a type of real estate development where landowners sold the "air" space above their property. Thus the terminal was the culmination of major economic, technological, societal, and cultural changes that had taken place in America's most important city. Its rivalry with the Pennsylvania Railroad would lead to great things for the public and itself. That rivalry produced not only Grand Central Terminal but the late, great Pennsylvania Station. The twin stations helped bring New York up to date on its infrastructure as the city entered the twentieth century.

In the 1960s and 1970s, even though the terminal still served as a public space for grand celebrations and momentous protests, its luster was fading. The wear and tear of running and maintaining such a structure for so many people became a drain on the New York Central. A heavily regulated rail industry could not compete with federally funded highways, airports, and suburban development. New York City lost population, not only to suburbanization but also to highway development and poorly designed urban renewal. A vicious cycle created downward pressure on neighborhoods outside the core, similar to the pressures facing Grand Central itself. Historic buildings were demolished in favor of new ones built in the core, and others suffered from neglect. Penn Station fell, and Grand Central seemed next on the list.

If New York City could not win the *Penn Central* case it probably would not be able to preserve *any* landmarked property because Grand Central Terminal, as Judge Breitel so aptly put it, was "no ordinary landmark." Even though that statement might seem paradoxical, it is true. Of all the protected landmarked buildings in New York City, Grand Central holds a special place in the life of New Yorkers. It functions as a grand gateway for hundreds of thousands of commuters as well as a lunchroom for office workers, a photo op for tourists, a marketplace for nearby residents, and a central place for iconic events; basically, it is Midtown's living room. The fight to save the terminal thus brought together a diverse battalion of celebrities, lawyers, real estate moguls, and judges.

The effort to save the terminal, culminating in the lawsuits, helped cement the legitimacy of landmark legislation in the United States and in New York in particular. In retrospect the case was generally straightforward. Grand Central was an exceptionally well-known building. It was definitely a landmark before buildings gained any legal status. While the Penn Central Railroad lost a potential revenue stream, it was still able to use the terminal as a train station and retail development. The US Supreme Court determined that more money could be made there. The Court had already ruled in *Breman v. Parker* that municipalities could make land-use decisions based on beauty and aesthetic considerations. New York City didn't need to argue that landmarks make the city more beautiful and increase economic development, tourism, and business overall because it was obvious that Grand Central did these things. The city did need to argue that individual landmark designations throughout the city could act as a landmark district as part of an overall land-use scheme. Each landmark was part of the whole, and the process was straightforward with many opportunities for judicial relief. The judicial relief argument impressed the justices who made a point of that in the majority opinion.

There are other reasons beyond mere landmarking why so many cities—such as Minneapolis, Atlanta, and San Francisco—invoke Grand Central Terminal when planning their new train stations: It was one of the first buildings that used ramps to help ease the flow of travelers. It still has the greatest number of track platforms of any station in the world. It hosted of the first fully electric train stations in the world. Its builders created the concept of air rights development. It is one of the greatest examples of Beaux-Arts architecture in the land. It is therefore fitting that Grand Central's Supreme Court case dramatically changed how cities look and how the law treats property rights.

New York City's preservation movement is well documented. Those involved in saving our landmarks today are part of a long and grand tradition. It is one that inspires, instructs, and calls us to remember that preservation, like the very sites it seeks to save, exists in time. There is a continually changing context to preservation's work. As the concept of public interest has emerged, part of an evolving governmental ethos, preservation of architectural monuments has moved from the edges of government activity to its forefront.

But preservation by its very nature limits what property owners can and cannot do with their property. American constitutionalism is built on a robust scaffolding of individual rights. Among these are the right to enjoy private property, to buy and sell, and to plan for future uses. Insofar as preservation constrains these rights, the conflict between preservation and ownership is inevitable.

CHRONOLOGY

February 2, 1913	Grand Central Terminal opens
October 19, 1954	*Berman v. Parker* case is argued before the Supreme Court and clears the way for the Bard Act
1955	New York State Senator MacNeil Mitchell introduces the Bard Act
April 2, 1956	The Bard Act is signed into law
1959	Municipal Art Society makes efforts to amend the city's zoning code, for "some kind of aesthetic zoning"
October 30, 1963	New York's Pennsylvania Station demolition begins
1965	The Bard Act is applied to create New York City's Landmarks Preservation Law
April 19, 1965	Mayor John Lindsay signs New York City's Landmarks Law
August 2, 1967	Landmark designation of Grand Central Terminal by Landmarks Preservation Commission
February 1, 1968	Pennsylvania and New York Central Railroads merger is complete
1968	The Bard Act is amended to define the types of places for legislative protection
June 19, 1968	A fifty-five-story skyscraper is proposed over the terminal concourse
September 26, 1968	Landmarks Preservation Commission denies the proposed skyscraper a certificate of appropriateness
January 1, 1969	Breuer II plan is submitted
August 26, 1969	Certificate of no exterior effect is unanimously denied to Breuer II
October 7, 1969	Penn Central Railroad files suit against New York City
January 17, 1975	Grand Central Terminal is added to the National Register of Historic Places
January 21, 1975	State Supreme Court (trial court) justice Irving H.

	Saypol invalidates the landmarks designation of the terminal
December 16, 1975	Landmark status of the terminal is reinstated by the Appellate Division of the State Supreme Court
June 23, 1977	New York State Court of Appeals upholds the Appellate decision
June 26, 1978	US Supreme Court upholds landmark status of the terminal
January 1, 1983	Metro-North Railroad (a division of the MTA) is formed
October 8, 1998	Grand Central Terminal is fully restored
November 2018	Grand Central Terminal to be bought by MTA
March 13, 2020	Grand Central MTA purchase finalized

BIBLIOGRAPHIC ESSAY

The most important cases are *Penn Central v. New York City*, 438 U.S. 104 (1978); *Penn Central v. New York City*, 42 N.Y. 2d 324 (1977); *Penn Central v. New York*, A.D. 2d 265 (1975); *Benenson v. United States* 548 F. 2d 939 (1977); *Goldblatt v. Hempstead*, 369 U.S. 590, (1962); *Pennsylvania Coal Co. v. Mahon*, 260 U.S. 393 (1922); *Euclid v. Ambler Realty Co.*, 272 U.S. 365 (1026); *Hadacheck v. Sebastian*, 239 U.S. 394 (1915); *New Orleans v. Dukes*, 427 U.S. 297 (1976); *Young v. American Mini Theatres, Inc.*, 427 U.S. 50 (1976); *Village of Belle Terre v. Boraas*, 416 U.S. 1, 9–10 (1974); *Berman v. Parker*, 348 U.S. 26, 33 (1954); *Armstrong v. United States*, 364 U.S. 40 (1960); *United States v. Causby*, 328 U.S. 256, 262 (1946); *Lutheran Church in America v. City of New York* 35 N.Y.2d 121 (1974); *Matter of Trustees of Sailors' Snug Harbor v. Platt* 280 N.Y.S.2d 75 (1968); *Maher v. City of New Orleans*, 371 F. Supp. 653 (E.D. La. 1974); *Salamar Bldrs. Corp. v. Tuttle*, 325 N.Y.S.2d 933 (1971); *French Investing Co. v. City of New York*, 385 N.Y.S.2d 5 (1976); *Queenside Hills Realty Co. v. Saxl*, 328 U.S. 80 (1946); *Atlantic Coast Line R.R. Co. v. North Carolina Corporation Commission*, 206 U.S. 1 (1907); *Puget Sound Traction, Light & Power Co. v. Reynolds*, 224 U.S. 574 (1917); and *U.S. v. Fuller*, 409 U.S. 488 (1973).

Later cases influenced by *Penn Central* include *Agins v. City of Tiburon*, 447 U.S. 255 (1980); *Nollan v. California Coastal Commission*, 479 U.S. 913 (1986); *Keystone Coal v. Debenedictis*, 480 U.S. 470 (1987), *First English Evangelical Lutheran Church of Glendale v. County of Los Angeles*, 482 U.S. 304 (1987); *St. Bartholomew's Church v. New York*, 728 F. Supp. 958 (S.D.N.Y. 1990); *Florida Rock v. United States*, 189 F.3d 1355 (1999); and *Lingle v. Chevon* 544 U.S. 528 (2005).

Oral argument in *Penn Central* is available at https://www.supremecourt.gov/pdfs/transcripts/1977/77-444_04-17-1978.pdf. Additional comments include Daniel M. Gribbon, "Appellants Reply Brief," April 1978; L. Kevin Sheridan, Leonard Koerner, Counsel, "Appellees Motion to Dismiss," W. Bernard Richland, Corporation Counsel of the City of New York, Attorney for Appellees, November 16, 1977, and materials appended to the New York Preservation Archives Project discussed below.

The essential source for memoirs and interviews with participants is the New York Preservation Archive Project, at http://www.nypap.org/oral-history/. When not otherwise noted in the text, recollections came from this collection. Especially valuable were retrospectives, among which were "Leading the Movement—Interviews with Preservationist Leaders in New York's Civic Sector," featuring the reminiscences of John Belle and John Beyer. The reminiscences of Lorna Nowvé provide a broad perspective on the climate of the preservation movement in New York City at the time of her involvement. She discusses the role of the Municipal Art Society and its then subsidiary, the Historic Districts Council, in preservation battles, and recounts her experiences organizing rallies to save Grand Central Terminal.

The reminiscences of Fred Papert are especially important. Papert discusses the publicity campaign that preservationists mounted as they fought court battles over Grand Central Terminal in the 1970s, focusing in particular on the involvement of Jacqueline Kennedy Onassis. So too was "Through the Legal Lens: Interviews with Lawyers Who Shaped NYC's Landmarks Law," which includes interviews with Virginia Waters, who helped to develop key strategies for the Landmarks Preservation Commission, and Michael Gruen, who discusses his role in the development of some of the legal mechanisms that enable preservation and gives his perspective on the volunteer-driven preservation movement of the 1970s. The Legal Lens series also features the reminiscences of Leonard Koerner, Seymour Boyers, and Jack Kerr. Kerr speaks about his experiences working on *Penn Central*, and the conversation then ranges to how he became interested in preservation law, significant cases, and his current activities in historical preservation. A few of the cases he worked on for the Landmarks Conservancy, St. Vincent's Hospital's claim to the Landmarks Preservation Commission, and *St. Bartholomew's Church v. City of New York*, helped to establish the parameters of the then new Landmarks Preservation Law, and how it is applied today.

The interview with Jennifer Raab is part of the Leading the Commission: Interviews with the Former Chairs of NYC's Landmarks Preservation Commission oral history project, which also includes recollections of Anthony C. Wood and Frank Gilbert. The latter interviews are part of the New York Preservation Archive's Project's collection of individual oral history interviews. Frank Gilbert was the first secretary of the Landmarks Preservation Commission (LPC) and then became its executive director. Gilbert draws on archives to recount his memories of the early days of the LPC. Topics covered include several early designations, including Astor Library, Friends Meeting House, and Sailors' Snug Harbor. He also describes an early hardship application that led to the demolition of the landmarked Manhattan Club, a court decision upholding the designation of *Sailors' Snug Harbor*, and a court decision striking down the designation of the *Morgan House*. The interview touches on legislative matters as well, including a 1968 amendment to the Bard Act, and the 1973 amendments to the city's Landmarks Law. In the second half of the interview, Gilbert provides detail about the proposed office tower above Grand Central Terminal that led to a legal battle over the LPC's decision. After leaving the LPC, he took up a position with the National Trust for Historic Preservation, where he continued his involvement in the Grand Central Terminal litigation.

A crucial source is the oral history interview with Harmon Goldstone on the Brian Lehrer radio show, at http://www.wnyc.org/story/interview-with-harmon-goldstone-chairman-of-the-landmarks-preservation-commission. I deeply appreciate Rebecca in the listener support services at WNYC for the transcription of the radio interview for me.

One should also consult the NYC Landmarks Preservation Commission website, http://www1.nyc.gov/site/lpc/about/about-lpc.page, for basic information including mission statements, brief histories, and a number of current landmarks. The Landmarks Preservation Commission Grand Central Terminal Designation Report, August 2, 1967, Number 2, LP-0266, traced the first steps.

Peter L. Bernstein's *The Wedding of the Waters: The Erie Canal and the Making of a Great Nation* (New York: Norton, 2005) was the source for much of the Erie Canal discussion. Alfred D. Chandler, *The Visible Hand: The Managerial Revolution in American Business* (Cambridge, MA: Harvard University Press, 1977), is a classic on corporations in the nineteenth century. T. J. Stiles, *The First Tycoon: The Epic Life of Cornelius Vanderbilt* (New York: Knopf, 2009), is the best work on Vanderbilt.

General works on the terminal and the preservation movement include John Belle and Maxine Rhea Leighton, *Grand Central: Gateway to a Million Lives* (New York: Norton, 2000), a chronicle by the director of the restoration. Also see Deborah Nevins, ed., for the Municipal Art Society of New York, *Grand Central Terminal: City Within the City* (New

York: Municipal Art Society, 1982), on the history of Grand Central Terminal and the Municipal Art Society's role in landmarking and litigating the landmark court case. Anthony W. Robins and the New York Transit Museum, *Grand Central Terminal: 100 Years of a New York Landmark* (New York: Stewart, Tabori & Chang, 2013), is a history of the terminal focusing on it as a "town square" of New York that contains contemporary newspaper accounts of the time. Anthony C. Wood, *Preserving New York: Winning the Right to Protect a City's Landmarks* (New York: Routledge, 2007), is a triumphalist account of the LPC. Robert A. Levy and William H. Mellor, *The Dirty Dozen: How Twelve Supreme Court Cases Radically Expanded Government and Eroded Freedom* (New York: Sentinel, 2008), includes a critique of the decision.

Kurt C. Schlichting, *Grand Central Terminal: Railroads, Engineering, and Architecture in New York City* (Baltimore: Johns Hopkins University Press, 2001), discusses the architecture of Grand Central and the engineering of the building and Terminal City. The work includes accounts by engineers, architects, and developers as well as a summary of the 1990s restoration. William D. Middleton, *Grand Central... The World's Greatest Railway Terminal* (San Marino, CA: Golden West Books, 1977), written just before the Supreme Court case was decided, is the perfect time capsule of advocates' mood before the building was finally saved. Sam Roberts, *Grand Central: How a Train Station Transformed America* (New York: Grand Central Publishing, Hachette Book Group, 2013), is a comprehensive overview on the history of Grand Central, the landmark case, and the people who use the station. Anthony M. Tung, *Preserving The World's Great Cities; The Destruction and Renewal of the Historic Metropolis* (New York: Clarkson Potter, 2001), has just a small section on New York and Grand Central, but the author makes the strong case that preservation and New York politicians came together and saw the value of buildings and places that they did not see before the 1960s.

The web was a readily available source of original and reprint journalism on the people involved in the preservation movement, the railroad, and the city. Among those used for this volume were citylab.com and the Congressional Budget Office's "Regulatory Takings and Proposals for Change" at the Environmental Policy Project website.

The New York Times covered the story from start to finish. Its reportage is available on the paper's timeline, online. Persons quoted or featured in the stories, along with the dates and other information, appear in the text. *The Washington Post, New York Magazine, Forbes, Christian Science Monitor, Town and Country*, and *New Yorker* also followed the story. Other journals and magazine articles on the subject are cited in the text. The author has a full list of web addresses available online. Materials on the judges and justices was taken from the obituary files of the papers, as well as from standard reference works like Melvin I. Urofsky, ed., *Biographical Encyclopedia of the Supreme Court* (Washington, DC: CQ Press, 2006); Roger K. Newman, ed., *Yale Biographical Dictionary of American Law* (New Haven, CT: Yale University Press, 2009); and John R. Vile, ed., *Great American Judges*, 2 vols. (Santa Barbara, CA: ABC-CLIO, 2003).

Law scholars did not neglect the case. The gold standard is James A. Kushner et al., *Land Use Regulation*, 5th ed. (Burlington, MA: Aspen, 2017).

Shortly after the decision came down, legal academics rushed to their pens. See Richard Wolloch, "*Penn Central v. City of New York*, A Landmark Landmark Case," 6 *Fordham Urban Law Journal* 667 (1978); Herbert Gleason, "Implications of the Grand Central Terminal: Litigation and Likely Effects on State and Municipal Government Programs," 1 *Pace Law Review* 3 (1981), part of the Symposium on Historic Preservation Law; Norman Marcus, "The Grand Slam Grand Central Terminal Decision: A Euclid for Landmarks, Favorable Notice for TDR and a Resolution of the Regulatory/Taking Impasse," 7 *Berkeley Ecology Law Quarterly* 731 (1979); Carol Clark, "Albert S. Bard and the Origin of Historic Preservation in New York State," 18 *Widener Law Review* 323; Thane DeNimmo Scott, "Alas in Wonderland: The Impact of *Penn Central v. New York* upon Historic Preservation Law and Policy," 7 *Boston College Environmental Affairs Law Review* 317 (1978); and Joseph P. Tomain, "Elimination of the Highest and Best Use Principle: Another Path Through the Middle Way," 47 *Fordham Law Review Volume* (1978).

Later assessments include Sheldon Lobel and Scott S. Markowitz, "*Penn Central*: Was It Really a 'Euclid' for Landmarks?," 204 *New York Law Journal*, July 16, 1990; James A. Kushner, "Property and Mysticism: The Legality of Exactions as a Condition for Public Development Approval in the Time of the Rehnquist Court," *Florida State University Journal of Land Use and Environmental Law* 8 (1992), 53–173; Eric R. Claeys, "The Penn Central Test and Tensions in Liberal Property Theory," 21 *Harvard Environmental Law Review* 339 (1997); Gideon Kanner, "Making

Laws and Sausages: A Quarter-Century Retrospective of Penn Central Transportation Co. v. City of New York," 13 *William & Mary Bill of Rights Journal* 679 (2005); "Looking Back on Penn Central: A Panel Discussion with the Supreme Court Litigators," 15 *Fordham Environmental Law Review* 287 (2004); John D. Echeverria, "Is the Penn Central Three-Factor Test Ready for History's Dustbin?," 52 *Land Use Law & Zoning Digest*, 1 (2000); and Robert M. Washburn, "Reasonable Investment-Backed Expectations as a Factor in Defining Property Interest," 49 *Journal of Urban and Contemporary Law Volume* 63 (1996). John Romayne, "How Far Is Too Far?," 53 *Planning Commissioner's Journal* 1 (2004), crosses over the boundaries between law and planning. Steven J. Eagle, "The Four-Factor Penn Central Regulatory Takings Test," *Penn State Law Review* 118 (2014), 602–646, found the decision "incoherent" (646). Richard Epstein's *Takings* (Cambridge, MA: Harvard University Press, 1985) is the most thorough-going and powerful critique of the case and its foundations.

Additional sources include California Research Bureau California State Library CRB Note, vol. 3, no. 1 (March 1, 1995), Overview of New York City's Fiscal Crisis Prepared by Roger Dunstan California Research Bureau, California State Library, https://www.library.ca.gov/crb/95/notes/v3n1.pdf.

The New York Public Library Humanities and Social Sciences Library Manuscripts and Archives Division houses the Albert S. Bard Papers. See https://web.archive.org/web/20120329012603/http://legacy.www.nypl.org/research/chss/spe/rbk/faids/bard.pdf.

A last but hardly least important source is Benjamin Baccash, "Enforcement and the New York City Landmarks Law: Past Present and Future" (MA thesis, Columbia University, 2010), an inside look at the strengths and weaknesses of the commission

INDEX

Action Group for Better Architecture in New York (AGBANY), 82, 93, 94, 95
advertisements, at Grand Central Terminal, 56–58, 233–34
African Americans, home locations of, 103
air rights
    conditions of, 169
    defined, 46–47
    Grand Central Terminal and, 37, 46–47, 49, 120
    lawsuit decision regarding, 133
    in New York City, 51–53
    transfer of, 174
    wrongs and, 51–53, 109–20
Albany, New York, 29
American Institute of Architects, 20, 58, 72, 87, 93
American Institute of Planners, 72
American Radiator Building, 130
Amtrak, 97, 234
Amtrak Improvement Act of 1974, 165–66
Appellate Court
    bench of, 159–60
    influence of, 221
    on Landmarks Preservation Law, 167
    opinion of, 165
    oral arguments in, 159
    ruling of, 163–64, 184
    standards from, 166
    See also *Penn Central v. New York City*
Associated Architects of Grand Central Terminal, 31
Atlanta, Georgia, 244
Atlantic Coast Line R.R. Co. v. North Carolina Corporation Commission, 183

Auchincloss, Louis, 22, 142
automobile industry, railroad competition from, 50–51

Baccash, Benjamin, 240
balancing tests, 229
Baltimore, Maryland, 5, 13
Baltimore and Ohio (B&O) Railroad, 8, 13, 14, 29, 41
Bar Association of New York City, 70
Barclay Hotel (NYC), 174, 230
Bard, Albert, 1, 67, 69, 70–72, 73, 76
Bard Act, 72–80, 87
Barwick, Kent L., 109, 121, 130, 135–36, 137, 235, 237
Battery Park (NYC), 80
Bauer, John I. H., 117
Bayley, John Barrington, 90–91
Beacon Hill (Boston), 67
Beame, Abraham D., 137–38, 145, 156, 170
Beaux-Arts architecture, vii, 31, 32, 35, 36, 43, 53, 106, 237
Beckelman, Laurie, 143
Belle, Albert, 227
Belle, John
    on appeal, 145, 146
    on concourse, 59
    on Grand Central Terminal decline, 66, 232
    on Grand Central Terminal renovation, 237, 238
    on lawsuit, 125
    legacy of, 60
    on Penn Central Railroad building, 116
    on *Penn Central v. New York City* decision, 231
    on preservation, 65
    on restoration, 236
    on Supreme Court opinion, 223
Bellusch, Pietro, 62

beneficial use test, 177
Benenson v. United States, 184
Benkard, James W. B., 171
Berman v. Parker, 69, 72–73, 74, 181, 195
Bernstein, Leonard, 237
Bernstein, Peter, 4
Bernstein, Richard, 130–31
best use doctrine, 16
Beyer, John, 237–38
Beyer Blinder Belle, 235, 236
Biddle, James, 141
Billboard Advertising Commission, 71
Biltmore Hotel (NYC), 48, 117, 122, 128, 133, 144, 174, 230, 231
Blackmun, Harry A., 154, 189, 190, 192, 197, 211
Blake, Peter, 115, 135
Blaustein, Frank, 90
Board of Estimate (NYC), 103–4, 169–70
Board of Standards and Appeals (NYC), 58
Bolisi, James O., 63
Boston, Massachusetts, 5
Botein, Bernard, 128–29
Boutin, Bernard, 140
bowling alley, proposal for, 57–58, 161
Boyle, Marsilia, 232
Brandeis, Louis D., 197
Breakers, 21–22
Breitel, Charles D., 171–72, 173–74, 176, 177–78, 193, 201, 206, 214
Breman v. Parker, 243–44
Brennan, William J., Jr., 154, 189, 190–92, 206, 208, 211–12, 216, 220–21
Breuer, Marcel, 111–15, 116, 117–18, 122
Breuer II Revised, 116–19
Brewer, David J., 197
brick kiln industry, 181
Brooklyn Bridge, 62, 102, 166, 198
Brooklyn Heights, 75, 80–81, 82, 84, 98
Brooklyn Heights Historic District (NYC), 102
Broome Street (NYC), 81
Brothman, Abraham, 126

Buffalo, New York, 5, 7, 8, 9, 10, 11
Bull Run battlefield, 203
Burger, Warren E., 154, 185, 189–90, 198, 203–4, 205, 210, 216
Burlington Railroad, 50
Burnham, Alan, 101–2
Burnham, D. H., 31
Byard, Paul Spencer, 136, 146, 180

Capers, Virginia, 145
Caracalla (Emperor), 43
Carey, Hugh, 135
Carlhian, Jean Paul, 117
Carnegie Hall (NYC), 61, 85, 107
Caro, Robert, 80
Carpenter, Barton, 192–93, 208, 225
Carpenter, David, 191, 192–93, 206–7, 208–9, 225, 226
Carter, Jimmy/Carter administration, 187
Cassatt, Alexander, 41, 42, 46
Cassett, Mary, 41
Castle Clinton, 80
Cavaglieri, Giorgio, 79, 95, 117
Cavett, Dick, 144–45
Central Park, 85, 237
Central Park Association, 70
Central Twentieth Century Limited, 54
Chandler, Alfred D., Jr., 10–11
Charleston, South Carolina, 221
Chemical Bank (NYC), 53
Chicago, Illinois, 8, 14
Chicago World's Fair, 31
Chrysler Building (NYC), 48–49
Chrysler Corporation, 56
Church of Saint Michael, 45
Cincinnati & St. Louis Railway, 14
Citizen's Union, 58, 70, 161
City Beautiful movement, 31, 32, 48
City Club of New York, 70, 161
City Planning Commission (NYC), 82–83, 84, 94, 101, 104, 113, 169–70, 201
Civil Rights Act, 64

Clark, Horace, 12
Clark, Tom C., 195
Cleveland, Ohio, 8
Clinton, DeWitt, 4
Cobb's Corner (NYC), 118
College Hill (Providence), 67
Committee for the Preservation of Structures of Historical and Esthetic Importance, 85, 97
Committee on City Development (Fine Arts Federation), 74
Committee on Historic Architecture, 69
Committee on Landmarks (City Planning Board), 73
Committee to Save Grand Central, 141, 143–44
Commodore Hotel (NYC), 48, 117, 174, 230
commuter railroads, 15–16, 55. *See also specific railroads*
Connecticut Transportation Authority (CTA), 129
conservation, importance of, 61
Conway, E. Virgil, 238
Cook County, Illinois, 8
Costonis, John, 105
Coulan, Jules Alexis, 36
Court of Honor, 48
crime, in New York City, 64
Cushing, Richard, 141

Dana, Mrs. Richard Henry, 79
Davey, Marsden, 30
Davies, J. Clarence, 101
Davies, John V., 42
Davis, Richard Harding, 21
Delaware, Lackawanna & Western (DL&W) Railroad, 41
Depew, Chauncey, 23
Depew Place, 23
D'Esposito, Joshua, 47
Dewey, Ballantine, Bushby, Palmer & Wood, 125, 132
DeWitt Clinton (locomotive), 5

Diamonstein-Spielvogel, Barbaralee, 68
District of Columbia, 64, 69. *See also specific locations*
Donovan, William J., 78–79
Douglas, William O., 69, 72, 74, 181, 210
Dow Jones Industrial stock market, 157
Drabkin, Murray, 128
Drew, Daniel, 8, 12
Droege, John, 38
du Pont, Henry, 139

Eagle, Steven J., 222, 229
Easterbrook, Frank, 188
East River, 3
Echeverria, John D., 221–22, 226
École des Beaux-Arts (Paris), 32
Edward S. Gordon Company, 234
Eisenhower, Dwight D./Eisenhower administration, 51, 139, 191
electricity, 30
electric traction engine, 27
Electric Train Commission, 30
electric trains, 41
Elliott, Donald K., 114
Ellis Island, 236, 240
Emergency Financial Control Board (EFCB), 135
Emery Roth & Sons, 60, 62–63
Emmet, Robert, 6
Emmet, Thomas, 6
Empire State Building (NYC), 59
Epstein, Richard, 226
Erie Canal, 3, 4–5, 12–13
Erie Railroad, 8, 10, 13, 14, 41
Euclid v. Ambler Realty Corp, 72–73, 227, 228
Europe, preservation authorities in, 240
Exchange Place Terminal, 14, 40

federal government
 brief of, 182, 183, 187, 202
 deference to, 224

{ *Index* }   255

federal government, *continued*
  Grand Central Terminal and,
    144–45
  growth of, 139
  Historic American Buildings
    Survey and, 165
  litigation interest of, 188
  Metropolitan Transportation
    Authority (MTA) and, 237
  police power and, 202
  preservation role of, 202
  regulatory powers of, 202–3
  suburban America and, 51
Fellheimer, Alfred, 55
Felt, Irving Mitchell, 97
Felt, James, 82, 83–91, 97, 98
Fifth Amendment, 1, 124, 161, 167, 175,
  192, 197–98, 217, 218, 222
Fifth Avenue (NYC), 28
Fifty-First Street (NYC), 52
Fifty-Second Street (NYC), 51
Fifty-Seventh Street (NYC), 47
Fine, Susan E., 235, 237
Fine Arts Committee, 139
Fine Arts Federation, 58, 70, 74, 88
Finley, David, 139
Fisher, William, 89
Fisk, Jim, 12
Fitch, James Marston, 117
floor area ratio (FAR), 122–23
Flushing Meadow Park, 95
Fly, James L., 56
Ford, Gerald/Ford administration,
  156, 157–58, 189
Forty-Fifth Street (NYC), 51–52
Forty-First Street (NYC), 47
Forty-Second Street (NYC), 6, 16,
  31–32, 33, 46, 48–49, 113, 151
Fourteenth Amendment, 124, 161, 167,
  175, 224
Fourth Avenue Improvement (NYC),
  26
Fowler, Glenn, 110
France, comparison to, 106
Frankfurter, Felix, 193, 210

Freedman, Doris, 144
French, Daniel Chester, 102
French Gar d'Orsay, 27
French Investing Co. v. City of New York,
  172
Friedman, Stanley M., 137
Friendly, Henry, 193
fuel factory, function of, 16
Fuller v. United States, 204–5

Gare d'Orsay, 41
Garnier, Charles, 36
Garrison, William Lloyd, 9
Garvin, Alexander, 221
Gayle, Margo, 117
GCT Venture, 237
General Services Administration
  (GSA), 140
General Tire & Rubber, 52
gentrification, 103
Georgetown (Washington, DC), 67
Gilbert, Bradford L., 24–25
Gilbert, Cass, 102
Gilbert, Frank
  on appeal, 165
  on Bard Act, 75–76
  on Brooklyn Heights, 103
  on Charles Breitel's decision, 174
  on financial report, 162–63
  on Grand Central Terminal, 107–8
  on Kodak sign, 233
  on Landmarks Preservation
    Commission, 101, 106, 118–19, 122
  on lawsuit, 124, 127, 128, 130, 131,
    132–33, 134
  on Penn Central Railroad
    building, 115, 117–18
  on restoration, 104
  on Supreme Court case, 182, 196
  on Supreme Court decision, 211,
    220–21
Gilchrist, Agnes Addison, 91
Gilded Age, 22, 23
Gill, Brendan, 79, 136
Gilmartin, Gregory, 39, 143

Gimbel's, 92
Giuliani, Rudolph, 240
Goldberger, Paul, 111, 136, 230
Goldblatt, Herbert W., 167
Goldblatt v. Hempstead, 167, 181, 195, 213
Goldstein, Diana (Kirsch), 93
Goldstein, Nina Gershon, 145, 162–63, 170
Goldstein, Tom, 171
Goldstone, Harmon
  on Albert Bard, 71–72, 78
  background of, 58, 86
  Landmarks Law and, 83
  on Landmarks Preservation Commission (LPC), 89, 90, 101, 109, 115–16, 117, 120–21, 122, 131
  on lawsuit, 129
  leadership of, 85
  on Marcel Breuer, 112–13
  on Municipal Art Society, 68, 79
  New York Preservation Archive and, 121
  on Penn Central Railroad building, 115–16, 117
Goodman, Benny, 145
Goodwin, Thomas, 227
Gould, Jay, 12, 17
grain, railroad shipment of, 9
Gramercy Park, 84
Grand Central Bowl, 57
Grand Central Depot
  accident at, 21
  acclaim for, 18, 19, 20
  criticism of, 20, 25
  description of, 23–24
  design of, 17–18, 20, 24–25
  electricity introduction in, 27
  extension of, 23
  growth of, 20–21
  lobby of, 18
  location of, 18
  opening of, 19
  overview of, 16–22
  photo of, 148
  political support for, 17
  smoke in, 26, 28–29
  statistics of, 19, 21, 28
  value of, 19
  waiting room in, 18, 19, 24, 25
  as writing inspiration, 21
Grand Central Palace (NYC), 48, 52
Grand Central Partnership, 235
Grand Central Station, 28, 148, 149, 150
Grand Central Terminal
  acclaim for, 38
  advertisements and, 56–58
  air rights of, 37, 46–47, 49, 120
  arches of, 35–36
  as bidirectional, 34
  bowling alley and, 57–58
  building influence of, 244
  ceiling design of, 35, 236–37
  ceremony at, 155
  chronology of, 245–46
  communications displays at, 241
  completion of, 37
  concourse of, 34, 35, 59, 61–62, 152, 232, 239
  condition of, 230, 231
  construction of, 35
  contributions of, 174
  costs of, 164, 218–19
  crime in, 65
  decline of, 54, 230, 231, 243
  design proposal of, 231
  electrification and, 34
  features of, 33
  financial return of, 167
  following *Penn Central v. New York City* case, 230–41
  grand entryway of, 36
  homeless population in, 231–32, 233, 234
  illustration of, 153
  Kodak sign in, 233–34, 236
  landmark status of, 106–8, 130, 165, 166, 183, 199, 215
  lawsuit of, 39–40
  location of, 33

Grand Central Terminal, *continued*
  as Midtown transportation hub, 45–46
  origin of, 11
  as pedestrian thoroughfare, 32
  Penn Station as compared to, 44
  Pennsylvania Railroad rivalry with, 242–43
  photo of, 151, 152, 155
  plans for, 30–33
  preservation planning for, 61–63, 73, 85
  proposals for, 62, 153
  protesting in, 65
  public hearing on, 107
  rallies at, 144–45
  ramps of, 34
  rededication of, 239
  regulation of, 172–73
  renovation of, 230, 231
  rental space of, 46
  reputation of, 37–39
  restaurants in, 239
  restoration of, 235–41
  revenue of, 37–39, 54, 59, 126, 235, 238
  reversal of fortunes for, 50
  significance of, 57, 163–64, 166, 168, 173, 176, 179, 242, 243
  skyscraper terminal and, 59–60, 63
  statistics of, 54
  structure of, 33
  symbolism of, 144
  tax benefits and, 59
  train traffic in, 239–40
  vision for, 3
  waiting room in, 43
  working, 33–37
  zoning compliance of, 218
Grand Central Terminal Revitalization Plan, 237
Grant, Ulysses S., 8
Gratz, Roberta B., 130, 141
Gray, Christopher, 233–34
Graybar building (NYC), 48

Great Depression, 64
Great Lakes, Hudson River and, 4
Greenwich Village, 75, 77, 81–82, 84, 98
Greenwich Village Historical District, 102, 103
Gribbon, Daniel M., 185, 193, 194–96, 197–98, 204–5, 207, 225, 226, 228
Grimes, Tammy, 170
Grogan, Louis V., 7
Gropius, Walter, 62–63
Gruen, Michael, 87, 105
Gruen, Victor, 58
Grundy, Owen, 77–78
Gruzen & Partners, 231
Guinzburg, Tommy, 141

Hadacheck v. Sebastian, 181, 213
Hamilton, Alexander, 205
Hamlin, Talbot, 69
Hardy, Hugh, 141
Harlem, New York, 7, 64
Harlem Railroad, 5–6, 7, 8, 11, 15, 18, 19
Harlem River, 3
Harmon, Yvette, 127
Harnett, Joel, 142
Harriman, Averell, 74
Harris, Harold J., 56
Harrisburg, Pennsylvania, 13, 29
Harry Weese & Associates, 235
Haskell, Douglas, 59
Haynes, O'Brien, 91
Hellenbrand, Samuel, 117
Hempstead, New York, 167, 181
Hercules, 36
heritage conservation, importance of, 61
Hilton Hotel Corporation, 198
Hiss, Alger, 126
Historical Society of the District of Columbia Circuit, 194
Historic American Buildings Survey, 165
Historic City Committee, 240
Historic Preservation Enabling Act, 72–80, 87

Hoff, Olaf, 36
Holmes, Oliver Wendall, 219
homeless population, 231–32, 233, 234
Hone, Philip, 67–68
Honest Ballot Association, 70
Hotel Belmont (NYC), 52
Hotel Marguery (NYC), 53
Housing and Urban Development (HUD), 111
Hoving, Thomas P. F., 142
Huckle, Samuel, Jr., 25
Hudson Railroad (New York & Albany (Hudson) Railroad), 7
Hudson River, 3, 4, 41, 45
Hudson River Railroad, 8, 10
Hughes, Charles, 117
Hunt, Richard Morris, 32, 36
Huxtable, Ada Louise, 58, 96, 114, 136–37, 230
Hyatt Hotel Corporation, 230

Interborough Rapid Transit (IRT) subway, 33, 45–46
Interstate Highway Act, 51

Jackson, Kenneth, 66
Jacobs, Charles M., 42
Jacobs, Jane, 67, 82
James A. Farley Post Office, 98
Janitorial Workers, 92
Janney, Eli, 23
Jayme, William, 79
Jefferson Market Courthouse (NYC), 61
Jersey City, New Jersey, 14
Johnson, Lyndon, 191
Johnson, Paul, 39
Johnson, Philip, 141, 170, 237
Johnstown, Pennsylvania, 13
Joint Committee on Design Control, 72
Jonnes, Jill, 43
J. P. Morgan Library, 131
Juniata River, 13

Kansas City, 8
Katte, Walter, 24
Keally, Francis, 88
Kellerman, Regina, 91
Kennedy, John F., 61, 64, 138, 191
Kennedy Onassis, Jacqueline
  appeal and, 170
  ceremony for, 155
  on Grand Central Terminal restoration, 236
  influence of, 228
  intervention by, 138–43
  introduction to, 1
  Lafayette Square and, 139–40
  Landmarks Preservation Law and, 67
  leadership of, 143
  legacy of, 239
  Municipal Art Society and, 141–42, 143
  Pennsylvania Avenue and, 140
  photo of, 154
  praise for, 141
  White House renovations and, 138–39
Kerr, Jack, 146, 159, 180, 220
Ketchum, Morris, Jr., 94
Keystone Bituminous Coal Association v. Debenedictis, 228
Kimball, Fiske, 44
King, Martin Luther, Jr., 64
Klein, Robert, 145
Koch, Edward, 117, 137, 142, 144, 156, 240
Kodak, Eastman, 56
Kodak sign, 56, 233–34, 236
Koerner, Leonard
  brief of, 180
  on Charles Breitel's decision, 174, 175, 177–78
  on *Goldblatt v. Hempstead*, 181
  on *Maher v. City of New Orleans*, 181–82
  oral argument of, 170, 194, 198–202, 207
  on oral arguments, 194

Koerner, Leonard, *continued*
  on Penn Central Railroad, 197
  on *Penn Central v. New York City*
    impact, 225
  on preparation of the case, 185–87
  on Supreme Court case, 205, 206
  on Supreme Court decision,
    219–20
  on the trial, 127–28, 134
Kupferman, Theodore R., 159, 163

LaFarge, L. Bancel, 79, 94
Lafayette Square (Washington, DC),
  139–40
Lake Shore Railway, 11–12, 14
Landmark Express, 154, 194
landmark movement, rise of, 81
landmark property status
  certificates for, 104
  compensation and, 228
  conditions of, 120
  costs of, 219
  decision of designation of, 212
  investment backed expectation
    and, 220
  as land-use tool, 179
  purchase decline potential and,
    226
  quality of life and, 221
  reasonable return on investment
    of, 105
  requirements for, 104
  single designation of, 213, 217
  spot zoning of, 180
  tax relief and, 105
  transfer of development rights
    and, 105
  zoning and, 216
Landmarks Preservation Commission
  (LPC)
  air rights and, 169
  certified letters from, 107
  challenges to, 105
  changes to, 109
  cost burden from, 218
  demoralization of, 131
  designing by, 102
  exhibit of, 136–37
  function of, 88, 101, 104
  on Grand Central Terminal
    renovation, 238
  landmark conditions of, 120
  landmark list of, 86, 102, 105–6, 201,
    240
  lawsuit against, 124–25
  leadership of, 88–89
  limitations of, 122
  members of, 101
  mission of, 89
  moderation by, 98
  modification regulation by, 103
  opposition to, 104
  organization of, 101
  origin of, 67, 86
  Penn Central Railroad and, 110,
    114, 118–19, 169
  Penn Station and, 92–93, 98
  permanent status of, 90–91
  powers of, 122–23, 124
  procedures of, 200
  proposal to, 90
  public hearing of, 115, 116
  qualifications of, 199–200
  Real Estate Board of New York
    and, 107
  research work of, 91
  standards of, 215
  success of, 175, 240
  in Supreme Court discussion,
    207–8
  Supreme Court hearing and, 179
  trepidation at, 115–16
  trial of, 125–32
  victory of, 224–25
Landmarks Preservation Law
  advancement of, 83
  arbitrary action and, 205
  compensation proposal for, 214–15
  comprehensive plan of, 212
  conditions of, 100, 102, 172

cost of, 217
countrywide usage of, 214
criticism of, 213
discrimination of, 167–68
impacts of, 242
importance of, 100–101
land-use decision and, 212
limitations of, 213
majority of, 166
nonmonetary value of, 224
police power and, 162
property usage function of, 211–12, 215
quality of life and, 221
signing of, 100
structure application of, 214
taking of private property and, 211
vice of, 198
land-use regulation, 146, 199, 212
Lansburgh Apartments, 140
Law Department (NYC), 158–71
Learned Hand, Billings, 193
Lee, Robert E., 8
Lehigh Valley Railroad, 41
Lehman Brothers, 157
Lewis, George, 117
Lexington Avenue (NYC), 47
Lhota, Joseph, 239
Lincoln Building (NYC), 52
Lindsay, John V., 64–65, 94, 159
Lipsett, Morris, 96
Lobel, Sheldon, 226
Long Island, 3
Long Island Rail Road (LIRR), 42, 55, 97, 233, 239–40
Los Angeles, California, 181
Low, Seth, 48
Lupiano, Vincent A., 161, 168–69
Lutheran Church in Amer. v. City of New York, 166, 198
Lutheran Church of America, 130–31
Lyness, Russell, 89

Macy's, 92
Madison Avenue (NYC), 47
Madison Square Garden, 17, 92, 96–97, 108
Madison Square Garden Corporation, 95
Maher v. City of New Orleans, 181–82, 184
Malcolm X, 64
Malkin, Peter, 235
Mallamud, David, 142
Manhattan Hotel (NYC), 48
Marble House, 21–22
Marcus, Norman, 171–72, 221, 227–28
Markewich, Arthur, 160
Marshall, Thurgood, 154, 189, 191, 195–96, 199–200, 210, 211
Marshall, William, Jr., 141
Mason, John, 6
Massengale, John, 39
Matter of Trustees of Sailors' Snug Harbor v. Platt, 166
McCree, Wade, 187
McFadden, John, 234
McGrath, Dorn, 140
McKim, Charles, 32, 41, 42
McKim, Mead & White, 17, 31
McMahon, Dennis, 20
McMilen, Loring, 89
Meadowlands, 96
Medford, Kay, 170
Meeks, Carol L. V., 50
Menapace, Ralph, 146, 158–59, 180
Mendelson, Bradley C., 234
Mercury (god), 36, 37
Merrill Lynch, 56
MetLife Building, 63, 107
Metro-North Railroad, 55, 231, 232–33, 234, 239–40
Metropolitan Museum of Art, 107, 166
Metropolitan Transportation Authority (MTA), 129–30, 144, 161, 163, 169, 170, 233, 235–36, 237
Meyerson, Bess, 145
Michelman, Frank, 192
Michigan Southern Railroad, 14
Midtown Manhattan, 53, 64

Miner, Dorothy, 146, 170, 180, 186–87, 194, 225
Minneapolis, Minnesota, 244
Mitchell, MacNeil, 74–75, 94
Mohawk River Valley, 4
Monaghan, Henry, 192
Montana Apartments, 52
Montgomery, Charles, 139
Monticello, 67
moot court, 188
Morgan, J. Pierpont, 22
Morgan House, 130–31
Morris, Newbold, 95
Morrone, Francis, 38–39
Moses, Robert, 67, 73, 77, 80–83, 101
Mount Vernon, 67
Municipal Art Society
   Albert Bard and, 70
   at appeal, 159
   brief of, 161
   committees of, 122, 137, 138
   criticism of, 144
   Grand Central Terminal renovation and, 237
   Jacqueline Kennedy Onassis and, 141–42, 143
   Landmark Express of, 193–94
   on lawsuit, 128–29
   limitations of, 79
   preservation work of, 61, 68, 87
   resolution of, 76, 80
   respect for, 225
   structure list of, 79, 81, 84, 86
Municipal Assistance Corporation (MAC), 135
Murphy, Francis T., 159, 163, 164, 165, 167, 168
Murtagh, William J., 144
Muskin, Victor, 127

Napoléon III, 18
Nast, Conde, 48
National City Bank (NYC), 48
National Environmental Protection Act, 202
National Historic Preservation Act (NHPA), 106, 141
National Press Club, 157–58
National Roadside Council, 70, 71
National Theater (Washington, DC), 140
National Trust for Historic Preservation (NTHP), 58, 161, 185, 189, 194
Nespole, James, 127
Nessen, Ron, 157
Nevins, Allan, 52, 174–75, 225, 229
Newburgh-on-Hudson, 67
new federalism, 223
New Haven Railroad (New York, New Haven & Hartford Railroad), 15, 18, 19, 34, 37–38, 60, 62, 109–10
New Jersey, 3
Newman, William H., 40
New Orleans, Louisiana, 67, 68, 184–85, 221
New Orleans v. Dukes, 184–85
Newport, Rhode Island, 5, 21–22
New York Board of Trade, 92
New York Central Building, 48, 52
New York Central Railroad (NYCRR)
   in Chicago, 14
   dominance of, 8
   electrification of, 30
   expansion of, 11
   freight of, 11
   at Grand Central Depot, 18, 19
   on Grand Central Terminal decline, 54
   Great Steel Fleet of, 50
   legacy of, 242
   location of, 8, 10
   map of, 150
   monopoly of, 3
   office building of, 53
   origin of, 13
   Pennsylvania Railroad merger with, 108

Pennsylvania Railroad *versus*, 40
professionalism of, 16
proposals for, 62
revenue decline of, 54, 58
revenue of, 46
reversal of fortunes for, 50
salaries of, 10
stations of, 29
stockholders meeting of, 10
stock of, 11
streamliners of, 50
ticket windows for, 34
track locations of, 26
New York City (NYC)
air rights in, 51–53 (*see also* air rights)
architectural style of, 53
bankruptcy aversion of, 156–58
commercial dominance of, 5
crime in, 64, 232
decline of, 63–66, 156
demolition in, 97
economy of, 4
financial challenges of, 134–35, 156, 219, 243
Fourth Avenue Improvement in, 26
growth of, 3
harbor of, 3
hotels in, 48 (*see also specific hotels*)
landmark districts of, 102–3
location of, 3
migration to, 3
as Nieuw Amsterdam, 3
origin of, 3
political ascendancy of, 5
preservation efforts in, 67
quality of life in, 65
railroad track maze in, 25–26
real estate market in, 48, 108–9
redevelopment in, 52, 67–68
reimagined cityscape of, 45–49
riots in, 64
skyscrapers in, 52–53
smoke in, 26

transferable development rights program of, 216
as transportation hub, 3
urban redevelopment in, 44–45
zoning law in, 51, 52–53, 84–85
See also specific locations
New York City Transit Authority, 233
New York Community Trust, 79
New York Court of Appeals
appeal to, 170
case to, 171–78
erroneous finding of, 204
influence of, 221
leadership of, 159–60
Morgan House and, 130–31
Supreme Court and, 193
See also specific cases
New York Knicks, 108
New York Landmarks Conservancy Board, 159
New York Port Authority, 70
New York Preservation Archives Project, 180, 185–86
New York Public Library, 62, 166, 198
New York Rangers, 108
New York State Landmarks Preservation Law, 67
New York State Office of Parks and Recreation, 144
Nixon, Richard M., 160, 189–90
NJ Transit, 97
nonprofit test, 177
Northeast Corridor, 14
Nowvé, Lorna, 143

Orbach, Jerry, 170
Old Stock Exchange (Chicago), 165
Onassis, Aristotle, 141
Ouroussoff, Nicolai, 238–39
Outdoor Advertising Association of America, 71

Pacific Legal Foundation, 184
Palace of Progress, 78–79
Pan Am Airways, 63

Pan Am Building, 107, 110, 115, 119, 125, 163
Panic of 1857, 7
Papert, Fred, 142, 143, 145
Paris Exposition Universelle, 27
Parish, Mrs. Henry, II, 138–39
Park Avenue (NYC)
    air rights and, 51–52
    Beaux-Arts jewel in, 35
    fame of, 52
    millionaires at, 48
    property values of, 47, 176–77
    rebuilding plan of, 59
    remake of, 52
    structures of, 52
Park Avenue Tunnel, 28–30
Partnership for the Homeless, 234
Patton, D. Kenneth, 131
Pearsall, Otis Pratt, 81, 98
Pei, I. M., 59, 60, 117
Penn Central Railroad
    accusations of, 197
    air rights and, 110, 174
    bankruptcy of, 129
    Biltmore Hotel and, 133 (*see also* Biltmore Hotel (NYC))
    Breuer II Revised of, 116–19
    building plans of, 110–12, 113–14, 116–19, 126–27, 196–97
    compensation proposal for, 197, 214–15, 222
    costs of, 164, 218–19
    criticism of, 113–15, 117, 137
    development rights of, 121–22, 168
    discrimination of, 167–68, 186
    Grand Central Terminal contributions to, 174
    lack of evidence by, 213
    Landmarks Preservation Commission (LPC) and, 169
    lawsuit of, 124–25
    Metropolitan Transportation Authority (MTA) and, 129–30, 161, 163, 169
    as monopoly power, 178
    origin of, 108
    praise for, 115
    primary interest of, 215
    property selling by, 230
    revenue of, 109, 169
    "Statement of Revenues and Costs" of, 163, 165
    submission flaws of, 173
    syllogism of, 207
    trial of, 125–32
Penn Central Transportation Company, 13, 176
Penn Central v. New York City
    amicus brief for the United States of, 183
    appeal of, 145–46, 158–71
    brief for, 180
    calculations in, 192
    conferences of, 191–93
    criticism of, 135–37
    decision of, 132–34
    drafts of, 191–93
    federal government brief of, 183, 202
    filing of, 124–25
    friends of the court briefs and, 182–85
    immediate impact of, 224
    impacts of, 242
    Landmark Express at, 193–94
    legal framework from, 1
    as lodestar of landmark law, 224
    long-term impact of, 227–29
    Municipal Arts Society brief of, 194
    National Trust for Historic Preservation (NTHP) brief of, 185, 194
    new federalism and, 223
    in New York City Court of Appeals, 171–78
    oral argument in, 193–205
    Pacific Legal Foundation brief of, 184
    precedent in, 180

preparation for oral argument in, 185–89
principle of takings and, 185
qualifications in, 212
reactions to decision of Supreme Court in, 219–27
solicitor general brief of, 206
State of California brief of, 184
State of New York brief of, 184–85, 194
Supreme Court justices of, 189–91
Supreme Court majority opinion of, 210–16
Supreme Court team for, 180
takings test in, 212
trial of, 126–32
waiting for Supreme Court ruling of, 205–9
Penn Station
architectural influence of, 43
concourse of, 43–44
cost of, 43
decline of, 79
demolition of, 80, 81, 95–96
design of, 43
features of, 43
Grand Central Terminal as compared to, 44
legacy of, 243
location considerations for, 42
loss of, 91–99
origin of, 29
overview of, 40–44
razing of, 80
significance of, 98–99
structure of, 43
threat to, 61
tunnels of, 45
Pennsylvania Avenue (Washington, DC), 140
Pennsylvania Canal, 13
Pennsylvania Railroad (PRR)
acquisitions of, 14
construction of, 13–14
cost of, 44

decline of, 91–92
depot of, 29
dominance of, 8
economic stance of, 12
Erie Canal and, 12–13
facilities and equipment of, 40–41
New York Central merger with, 108
New York Central *versus*, 40
origin of, 13
overview of, 12–14
revenue decline of, 54–55
routes of, 13, 40
station of, 151
streamliners of, 50
success of, 40
terminals for, 31
urban redevelopment and, 44–45
Pennsylvania Station (Manhattan), 31
Peoples Line steamboats, 8
Perlman, Alfred E., 62
Philadelphia, Pennsylvania, 5, 13
Philadelphia & Reading (Reading) Railroad, 41
Philadelphia & Trenton Railroad, 14
Pittsburgh, Fort Wayne & Chicago Railroad, 14
Pittsburgh, Pennsylvania, 8, 13, 29
plaque program, 79
Platt, Geoffrey, 74, 79, 83, 89, 93, 101, 109
Plaza Hotel (NYC), 110
Plimpton, Francis T. P., 129
Plimpton, George, 136
police power, 162, 202
Poole, C. W., 20
porters, role of, 54
Posner, Richard, 188
post-World War II era, reversal of fortunes in, 50
Powell, Adam Clayton, 126, 207, 211
Powell, Lewis F., Jr., 154, 189
Prapert, Fred, 133
precedent, importance of, 180–81
Prentice, T. Merrill, Jr., 142

preservation
   Bard Act and, 72–76
   examples of, 67
   federal government's role in, 202
   of Grand Central Terminal, 61–63, 73
   legal standing of, 224
   limitations of, 244
   local governance of, 240
   loss of Penn Station and, 91–99
   nonmonetary value of, 224
   pragmatism in, 238
   statistics of, 67
property/property rights
   beneficial use test on, 177
   best use doctrine for, 16
   compensation and, 205, 214–15
   complexity of, 219
   conditions of, 1
   economic viability and, 200
   highest and best use concept of, 204–5
   naked deprivation of, 222
   nonprofit test on, 177
   proportionality and, 217
   proportionality calculus and, 218
   public interest test on, 177, 229
   reasonable return test on, 177
   rental value and, 164–65
   social benefit and public interest in, 214
   social investment test on, 177
   takings of, 198
   test for, 167
proportionality calculus, 218
Proportional Representation Committee, 70
protesting, in Grand Central Terminal, 65
public interest test, 177
public nuisance law, 217–18
Public Service Commission, 161
Puget Sound Traction, Light & Power Co. v. Reynolds, 183–84
Pullman, George, 7

Purdy, Lawson, 73
P. W. Grosser Consulting, 53

Queenside Hills Realty Co. v. Saxl, 181
Quill, Mike, 64–65

Raab, Jennifer J., 239
railroads
   accidents of, 7
   automobile industry competition with, 50–51
   commuter lines of, 15–16
   dangers of, 6, 16, 25, 26–27, 29–30
   dependence on, 8
   description of, 9
   early years of, 6
   electric traction engine of, 27
   expansion of, 9, 22–23
   fare of, 6–7, 15
   gauge of, 8–9, 22–23
   government dependence of, 173–74
   horsepower and, 6, 16
   hubs for, 8
   innovations of, 23
   lines of, 5
   maturation of system of, 8–9
   popularity of, 5
   principal duty of, 47
   regulation of, 22
   sleeping car of, 7
   smoke from, 26
   statistics of, 23
   time zones of, 22–23
   train length of, 28
   transcontinental, 10
   See also specific railroads
rallies, at Grand Central Terminal, 144–45
Rand, Reminton, 48
Randall, Tony, 145
Rankin, Lee, 118, 121
Ravitch, Richard, 232–33
RCA Building (NYC), 119
Reading Terminal, 29
Reagan, Ronald, 189

Real Estate Board of New York, 92, 107, 120
Real Estate Record & Builders Guild, 18
reasonable return test, 177
Redevelopment Act (District of Columbia), 69
Reed, Charles H., 31, 40
Reed, Henry Hope, 77, 91
Reed & Stem, 31–33, 39–40
Rehnquist, William H.
  background of, 190
  case opinion of, 200, 201, 204–5, 216
  as conservative, 189
  dissent of, 185, 216, 218–19, 223
  on the Fifth Amendment, 197–98
  influence of, 227
  new doctrine and, 223
  photo of, 154
  processes of, 210
Remington, William, 126
restoration, process of, 103
Rezin, John, 96
Richland, W. Bernard, 137, 170–71
Richmondtown, 84
Riverdale, 84
Roberts, Samuel, 117, 231, 233
Robertson, Jack, 128
Robertson, Jaquelin T., 114
Robins, Anthony W., 38, 57, 63–64
Rochester, New York, 5, 29
Rockefeller, Nelson A., 160
Rockefeller Center, 62
Roe v. Wade, 190
Rogers, Elizabeth Barlow, 237
Rohatyn, Felix, 135
Rome, demolition in, 97
Roosevelt Hotel (NYC), 48, 117, 174, 230
Rose, Billy, 78
Rosenberg, Julius and Ethel, 126
Rosenblatt, Arthur, 117
Rosenman, Samuel I., 129
Ross, Harold, 56
Roth, Richard, 115

Rowland, Virginia, 56–57
Rubinow, Ray, 82, 94
Rudolph, Paul, 142

Sachs, Alice, 94
Saddy, Morris, 110
Sadowsky, Edward, 93–94
Salamar Bldrs. Corp v. Tuttle, 167
Sanders, James, 42
San Francisco, California, 244
Santa Barbara, California, 221
Santa Fe, New Mexico, 221
Saypol, Irving, 125–34, 145–46, 162
Schaap, Dick, 65
Schiffer, Lois, 188–89
Schlesinger, Arthur, Jr., 139–40
Schlichting, Kurt C., 30, 40, 53
Schwartz, Allen G., 180, 186, 194
Scientific American (magazine), 19, 23
Scott, Thane, 226
Scully, Vincent, 97, 127–28
Seagram's House, 52
Seelye Stevenson Value & Knecht, 235
Seventh Avenue (NYC), 43
Seymour, Whitney North, Sr., 79, 129, 158–59
Shanker, Albert, 157
Sheridan, L. Kevin, 175, 180, 186
Shipler, David K., 114
Short, Bobby, 170
Siegel, Norman, 233
skyscrapers, proposal and development of, 52–53, 59–60, 63, 108–9, 110–12
sleeping car, 7
Sloan, Peter, 146
Sloat, M., 15
Smith, Peter, 234
Smith, Robert L., 65–66
smoke, 26, 28–29
Snook, John B., 17
Soboloff, Simon E., 72
social investment test, 177
Southern Railway, 22

Spatt, Beverly Moss, 137, 146, 170, 175
spot zoning, 180. *See also* zoning ordinances
Standard Oil, 71
Stangl, Peter, 232–33, 235
State Appellate Court, 159
State Historic Preservation Office (SHPO), 238
Staten Island, 3, 84
Statue of Liberty, 102, 198, 240
St. Bartholomew's Church, 159
Stecse, Edward, 68–69
Stein, Gertrude, 159
Stem, Allen H., 31
Stem, Robert A. M., 39
Stevens, Harold Arnoldus, 159–60, 163
Stevens, John Paul, III, 154, 185, 189, 190, 201, 202–3, 209, 216, 222–23
Stewart, Potter, 154, 189, 191, 201, 207, 222
Stiles, T. J., 11, 17
Stone, Harlan, 210
St. Pancras Station (London), 17
St. Paul's Chapel (NYC), 106
streetcars, electric, 27
Stringer, Lee, 54
Stuart, James, 3
suburbs, growth of, 51
Sullivan, Louis, 32
Supreme Court
   appeal to, 175
   on *Berman v. Parker*, 69
   clerk role in, 192–93
   conferences of, 191–93
   courts of appeal as compared to, 179
   dissent of, 216–19
   divisions of, 223
   drafts of, 191–93
   friends of the court briefs and, 182–85
   justices of, 189–91
   lines of argument for, 179
   majority opinion of, 210–16
   New York Court of Appeals and, 193
   oral argument in, 193–205, 206
   photo of, 154
   preparation for oral argument in, 185–89
   processes of, 210
   reactions to decision of, 219–27
   time allotment in, 187
   waiting for response of, 205–9
   Warren Court in, 189
Supreme Court of New York, 124
Susquehanna River, 13
Sutton, Percy E., 142
Symes, Jim, 92
Syracuse, New York, 5, 77

Tankel, Stanley, 89
taxation, on landmark properties, 105
Taylor, Jack, 236–37
Teacher's Retirement System, 156
textile industry, 10–11
Thompson, Barton, 222
Thompson, Hugh, 46–47
Thomson, John E., 13
Time (magazine), 114
time zones, 22–23
Todd, David, 117
Town & Country Magazine (magazine), 141
Train 118, accident of, 29–30
Transactions (journal), 46
Transportation (sculpture), 36
Transport Workers Union of America (TWU), 64–65
Travers, Mary, 145
travertine marble, 43
Trinity Church (NYC), 106, 119
Truman, Harry S., 62
Trump, Donald, 230
Tweed Courthouse, 132

Union Carbide Building (NYC), 53
Union General Properties (UGP) Ltd., 110, 113, 118, 126–27

Union Pacific Railroad, 50
unions, labor struggles and, 65
Union Station (Washington, DC), 31
United Canal & Railroad, 14
United Press International, 157
Upper East Side Historic District (NYC), 102
Upper West Side Historic District (NYC), 102
Urban Development Corporation, 230
urban spaces, people's interest in, 1
US Customs House, 102
US Post Office (NYC), 48
Utica, New York, 29

Van Alen, William, 48–49
Vanderbilt, Arthur T., II, 21
Vanderbilt, Cornelius
  background of, 5
  blaming of, 7
  death of, 21
  description of, 12, 21
  economic faith in, 8
  empire of, 10
  expansion of, 11
  financial contributions of, 11
  Grand Central Terminal building by, 16–22
  Hudson River Railroad of, 8
  leadership of, 7
  legacy of, 39, 242
  photo of, 147
  political support for, 17
  professionalism of, 16
  railroad of, 5–12
  railroad purchases of, 10
  vision of, 3
  worth of, 21
Vanderbilt, Cornelius, II, 21–22
Vanderbilt, Maria Louisa, 12
Vanderbilt, William H., 8, 11, 19, 21, 31, 36, 39
Vanderbilt, William K., 21–22
Vanderbilt Avenue, 232
Vanderbilt Hall, 57

Van Derpool, James, 89, 99, 102
Van Voorhis, John, 168–69
viaduct, 35, 39, 53
Vieux Carré (New Orleans), 67
The Villager (magazine), 84

Wachtler, Sol, 171
Wagner, Robert F.
  on Grand Central Terminal, 142–43
  introduction to, 1
  Landmarks Preservation Law and, 67
  on lawsuit, 128–29
  leadership of, 62
  New York City Landmarks Preservation Law and, 100
  overview of, 83–91
  Penn Station and, 93, 94, 95
  at rally, 145
Wagner, Walter F., Jr., 115
Wald, Patricia M., 187–89, 202, 203–4, 206, 222–23, 226–27
Waldorf-Astoria (NYC), 117
Walker, Ralph, 140
Wall Street Journal (newspaper), 226
Walton, William, 140
Warnecke, John Carl, 141
Warner (Washington, DC), 140
Warren, Earl, 189, 210
Warren, Whitney, 31, 35, 36, 38, 239
Warren & Wetmore, 31, 32–33, 39–40
Washington, DC, civil rights movement in, 64, 69. *See also specific locations*
Washington, George, 67
Washington Arch (NYC), 119
Washington Post (newspaper), 140
Washington Square Park (NYC), 81–82
Webb & Knapp, 59
Webster, Bethuel M., 129
Weinberg, Robert, 58, 73, 88, 95
Wellington, Margot, 175–76
Westchester, New York, 15

{ *Index* }

Western Electric Company, 48
Westinghouse, George, 23
Wetmore, Charles, 31, 40
Wharton, Edith, 21, 26
wheat, railroad shipment of, 8
Whelcon, Clark, 65
White, Byron R., 154, 189, 191, 200, 204, 211
White, E. B., 54
White, Norval, 94
White, Stanford, 31, 102
White House, restoration of, 138–39
White Penn Station, 17
Whitman, Walt, 68
W. H. Vanderbilt (engine), 8
Wilbur Smith and Associates, 113
Wilgus, William J., 25, 30, 33, 37, 46, 47–48, 109–10
Willard Hotel (Washington, DC), 184, 227
Williams, Frederick, 117
Williamsburg, Virginia, 221
Winterthur Mansion, 139
Wolfson, Erwin, 62
Wolloch, Richard, 176–77
Wood, Anthony C., 74, 100

Wood, John, 132–33, 163
Woodbridge, Frederick F., 89, 94
World's Columbian Exposition, 48

Yale Club (NYC), 48
Yarborough, Ralph, 106
Yippies' Festival of Life, 65
Young, Robert R., 54, 59
Youngman, Henny, 145

Zax, Leonard A., 227
Zeckendorf, William, 59, 78–79
zoning ordinances
    analogy of, 214
    differential impact of, 213
    discrimination in, 172, 212
    Fifth Amendment and, 217
    landmarking and, 216–17
    as land-use tool, 199
    restrictions in, 216–17
    return on the property and, 179
    risk of, 162
    spot, 180
    See also specific properties
Zoning Resolution, 104, 105
Zuccotti, John, 138.

www.ingramcontent.com/pod-product-compliance
Lightning Source LLC
Chambersburg PA
CBHW030338240426
43661CB00052B/1672